PSYCHOTHERAPY WITH OLDER ADULTS

Second Edition

D1025230

This book is dedicated to the memory of my father,
Jack Allen Knight, Sr. (1894-1976).
Listening to his reminiscences laid
the groundwork for my career.

PSYCHOTHERAPY WITH OLDER ADULTS

Second Edition

Bob G. Knight

SAGE Publications
International Educational and Professional Publisher
Thousand Oaks London New Delhi

For information address:

SAGE Publications, Inc.
2455 Teller Road
Thousand Oaks, California 91320
E-mail: order@sagepub.com

SAGE Publications Ltd.
6 Bonhill Street
London EC2A 4PU
United Kingdom

SAGE Publications India Pvt. Ltd.
M-32 Market
Greater Kailash I
New Delhi 110 048 India

Printed in the United States of America

Library of Congress Cataloging-in-Publication Data

Knight, Bob G.
    Psychotherapy with older adults / author, Bob G. Knight.—2nd ed.
        p. cm.
    Includes bibliographical references and index.
    ISBN 0-8039-5401-8 (acid-free paper). — ISBN 0-8039-5402-6 (pbk.:
    acid-free paper)
    1. Geriatric psychotherapy. 2. Aged—Mental health. I. Title.
    RC451.4.A5K59 1996
    618.97'68914—dc20   95-50151

96 97 98 99 10 9 8 7 6 5 4 3 2 1

This book is printed on acid-free paper.

Sage Production Editor: Diane S. Foster

Contents

Preface to the Second Edition

The typescript for the first edition of *Psychotherapy With Older Adults* was completed 10 years ago, shortly before my daughter Carmen was born. As I complete this one, she is on the verge of entering fifth grade, and we are preparing for a sabbatical in Great Britain at the University of Sheffield and Community Health Trust at Sheffield.

The publication of the first edition has started a long process of discussion with others about psychotherapy with older adults. I have accumulated more experience in doing psychotherapy with older adults, consulting with others about therapy, teaching graduate students at the University of Southern California, and teaching continuing education sessions in a wide variety of settings. A key question in all of these discussions has been whether psychotherapy with older adults is similar to work with younger clients. If it is different, the next question is how it is different.

Some years ago, my wife Patty accompanied me to a talk I gave to a local psychology association. When I asked what she thought, her response was that I had said that working with older adults was like working with younger ones, with a few exceptions. She named the exceptions and then noted that all those exceptions added together sounded quite different. She was right, and in many ways this book represents my effort to be more clear about what the differences are and when they do, and do not, make much difference.

The first chapter of this volume outlines my perspective on the potential differences in working with older adults: maturation through adult life, specific challenges such as grief and chronic illness, cohort differences, and the context in which older adults live. The next chapters describe adaptations in therapeutic work with older adults based on these factors (Chapter 2), building rapport with older adults (Chapter 3), and transference and countertransference issues with the elderly (Chapter 4). These chapters provide the basis for understanding the perception that working with older clients is different and can provide a framework for understanding the older client that precedes making initial contact and beginning the assessment process.

Assessment with older adults is different and more difficult than assessment with younger adults. The frequent coexistence of physical and social problems along with psychological ones and the greater prevalence of dementing illnesses among the elderly provide complexity. Many mistakes seem to be rooted in failing to see interrelationships between psychological and physical problems or between psychological and social problems, often due to either/or thinking on the part of the therapist. Many other mistakes are due to failing to recognize the problems that older adults share with younger ones: depression, anxiety, alcohol abuse, marital distress, family problems, and so forth. The discussion of assessment in Chapter 5 is intended to be introductory; the reader will need more reading and more training in assessing older adults to function adequately. Suggestions for additional readings appear at the end of the chapter.

One major departure from the first edition is the addition of specific chapters on grief work (Chapter 6), chronic illness (Chapter 7), and the life review process (Chapter 8). Again, these are introductory summaries, and the reader should read further in the additional readings and other resources. In the life review chapter, I have integrated aspects of the contextual, cohort-based maturity/specific challenge model with traditional views of the life review and have suggested some ways to apply these concepts and to decide how to handle the total amount of autobiographical material that exists with older adults.

In the final chapter (Chapter 9), I offer some notes on ethical issues in working with older adults and some thoughts on the future of psychotherapy with older adults. As in the first edition, my attempt has been to write about therapy in a way that cuts across therapy systems. It may be a measure of my success that one reviewer described me as following psychodynamic, behavioral, social learning, family systems, and casework models all in the course of a three-page review. As I note in the last chapter, I have grown to see my perspective on therapy within an integrative psychotherapy framework.

Because integrative therapists often show clear signs of their origins, it may be helpful to know that my first exposure to counseling as an undergraduate was Rogerian. That training was reinforced by my first research interviewing experience with older adults, which used nondirective interviewing techniques. My training at Indiana University was intentionally cognitive-behavioral. My advisor Leon H. Levy was in turn a student of George Kelly; consequently, my cognitive approach is more similar to personal construct therapy than to Beck or Ellis. I was also taught psychotherapy by Kenneth Heller, a coauthor of the classic Goldstein, Heller, and Sechrest book that argued for using all of psychology (and especially social psychology) as a knowledge base for therapy. These roots are evidenced in my use of gerontology as a knowledge base for psychotherapy with older adults and in my concern for understanding older adults within their specific social contexts.

I have always read psychodynamic literature about older adults and have found the writing on the relationship of client and therapist compelling, if not always consistent with views of normal aging that were emerging in gerontology. I have at times been supervised by psychodynamic and gestalt therapists. Their focus on emotion as such has often been helpful in finding out what is really bothering a client. While we wait for a theoretical synthesis of psychotherapy, it is my view that one should know how to operate in two or more systems and to use the one that best fits the client's problems and the client as a person.

It has been my intent to refrain from taking sides about the modality of therapy as well. That is, I am as fond of group, couple, and family sessions as I am of individual work. It has surprised and perplexed me that my work is usually seen as being only about individual psychotherapy.

It is my hope that this volume will provide a coherent introduction to psychotherapy with older adults and to scientific gerontology as a potential knowledge base to draw from as we attempt to understand normal aging and the problems of later life. Without such a knowledge base, we are left with what we know, and with what we think we know, on the basis of personal experience and professional experience with the few older clients which come our way. Such experiences, though clearly compelling, are likely to lead to misunderstanding the aging process and to misunderstanding older people in ways that will harm some of the older clients whom we seek to help.

Good luck with your older clients!

Acknowledgments

There are far too many people who should be acknowledged to be recognized in this short space. Terry Hendrix at Sage Publications kept after me for years about revising this book until I agreed to do it, and I thank him for it. The thinking and reading that went into this edition have been very rewarding for me. Christine Smedley at Sage talked me through the actual revision process.

In different ways, Margaret Gatz, Steven Zarit, Michael Smyer, George Niederehe, Sandra Powers, Fiona Goudie, Martha Storandt, Sara Qualls, Elizabeth Zelinski, and other colleagues have said or written things about the first edition that have helped me see it in a different light and so have influenced the second edition. Gerald Davison and Sandra Powers reviewed earlier drafts of this manuscript, and their assistance is gratefully acknowledged.

I have had the great good fortune to work in two outstanding interdisciplinary centers for psychotherapy with older adults: Ventura County Senior Outreach Services (in California) and the University of Southern California's (USC's) Tingstad Older Adult Counseling Center. The generosity of Hortense O. Tingstad in supporting the counseling center and of Merle H. Bensinger in supporting the professorship which I hold at USC's Andrus Gerontology Center is gratefully acknowledged. Both have been inspirations with regard to the potential for aging well and for meeting the challenges of later life successfully.

On a more personal note, I would like to acknowledge the love and support of my wife Patty as well as her insights and wisdom with regard to life itself. In different ways, my late father (who would be 101 this year if he were still alive), my mother (who turned 65 last month), and my daughter (who will be 10 when this book is published), have taught me about growing up throughout life.

1

Gerontology for Psychotherapists

The Contextual, Cohort-Based,
Maturity/Specific Challenge Model

Mrs. G. is a 75-year-old woman who has come to see a psychologist on the advice of her granddaughter. The granddaughter has felt that Mrs. G. is depressed and that therapy might help because she herself had a good experience with therapy while at the state university. Mrs G. has been widowed 3 years and has never gotten over her grief. The past 2 months have included the anniversary of her husband's death, her 75th birthday, and the departure of a friend who has moved to another community. She has become more depressed, is losing weight, and complains of not sleeping soundly as well as not being able to remember things the way she used to. She is very unsure of what the therapist will do for her; her granddaughter has only been able to say that talking to the therapist will

AUTHOR'S NOTE: This chapter further develops ideas and duplicates material from the introduction and the concluding chapter of *Older Adults in Psychotherapy: Case Histories* (1992), which is published by Sage Publications. It also incorporates material published in *Generations* (1993) and reprinted as a chapter in M. Smyer (Ed.), *Mental Health and Aging* (Springer, 1993).

help. The waiting room reminds her of a doctor's office, and she thinks that perhaps she will get medication or the same kind of friendly but firm advice that her family physician (who died 10 years ago) used to provide. She knows that therapy has to do with mental health and worries that the psychologist will evaluate her and put her in the state hospital.

When the psychologist (Dr. Q.) comes to the waiting room, Mrs. G. is surprised that he is young. Furthermore, he is dressed in a style that Mrs. G. feels is not really professional. He looks surprised at Mrs. G.'s age and appears uncomfortable. When Mrs. G. wavers a little as she stands up from the waiting room couch, Dr. Q. unexpectedly and somewhat awkwardly grabs her to steady her, which annoys Mrs. G. and makes her feel more unbalanced for a second. Once in the therapy room, Mrs. G. has difficulty understanding Dr. Q., who tends to speak rather quietly and with an accent that marks him as being from out of state. At times Mrs. G. guesses what is being asked, and she is not sure how the answers are being taken because she cannot see the therapist's face very well. The room is dimly lit, and Mrs. G. has not replaced her glasses in 5 years because of the expense.

After an hour-long visit in which Dr. Q. and Mrs. G. have each become progressively more nervous, Mrs. G. leaves with the strong feeling that the doctor felt she is senile and with the advice that "it's normal to feel depressed at your age." She worries for the next 3 months about whether she will be able to afford the psychologist's bill. Although the clinic secretary said something about the fee's being based on income, no one told her what her fee would be. When no bill arrives, she concludes that the doctor saw her as a charity case and feels even more depressed. Her granddaughter urges her to see another therapist, but Mrs. G. refuses and secretly feels relieved that she was not sent to the state hospital geriatric unit.

In this story, Mrs. G. is unfortunately burdened with most of the problems that older people have in seeking therapy, but there are many like Mrs. G., and many who have only some of these problems and misconceptions. Older people have had less exposure to and informal education about psychotherapy and outpatient mental health services than the younger adults who make up the majority of therapists' caseloads.

Throughout much of older people's lives, "mental health" meant long-term stays for psychotic individuals in locked wards in state hospitals far from home. Very few of today's elderly went to college, and the ones who did are unlikely to have taken psychology classes. Novels and films about therapy and therapists were not common. Relatively few have known if any friends or family members sought therapy for other than extremely severe mental disorders. For all of these reasons, the elderly are unlikely to have any clear idea what outpatient therapy is and how it could be of help to them. If the therapist does not play an active role in educating the elderly client early in therapy, the client will fill in the gap with fantasies and with experiences based on visits to physicians or clergy.

Because not many therapists are trained to work with the elderly, it is also likely that the client will encounter a therapist who becomes nervous in dealing with an older client—a therapist who will be wondering, without knowing how to find out, if the client has Alzheimer's disease and who may feel that depression and even suicide are understandable responses to being old. Inasmuch as many elderly are hard of hearing and/or visually impaired, there are likely to be communication difficulties that will block the building of rapport and may strengthen the therapist's suspicion that the client is demented and could not benefit from therapy. In short, what could have developed into a therapeutic relationship that would have helped Mrs. G. to conquer her depression and establish a new life as a happier widow failed to develop at all. Mrs. G. has the added worry of the therapist's bill and a sense of being beyond help. With a little added work on the therapist's part, however, the experience could have been much different, and a successful therapy could have been started.

This book is motivated in large part by my observation that a growing number of psychotherapists are volunteering or being drafted to work with elderly patients. Because most training programs for therapists do not provide much knowledge or experience of older people, these therapists are often groping for clues to help them work with and think about older people. Those who are aware of the field of gerontology may find their time too limited to explore it in detail and are likely to find that scanning texts in the field leaves them feeling that works are too technical or too basic or are concerned largely with problems that the average psychotherapist finds irrelevant (e.g., changes in the ability to learn lists of nonsense syllables).

Gerontology is a multidisciplinary field of study to which scholars have traditionally come after completing training in one of the constituent disciplines. However, in the past 20 years or so, increasing numbers of persons have received degrees in gerontology. The constituent disciplines have included biology, medicine, nursing, psychology, social work, and sociology. In the past, services to the elderly were delivered mainly by social workers and nurses, joined in more recent years by planners in the aging network, nursing home administrators, rehabilitation and recreation therapists, paraprofessionals involved in senior centers and nutrition sites, and more recently physicians and psychologists.

The complex array of perspectives, persons, and disciplines in gerontology obviously generates a body of knowledge of considerable complexity that cannot be well summarized in a large book, much less a short chapter. However, there are within the discipline some general perspectives, trends in findings, and key sources of information that can present the therapist with very different concepts of aging and of the elderly than he or she is likely to have gotten from coming of age in our culture. It is these novel ways of thinking about aging that are discussed in this chapter.

Psychotherapy with older adults has been done, discussed, and studied for about eight decades. In general, both the case studies and the controlled research on outcomes have been positive (Knight, Kelly, & Gatz, 1992). For the most part, people who have experience doing psychotherapy with older adults have described it as valuable for clients and rewarding for the therapist, whereas those who have not worked with older adults have argued that the aged cannot benefit from psychotherapy. Since the 1970s, writing about therapy with older adults has increasingly drawn upon scientific gerontology (Knight et al., 1992).

The early history of gerontology as a discipline was characterized by a split between researchers who were discovering that aging is a more positive experience than society presumably believed and practitioners who were struggling with the problems of selected elderly and who generalized the real problems of frail older adults to all aging persons. The loss-deficit model of aging, which portrays the normative course of later life as a series of losses and the typical response as depression, has been an integral part of the practitioner heritage.

On the other side, life span psychology has brought important conceptual and methodological advances to the study of adult development and aging. Chief among these has been the insistence on using longitudinal methods to study the aging process, as opposed to the inexact but common practice of comparing older adults and younger adults at one point in time and drawing developmental conclusions from the observation of differences between young and old people. The development of mixed designs that utilize aspects of cross-sectional and longitudinal methods has brought greater sophistication to the study of adult development and has called attention to two competing influences that are often confused with aging: cohort differences, which are the ways that successive generational groups differ from one another, and time effects, which can be related to social influences that affect everyone at about the same time or which can be specific to changes in the research study itself. In my own work on psychotherapy with older adults, I have attempted to bridge this gap between science and practice. In part, this attempt was motivated by my puzzlement over the discrepancy between the loss-deficit model followed by most practitioners prior to 1980 and the emerging view of life span developmental psychology of the 1970s, which focused on normal aging and was more positive. In recent years, this has led to my proposal of a contextual, cohort-based, maturity/specific challenge model (see Knight, 1992, 1993, much of which is repeated and expanded in this chapter; see Table 1.1). In this model, older adults are seen as more mature than younger ones in certain important ways but also are recognized to be facing some of the hardest challenges that life presents to adults, including adjusting to chronic illness and disability as well as frequent grieving for others. The special social context of older adults and the fact that they are members of earlier born cohorts raised in different sociocultural circumstances may require adaptations that are not dictated by the developmental processes of aging. In what follows, maturation is discussed first, followed by cohort differences and contextual factors as important potential sources of difference in working with older adults in therapy. Finally, specific challenges that are not unique to later life but are more commonly experienced in old age are introduced.

Maturity

COGNITIVE CHANGES WITH AGING

Slowing

The most pervasive cognitive change with developmental aging is the slowing that occurs in all cognitive tasks in which speed of response is a factor (Botwinick, 1984; Salthouse, 1985). Although reaction time can be speeded up in older adults by practice, exercise, and other interventions, the age difference is seldom completely eliminated. In a thorough review of this literature, Salthouse (1985) argued convincingly that the probable locus of slowing is in the central nervous system.

TABLE 1.1 The Maturity/Specific Challenge Model

Elements of Maturity	Specific Challenges	Cohort Effects	Contexts
Cognitive complexity	Chronic	Cognitive abilities	Age-segregated
Postformal reasoning	illnesses	Education	communities
Emotional complexity	Disabilities	Word usage	Aging services
Androgyny	Preparation	Values	agencies
Expertise	for dying	Normative life	Senior recreation
Areas of competency	Grieving for	paths	sites
Multiple family	loved ones	Social-historical	Medical settings
experiences		life experience	Long-term care
Accumulated			Age-based law and
interpersonal skills			regulations

Intelligence

Intelligence can be divided up in a number of ways. A useful two-factor distinction was proposed by Cattell and elaborated by Horn (see Labouvie-Vief, 1985, for a review). In the study of aging, fluid intelligence, which is usually measured by tasks that involve a speeded or timed component, shows clear evidence of change with developmental aging. Inferential reasoning (for example, as assessed by questions that ask what comes next in a series), is part of fluid intelligence in this sense. Crystallized intelligence, which is usually measured by the types of tasks most often associated with intelligence in adults, such as using a general fund of information or vocabulary or arithmetic skills, shows little change as a result of the aging process until age 75 or later (Schaie, 1983). Changes after 75 have been less frequently studied and are very difficult to untangle from changes that could be signs of the early stages of Alzheimer's disease or other dementing illnesses.

Rybash, Hoyer, and Roodin (1986) advanced some intriguing notions about the course of cognitive development across the adult life span. Drawing on the information-processing "mind as computer" metaphor, they argued that increased experience can be seen as operating like an "expert system" program. With the accumulation of experience, older adults have a considerable store of knowledge about how things are and how things work, especially in their individual area of expertise, informed by work experience and family experiences. In these expert domains, the more mature may tend to outperform the young. In contrast, the excess speed and energy of the young may be helpful in processing large amounts of new information without the aid of an expert system. In a somewhat related vein, Salthouse (1985) speculated that slowing with age could be due to older adults' having developed a machine language (the internal control language of the "mind as computer") that handles abstract material better and faster but at the cost of slowing down in the lower-level tasks typically measured in reaction-time experiments (e.g., speed of hitting a lever after hearing a tone).

Rybash et al. (1986) also argued for the existence of a postformal stage of cognitive development for more mature adults. Beyond the abstract thinking, deductive ability, and symbol manipulation of the formal stage, the postformal stage would include dialectical thinking, an appreciation of the truth of ideas depending on context or point of view, and the ability to perceive that two opposing viewpoints may each have elements of truth in them. They acknowledge evidence that many adults have not reached the formal stage and that both formal and postformal stages seem to be confounded with level of education. The notion is intriguing and consistent with clinical observation of greater complexity of thinking in older clients.

Learning and Memory

Memory is perhaps the most difficult topic in the study of cognitive changes in late life. In sharp contrast to the methodological sophistication of studies of intellectual change in aging, most memory studies are cross-sectional and so compare older adults with younger adults at one point in time, confounding aging effects and cohort differences. Longitudinal studies with the Wechsler Memory Scale show little developmental change in memory when health is statistically controlled (Siegler, 1983). In a more recent longitudinal study, Zelinski, Gilewski, and Schaie (1993) showed no evidence of age effects on longitudinal change in memory if reasoning (an aspect of fluid intelligence) was statistically controlled. Reisberg, Shulman, Ferris, de Leon, and Geibel (1983) identified older adults with memory problems and followed them over time. They reported that most older adults with memory changes, even changes that interfere with complex work or social activities, do not develop progressive memory loss. Although there are clearly increasing numbers of dementing older adults with each decade of life, the nature of the benign memory changes in normal aging is far less clear. The problem is methodologically challenging and has important implications for our understanding of normal aging and our ability to estimate the prevalence of disorders such as Alzheimer's disease in very late life. In general, what is known about memory now would suggest that even differences between current younger and older adults in memory performance are not large when the material is meaningful and relevant to the older adult and the older adult is motivated to learn (Botwinick, 1984; Craik & Trehub, 1982; Hultsch & Dixon, 1990; Poon, 1985). In contrast, younger adults do better on novel information and learning tasks with no intrinsic meaning (learning lists of nonsense words, for example).

An intriguing problem in this area is that older adults do not spontaneously use mnemonic aids. They can be taught to do so and thereby to improve their memory performance substantially. However, they have to be reminded to use the mnemonic aids at the next session (Botwinick, 1984). If this tendency to need prompting to use newly learned strategies generalizes to the therapeutic context, it is important, even if specific to current cohorts of the elderly.

Recent evidence has converged on a consensus that working memory typically declines with age (see Light, 1990, and Salthouse, 1991, for reviews). Working memory is the limited-capacity resource through which information must be processed before being registered in long-term memory. This limitation could influence the pace and effort of new learning and also affect language comprehension (Light, 1990). This finding would suggest still more reason to slow down and use simpler phrasing when working with older clients.

PERSONALITY AND EMOTIONAL DEVELOPMENT

There is much more available research on personality development in adulthood and later life than there was 9 years ago. The work of Costa, McCrae, and associates in the Baltimore Longitudinal Study on Aging (Costa & McCrae, 1988; McCrae & Costa, 1984) using self-report measures of personality and a nomothetic model of personality measurement has supported stability of personality across the adult life span, with the greatest certainty of stability from age 30 to age 60. Their sample is mostly male and middle class to upper-middle class. The dimensions on which they find stability include introversion/extroversion, neuroticism, openness to experience, dependability, and agreeableness. These results are not trivial: They support the concept that these personality dimensions are stable across years and even decades and that personality traits stay roughly the same through much of adulthood and into at least the early part of old age. Costa and McCrae also argued, on the basis of their data, against the concept that older adults become more hypochondriacal (1985) and against a normative midlife crisis. This concept of stability refers to correlational stability. Mean-level changes do occur, although Costa and McCrae (1988) did not consider them large enough to be of importance.

The Oakland Guidance Study of both men and women from age 7 to about age 60 used a very different methodology that included interviewer ratings rather than self-report and an active model of personality that led to the description of the relative salience of dimensions within the individual rather than the person's ranking in the group on predetermined scales (Haan, Millsap, & Hartka, 1987). They found stability for cognitive commitment, dependability, and outgoingness, dimensions that are conceptually similar to openness to experience, dependability, and introversion-extroversion in the studies by Costa and McCrae. They found the self-confident/victimized dimension (similar to neuroticism) to be stable across the adult years for men but not for women. In general, they found women to be more flexible than men in organization of personality across the life span. They concluded that despite considerable stability across many transitions, the organization of personality in late life was very different than that in childhood. They found childhood to early adolescence to be the most stable period of life, followed by considerable flux and reorganization in adolescence and early adulthood, followed by moderate stability in adulthood (the period for which Costa and colleagues have data). The transition into later life is quite stable for men but marked by considerable reorganization of personality for women.

These two research programs show remarkable convergence of the traits found to be stable in men, and the Oakland studies provide a rare report of empirical data on personality development in women. Field and Millsap (1991), in a follow-up on the Oakland/Berkeley studies, reported declines in energy level and a tendency to become somewhat more introverted as people aged into their 80s. Satisfaction (the inverse of neuroticism) remained stable, and agreeableness increased in the 70s and then remained stable. More guidance in what to expect of people as they develop past the age of 60 is clearly needed. Of interest to therapists, we also know that despite objective stability in personality, people report believing that they have changed and grown (Bengtson, Reedy, & Gorden, 1985; Woodruff & Birren, 1972).

Another intriguing discussion in the study of personality development is the question of changes in gender role and stereotypical gender-based attitudes across the life span. David Gutmann (1987), using projective testing in several cultures, has long argued that men and women cross over in later life, with women becoming more self-assertive and independent while men become more nurturing and caring. In a masterful review of the literature on self-concepts, Bengtson et al. (1985) concluded that findings were dependent on the method used to study the question: Objective personality measures tended to show more gender-stereotypical patterns in earlier cohorts, whereas self-concept measures (e.g., the Bem Androgyny Scale) showed more androgyny in the older respondents. These authors also noted that age-graded social roles and cohort effects were probable reasons for the reported differences and were very difficult to disentangle. There is, for example, some reason to believe that gender-based stereotyping in self-concept is strongest during the child-raising years and that androgyny may be more common both before and after these years. In work with older adults, one should keep an open mind about the possibility of naturally occurring change in long-held behaviors and beliefs about gender-related issues. In fact, contrary to the popular image of older adults as holding fast to traditional gender roles and values, there may well be a tendency for men to become more interested in children and relationships and for women to become more interested in self-assertion, politics, and career.

Emotional changes over the adult life span are a topic of considerable importance for psychotherapists working with older adults. Gynther (1979), in a review of MMPI research with older adults, noted that older adults are lower on scales associated with anger, impulsiveness, and confusion and argued that we may become less impulsive with maturity. At the psychobiological level, Woodruff (1985) concluded that older adults are more difficult to arouse but also have more difficulty returning to a state of calm once aroused. This finding might suggest a different time line for anxiety and anger in older adults than in younger ones. Schulz (1982) argued that the accumulation of experience leads to more complex and less extreme emotional experiences in later life. Each new experience reminds older adults of previous experiences that may have a mix of negative and positive emotional connotations, whereas earlier in life it is possible to have simpler and more intense reactions with little or no prior experience to moderate reactions to new events (falling in love) or losses (a friend's moving away).

Labouvie-Vief, DeVoe, and Bulka (1989) proposed a developmental model for the development of understanding and controlling the emotions. According to this model, one moves from a very simple physical reaction and naming of feelings in early adolescence to an integrated physical and emotional experience in midlife that is combined with an appreciation of situational determinants of the emotion and the reactions of others. Malatesta and Izard (1984), reporting on the study of facial expression of emotions, discussed evidence that older people's expressions convey elements of several feelings at once. As a cautionary note to younger adults working with the elderly, Malatesta and Izard also reported that younger people are much less accurate in identifying emotion in pictures of older faces. Taken as a whole, this body of work argues that emotionality in older adults is more complex and subtle than that of younger adults.

SUMMARY: EVIDENCE OF INCREASING MATURITY THROUGH ADULTHOOD

In a now-classic discussion of personality across the life span, Neugarten (1977) suggested that with age there is an increase in interiority, or a tendency to turn inward and to become more reflective, psychologically oriented, and philosophical about life. This change would, of course, make older adults more suited for psychotherapy.

Although speed of processing and other components of fluid intelligence decline with age, crystallized intelligence probably remains stable. Cognitive maturation throughout adulthood and into later life may also be characterized by the development of expert systems, dependent on the individual's experiences in adult life (Rybash et al., 1986) and by movement to a stage of postformal reasoning, with an appreciation of the dialectical nature of argument and social change and a greater appreciation that people hold differing points of view (Rybash et al., 1986).

On the emotional side, older adults have been seen as becoming less impulsive and driven by anxiety (Gynther, 1979) and more emotionally complex, with more complex reactions to events (Schulz, 1982) and with more complex experience of and ability to control emotional states (Labouvie-Vief et al., 1989). De Rivera (1984) argued for the development of a greater range of emotions and greater experience of the transformation of emotions as a likely outcome of increased experience throughout life.

Increased androgyny (Bengtson et al., 1985; Gutmann, 1987) can also be seen as increased psychological maturity. As one moves into the second half of life, behavior and social skills can become less constricted by sex-role stereotypes and therefore more fully human. At least in the context of heterosexual relationships, men and women learn skills and behaviors from one another over a period of decades.

The mechanism for such improvement can be as simple (and as complex) as the accumulation of life experiences, which can be understood as an increasingly complex database of human interaction. Breytspraak (1984) summarized sociological and social psychological thought on the development of the self and noted that social comparison processes, reflected appraisals, and the role of person-environment interactions provide input for a dynamically evolving self-concept. Assuming that such input is continual throughout life implies that with increasing years there is at least the potential for greater self-knowledge and the development of a more complex self (see also Markus & Herzog, 1991; Sherman, 1991).

Approaching the same conclusion from a somewhat different theoretical position, Bowen's family systems theory (see Hall, 1981) relates the development of the differentiated self to experience with one's family context. Bowen's concept of multigenerational transmission implies a general consistency from family of origin to family of marriage. Working with older families drives home the point that all older adults have experience of several family constellations: the family of origin, the family of marriage and small children, the extended family with adult children and grandchildren, and the dispersed family of later life. If one adds the knowledge gained of the spouse's family and the families of the spouses of the client's children, every older person can be something of an expert on family dynamics.

In summary, these trends in gerontological thinking suggest a potential for continual growth toward maturity throughout the adult life span. In this sense, *maturity* means increasing cognitive complexity, possibly including postformal reasoning; development of expertise in areas of experiential competence, including work, family, and relationships; androgyny, at least in the sense of acquiring role competencies and interests stereotypically associated with the opposite gender; and greater emotional complexity, with better comprehension and control of emotional reactions.

Cohort Differences

As described above, another dimension of our understanding of older adults from life span development is the separation of the effects of maturation from the effects of cohort membership. Much of social gerontology could be summarized as the discovery that many of the differences between the old and the young that society has attributed to the aging process are due, in fact, to cohort effects. Cohort differences are explained by membership in a birth-year-defined group that is socialized into certain abilities, beliefs, attitudes, and personality dimensions that will stay stable as that cohort ages and that distinguish it from those born earlier and later. For example, later born cohorts in 20th-century America have more years of formal schooling than earlier born groups.

Cohort differences in intellectual skills have also been identified. In general, Schaie's Seattle study shows that later born cohorts tend to be superior in reasoning ability. On the other hand, some earlier born cohorts (people who are now older) are superior in arithmetic ability and verbal fluency (Schaie, 1990). These findings illustrate the important point that the absence of developmental change does not necessarily mean that older people as they exist today are not different from today's younger people. They also show that some differences between cohorts favor the older cohort.

In studies of learning and memory, one aspect of the familiarity of materials to be learned is the discovery that older adults learn word lists better when the lists are made of "old words" (e.g., *fedora*) as opposed to "new words." This finding demonstrates that word usage changes over time and suggests that therapists need to consider using appropriate word choices when communicating with older adults (Barrett & Wright, 1981).

Costa and his associates found cohort effects in personality: For example, later born cohorts are less restrained and higher in dominance than persons born earlier in this century (Costa, McCrae, & Arenberg, 1983). In general, their results suggest that observed personality differences between young people and older adults are more likely to be cohort differences than differences due to aging as a developmental process.

With regard to changes in life satisfaction, Costa et al. (1987), using a very large national sample, found evidence that average levels of life satisfaction stay stable with aging and across cohorts but that earlier born cohorts tend to express both less positive and less negative affect.

In other domains, social change that occurs before or during our childhood years may be taken for granted, whereas that which occurs during our adult years will be truly experienced as change. These cohort differences are the reasons that older people seem "old-fashioned."

Cohort differences, though not developmental, are real. Working with older adults involves learning something of the folkways of members of earlier born cohorts, just as working with adolescents or young adults demands staying current in their folkways and worldview. During times of rapid social and technological change (e.g., the 20th century), cohort effects may overwhelm advantages of developmental maturation. Preparation to do therapy with older people has to include learning what it was like to grow up before we were born.

Understanding *aging* is about understanding maturation; working with *old people* is about understanding people who matured in a different era. Perhaps one of the most undeveloped aspects of understanding psychotherapy with older adults, the task of comprehending psychologically significant cohort effects is not essentially different in quality or difficulty from the task of learning to work with clients from other cultures or from the other gender.

The Social Context of Older Adults

Another complication for understanding older adults in psychotherapy is the need to understand the distinctive social milieu of older adults in the United States of the late 20th century. This context includes specific environments (age-segregated housing, age-segregated social and recreational centers, the aging services network, age-segregated long-term care, and so on), as well as specific rules for older adults (Medicare regulations, Older Americans' Act regulations, conservatorship law, and so forth). The network of aging services is yet another element of this context. An understanding of this social context that is based on both knowledge of what is supposed to be and experience of actual operations is important to the understanding of what older people say about their experiences in these settings. A danger of selective exposure of professionals to these environments for older adults is that many people who are expert about a given context (e.g., skilled nursing facilities) imagine that they are expert about older adults in general.

This type of work requires some knowledge of the social world of the elderly. Such knowledge does not have to be extraordinarily extensive but does need to go beyond the commonly believed but entirely false assumptions of many younger adults. The assumption that living in an age-segregated environment will lead to increased friendships is something that only a naive outsider to that world can believe. Many age-segregated environments are very intolerant of frailty and of social deviance of any sort (see Frankfather, 1977).

Each senior recreation center and meal site tends to have its own particular social ecology. Recommending that clients go to such places to find activity or friendship is risky if you do not know the particular range of activity or the degree of openness to newcomers at that site. In one locale where I worked, sites ranged from one that attracted retired professionals with a wide range of activities to one that served mostly former state hospital patients and had an environment similar to the day room in a chronic ward. An important part of initial rapport building has often been showing that I understand and agree with the client's perception of why finding appropriate activity or help has been so difficult.

Although this understanding is not terribly difficult to acquire, the lack of it among psychotherapists working with a general population may be one reason that older adults can seem difficult to understand. The formal network of health and social services for older adults and the formal distinctions between different levels can be learned in a lecture or two. Some informal visiting at such places can do a great deal toward providing a more experiential framework for understanding the environments of the elderly. These environments are unfamiliar territory for most younger adults.

We acquire some experience of school, work, military, sports, and family settings through our own lives, and this forms a background for understanding what other clients tell us. The settings of the elderly (senior recreation centers, retirement hotels, hospitals, nursing homes, doctors' offices, senior meal sites, volunteer programs, mobile home parks) are unfamiliar ground for most adults, including psychotherapists. Unfortunately, we often seem to confuse this unfamiliarity with the settings of older adults with an inability to understand older adults themselves. When older adults tell us strange things about the settings in which they live, we should perhaps be more ready to trust our psychotherapeutic skills in understanding others and in working within the client's point of view.

The Specificity of Challenges in Late Life

Practitioners working with older adults may well be thinking at this juncture that the view of aging presented here is overly optimistic. Our outline of evidence for increasing maturation has intentionally focused on normal development through the life span. Many elderly clients seeking help in therapy are struggling with problems that threaten psychological homeostasis at any point in the life span: chronic illness, disability, and the death of loved ones. These problems are not unique to late life but are more likely in the latter third of life. In addition, late life is not immune to the usual vicissitudes of all of life: disappointment in love, arguments with family members, and failing at the tasks we set ourselves. Finally, many people who have struggled with depression, anxiety, substance abuse, or psychosis all of their lives eventually become older adults who continue to struggle with these problems. The specific nature of these problems is important to the practice of psychotherapy with individual older persons. Just as the deficit side of the loss-deficit model ignores evidence for maturation, the perception that generic losses are normative in late life fails to do justice to the specific nature of the losses incurred. Clinical experience suggests that it matters whether what is lost is one's spouse, one's vision, or the use of one's legs. Recognizing the specificity of loss and reconceptualizing losses as challenges implies that some losses can be overcome through rehabilitation counseling, as well as adjusted to through grief counseling. Turning from a loss-deficit model to a maturity/specific challenge model also helps us to recognize when depression is not normative for a given life experience. For example, depression following retirement may be seen in this model as atypical (because many older adults enjoy freedom from the demands of work) and therefore in need of careful therapeutic assessment.

CHRONIC ILLNESS AND DISABILITY

Continued work with older adults and the writing of the case histories volume that is a companion volume to this one (Knight, 1992) have made it clear to me that working with emotionally distressed older adults very often means working with older adults who are chronically ill and/or physically disabled and who are struggling to adjust to these problems. In setting out to do psychological work with older adults, I found myself learning about chronic illnesses and their psychological impact, pain control, adherence to medical treatment, rehabilitation strategies, and assessment of behavioral signs of medication reactions. This work has taken me into hospitals, nursing homes, cardiac rehabilitation programs, and emergency rooms and to the bedside of many severely disabled older adults.

In doing this work, I have become acquainted with physicians and nurses and have learned how to talk to and with them. I have learned much about the limitations of medicine and about the demands that patients place on doctors. I have learned to think about hospitals and other medical settings as organizational systems inhabited by human beings but operating within distinctive social rules. I have come to appreciate my own expertise better by observing that many people with medical training are as uncomfortable with emotionality, psychosis, and suicidal threats as I am with blood, physical symptoms, and medical emergencies.

This aspect of working with older adults involves more specialized knowledge and specialized skills than other areas of psychotherapeutic practice, in which physical problems and the physical dimension of the person can be more safely ignored. The increased proportion of chronic illness and disability with each decade of life and the increased correlation of the physical and the psychological in later life make it impossible to function without the ability to discuss physical problems and to understand when a problem may have physical causes. This principle does not mean that every psychotherapist working with the elderly must be a physician. It does mean that we must be able to talk intelligently and cooperatively with physicians and with older clients who need to discuss the very real physical problems that they face.

The specific challenges part of this model differs from the loss-deficit model in that the loss-deficit model argued that the work of therapy with the elderly is adjustment to the natural losses of late life and grieving for them. This model is wrong on two counts. First, there is nothing especially natural about blindness or heart disease or cancer. The fact that they happen more frequently to older adults does not make these diseases and disabilities part of normal development. It certainly does not make the individual older person experience these problems as normal or as less of a crisis than they would be for a younger adult. Second, the loss-deficit model fails to suggest the next step of optimizing functioning. Rehabilitation may start by accepting the deficit in functioning, but it does not end there. The next step is to consider how life may be improved. The goal may not necessarily be a return to premorbid levels of functioning and mood, but there is always room for improvement over the initial level of mood and functioning. Issues in working with clients who have chronic illness or disability are covered in much more detail in Chapter 7.

GRIEF

In a similar manner, working with older adults in outpatient therapy often involves grief work. Although loved ones die throughout our lives, the experience is more common in later life. Older adults seeking help for depression frequently have experienced the deaths of several loved ones in the preceding months or years. Much of psychotherapy with older adults is grief work.

As was true for chronic illness and disability, older adults do not seem to experience grief as a normal and expectable part of later life. Losing a löved one, even a loved one who has been ill for some time, is often experienced as surprising and tragic. The loss may be experienced more deeply because of the length of the relationship.

Unlike the loss-deficit model, the maturity/specific challenge model goes beyond emotional grief work and the acceptance of loss to explore the question of what the remainder of the grieving client's life will be like. Grief work is not only about accepting loss but about finding a new way of living without the deceased in one's life. More detail about grief work with older clients is presented in Chapter 6.

In brief, the specific challenges part of this model recognizes the gravity of the problems faced by older adults. It emphasizes the specificity of the problems and assumes that problems in later life can be overcome. In fact, one of its implications is that work with older adults facing a specific problem should draw on the available knowledge about helping all adults with similar problems. Therapy with older adults should not become so specialized that techniques and concepts developed for other clients are not readily generalized to older adults and that techniques and concepts developed in gerontological counseling are not tried with younger adults as appropriate.

Summary

The contextual, cohort-based, maturity/specific challenge model portrays older adults in a complex light that draws upon scientific gerontology. The process of maturation is seen as making older adults more mature in some ways and as producing mild deficits in other cognitive processes. Cohort differences and the specially created social context in which many older adults live invite us to understand older adults in a specific context that changes as new cohorts become old and as the social environment of older adults changes over time in response to social, economic, and political influences. Finally, some of the problems faced by older adults are encountered more frequently in later life and have come to be identified with old age. Although the problems require specific expertise, they should not be overidentified with the age of the client: Younger adults have chronic illness, disabilities, and grief as well. In the next chapter, the discussion turns to the question of whether psychotherapy needs to be adapted when working with older clients. The four elements of the maturity/specific challenge model are used to structure that discussion as well.

2

Adaptations of Psychotherapy
for Older Adults

Discussions of psychotherapy with the elderly traditionally began with a discussion of the pessimism of therapists about working with older people. This pessimism was generally traced to Freud (1905/1953) and the psychoanalytic assumption that older people (over 50 years of age) had character structures that were too rigid to permit much change. Therapists were frequently accused of being prejudiced against or afraid of elderly people. Therapist prejudice was often seen as a major barrier to older people's receiving psychotherapy. These discussions generally concluded with some admonition that therapists ought to be more optimistic or at least less pessimistic about work with elderly patients.

A Basis for Optimism About
Psychotherapy With Older Clients

However, the uniformity of therapists' pessimism about older clients can be questioned even within the analytic tradition. Rather early on, Karl Abraham (1919/1953) argued for a more optimistic view of therapy with older clients, and Rechtschaffen (1959) cited several others who contributed to a more positive outlook. In other related traditions, bias against older clients has been even less prominent. Carl Jung (1933) discussed a positive developmental role for the second half of life within his theory of therapy. Erik Erikson (1963, 1968) also wrote of developmental tasks for the middle-aged and the older adult. As therapy has developed from psychoanalytic to psychodynamic and on to integrative orientations, assumptions of the importance of early childhood development and the lack of plasticity of early character structure have become less prominent. Therapy systems have tended to become more oriented toward understanding the person as she or he is now, toward setting and achieving relatively short-term and specific goals, and toward including an understanding of the social context within which the individual is embedded. In many ways, the evolution of therapy mirrors the changes that have been proposed for older adults (see Rechtschaffen, 1959). In short, the presumed pervasive pessimism about therapy has not ever been universally supported by therapists, and changes in therapeutic theory and practice have tended to make therapy more compatible with older clients. Moreover, there are numerous personal accounts from therapists of several schools describing successes in working with older clients (Knight et al., 1992; Rechtschaffen, 1959), as well as evaluative work on various kinds of therapeutic programs (Scogin & McElreath, 1994; Smyer & Gatz, 1983).

Behavior therapy, coming from a different tradition of the experimental study of learning and behavior change, has received increasing attention within the study of therapy with the elderly. By its very nature, behavior therapy is committed to a spirit of optimism about the possibility for change in older people. Behavior therapy conceptualizes behavior and the change of behavior in terms of environmental variables and the perception of the environment (see Carstensen & Edelstein, 1987; Hussian & Davis, 1985; Patterson et al., 1982; Teri & Lewinsohn, 1983; Wisocki, 1991). If one knows that the principles and techniques of learning theory work with cats, dogs, white mice, and goldfish, it is natural to assume that they also work with older adults, even frail or disabled ones (see Fisher & Carstensen, 1990, and Teri & Gallagher-Thompson, 1991, for reviews of behavioral approaches to working with demented older adults). Both psychotherapy and behavior therapy provide theory and practice that support a positive attitude toward work with the elderly.

More recently, controlled research studies have been completed that confirm the effectiveness of psychotherapy for depression in later life.

Recent meta-analyses show roughly equivalent effect sizes for psychological interventions (mean d = .78; Scogin & McElreath, 1994) and antidepressant medications (mean d = .57; Schneider, 1994) in the treatment of depression in older adults. Individual psychoeducational interventions and respite care have been found effective in reducing distress among family caregivers of dementia patients (mean d's of .58 and .63 respectively; Knight, Lutzky, & Macofsky-Urban, 1993). The studies that directly compare psychological interventions with medications have found psychological interventions to be equally effective or more effective on the basis of client self-reported mood and have found clients to be more likely to drop out of drug treatment (Beutler et al., 1987; Sloane, Staples, & Schneider, 1985). Psychotherapy does not have troublesome side effects that can produce unwanted changes in mood, cognition, and physical health in older adults. The effectiveness of mental health services with the elderly population has been established.

Do Therapists Avoid
Working With the Elderly?

If the notion that psychotherapy is ineffective with older adults is unfounded, what about the commonly held view that therapists are prejudiced against older adults and avoid working with them? My own research about therapist pessimism and prejudice suggested that the role of therapists' negative attitudes toward the aged in keeping the elderly out of therapy has been exaggerated and that at least in publicly supported mental health clinics the role of administrative policy is a much more important determinant (Knight, 1986a, 1986b). Changes in Medicare policy in the late 1980s provided confirmation of the view that Medicare reimbursement policy is a major determinant of the willingness of mental health providers to work with older adults (Gatz & Smyer, 1992; Knight & Kaskie, 1995).

Although there is clearly considerable variance in therapists' attitudes toward older people, which may affect other aspects of therapy, reluctance to initiate therapy with the elderly may have more to do with reimbursement policies and the fact that very few psychotherapists have any training background in working with older people (Gatz & Pearson, 1988). My impression from consulting with other therapists and from doing in-service training and continuing education is that reluctance to work with the aged comes more from perceived lack of expertise and anxiety when confronted with an elderly client than from ageist prejudice per se. The role of therapists' anxiety in affecting their work with the elderly is discussed in Chapter 4 as a countertransference problem.

Other important aspects of therapy that may be affected by therapists' pessimism and stereotypical thinking about the elderly include the assignment of a diagnosis and the therapist's expectation for the client's improvement. Dye (1978), Settin (1982), and Perlick and Atkins (1984), in separate studies of therapists, provided convincing evidence that age in itself influences diagnosis. The latter two studies used vignettes in which only the age of the client was varied and found that identical symptom descriptions were given a more severe diagnosis (organic brain syndrome or psychosis versus depression) when the client was older. Conceivably, other aspects of therapist behavior and various therapy process variables are also affected by therapists' attitudes. Although attitudes do not seem to play an important role in the exclusion of elderly clients from therapy, prejudices about older clients may significantly affect the quality of therapy.

Adapting Psychotherapy
for Work With Older Clients

As we have seen, several decades of clinical experience and a number of controlled research studies provide a basis for therapeutic optimism, and therapists do not all harbor some dark hatred of the old. Presumably there is a basis for moving beyond the question of whether therapy is possible with the aged to a consideration of whether therapy needs to be adapted for the aged. Drawing on the previous chapter's discussion of general findings in gerontology, the following discussion explores the changes that need to be made in therapy to maximize success with older clients. Adaptation might be required by developmental changes that take place during adulthood, cohort effects, or the special social circumstances of older adults. Each of these three sources of change carries different implications for the nature and scope of adaptation in therapy with older adults. The specific challenges of later life form a fourth basis for adaptation of therapy, one that is problem specific rather than client specific. These problem-oriented issues are elaborated in Chapters 6 and 7.

Developmental changes would affect all older adults and be relatively consistent over time. If most adaptations were due to development, then therapy with older adults might be different from therapy with younger adults, as therapy with children is. Changes due to cohort effects would differ with each cohort and would require that adaptations in therapy be constantly revised as each cohort became old. Adaptations based on cohort differences would imply that skills specific to work with a given cohort would remain useful with that cohort as it aged. However, therapy might have to adapt itself to new cohorts as they became adults, as well as be adapted to work with cohorts who missed the early development of therapy: the currently old. Adaptations due to the social circumstances of the elderly would be specific to those elderly who were defined by specific social circumstances: the retired, the widowed, those living in segregated housing, those living in institutions, and so on. These adaptations would need to respond to change in the social definition and context of the elderly.

MATURATIONAL ADAPTATIONS

In Chapter 1, the overview of gerontology suggested that some consistent developmental changes occurring with aging are the slowing of cognitive processing, changes in cognitive abilities and in memory performance, changes in emotional complexity, and the opportunity to have developed expertise in relationships. Much of maturation in adulthood is characterized by stability or positive change, with negative changes often being small, not important for socially significant functioning, and compensated for by use of other intact abilities. In addition, adult developmental change is far from consistent either across individuals or in any one individual's various characteristics. The potential impact of each of the consistently observed factors on the practice of psychotherapy is considered in the following discussion.

Slowing

The slowing of cognitive processes that occurs with normal aging, which is increased with many chronic diseases, can become a noticeable influence on communication between older and younger adults. As noted in Chapter 1, the smaller capacity of working memory in later life is likely to have a similar impact on processing conversation and written materials. It is especially noticeable if the younger professional is feeling rushed or tends to be mildly hypomanic, or if the older person has the additional slowing that comes with depression, hypertension, or other disorders with psychomotor slowing as a symptom. In any case, the recommendation is clear: If there appears to be some uncertainty in communication, the younger therapist should relax and slow down the pace of the conversation. Although this sounds easy and obvious, observation of younger people talking with older people suggests that the natural reaction to miscommunication is to become nervous and speak even faster. In the midst of a busy day, slowing down may require conscious effort, some deep breathing to relax, and some mental counting between the end of the therapist's sentence and the beginning of the client's response.

The impact of slowing in therapy is that the conversational flow of each session is usually slower than with younger adults, in both the pacing of sentences and the latency between therapist speech and client speech. Speaking quickly often leads to communication inaccuracy and the need to repeat. The therapist working with older clients will need to be more aware of pacing within sessions and may need to resist actively any internal tendency to speak quickly in response to time pressure, anxiety, or excitement.

If slowing were not compensated for in other ways, one would expect that therapeutic progress as a whole would be slower with older adults in terms of number of sessions required to reach therapeutic goals. To date, there are no systematic evaluations of length of therapy with older clients. Informal clinical reports describe all possible outcomes: that older people take more time, the same time, or less time to reach therapy goals. In the absence of systematic evaluations, it is not possible to say for certain whether these differences are due to the clients, the therapists, or the techniques used. My clinical experience has been that though individual sessions may "feel" slower, the course of therapy in number of sessions has not been different for the younger old. One study of therapist-rated change suggested that the old-old needed more sessions to achieve gains than the young-old (Knight, 1988).

Memory

As noted in Chapter 1, memory changes with normal aging (in the absence of diseases that impair memory functioning) seem to occur more in spontaneous performance than in capacity. Performance changes would, of course, also be of importance to the therapist. However, research is again reassuring in that memory for meaningful and well-organized material does not seem to decline and in some studies is superior to the memory of college students for similar meaningful and organized material (see Craik & Trehub, 1982).

The changes in the capacity of working memory in later life (Light, 1990) may also require some modification of communication style in the therapy setting. Working memory is the active processing capacity of memory, the number of things that can be actively held in memory and worked on at one time. This limited-capacity store may be slightly smaller in later life. If so, it may account for changes in comprehension of speech and in problem-solving abilities. Both of these changes could be compensated for by slowing the pace of speech, simplifying sentence structure, and presenting problems in smaller pieces. These changes may be important for cohort-based reasons as well. The therapist who tends to use a lot of jargon and make longer and complex interpretations will need to modify this style when working with older adults, especially the old-old.

There are, of course, also older people who suffer from memory-impairing diseases. In many cases, these individuals will be living in the community and may not be fully aware of their memory loss. There are also many older people who worry and complain about memory loss in the absence of objective memory impairment. These two facts make it essential that the therapist be able to assess memory loss accurately or be able to refer the individual to someone who can. This topic is explored further in Chapter 5.

Fluid Versus Crystallized Intelligence

To the extent that therapy mostly draws upon well-learned information about oneself and the world, there is not likely to be any effect of developmental aging on the therapeutic process. The tasks associated with fluid intelligence often have a timed component or involve visually mediated processing. Reasoning is usually associated with fluid intelligence. If reasoning declines with aging, the decline may have some impact on therapy. The required changes are likely to be similar to those that one might make working with less educated adults: That is, one may have to use more concrete examples and do more of the inferential work oneself rather than relying on the client to think through the implications of abstract interpretations. Taken together, the changes in speed of processing, working memory, and reasoning suggest that therapists may need to slow the pace of learning of new material in therapy and be prepared for repetition of new points. As is always true in psychotherapy, these changes are individualized and represent working at the client's level of ability. Therapists who have experience working with clients from a wide range of educational and intellectual backgrounds may not perceive the adaptations made with older adults as different from adaptations made between other types of clients.

Expertise and Greater Cognitive Complexity

The development of expertise through life experience will, in general, be an asset when working with older adults. Older clients often have expertise that is relevant to the problem that was brought to therapy. Their accumulated knowledge of people and relationships can be brought to bear on current relationship problems. Tapping into this expertise can be an adaptation for the therapist in a couple of ways. First, therapists working with younger adults may be more used to encouraging people to explore themselves to discover as yet untapped strengths. Switching to helping people recall and use already existing strengths is not more difficult but is different. Second, working with clients who have more experience and expertise than oneself is also a change of perspective for the therapist. It can be quite exciting for therapists who are open to learning from clients. It may be anxiety arousing for therapists who are uncertain of their own abilities.

When older adults do exhibit greater cognitive complexity and postformal reasoning, these attributes are likely to be helpful in therapy. An ability to appreciate the ebb and flow of change in life, to take the other person's viewpoint, and to appreciate differences in perspective based on cultural, religious, or family differences are all beneficial to the work of therapy. As with expertise, it can be unsettling to work with clients who may have more of these abilities than the therapist. There are times in working with older adults when they explain to you how they resolved a problem or when they explain their understanding of an interpersonal event to you because it is outside your comprehension. For example, my own understanding of how parents negotiate adult-to-adult relationships with grown children while still retaining the vivid memories of this individual as a child and a deeply felt sense of needing to protect him or her comes from clients who have explained it to me. In a similar way, much of what I understand about the differences between having a child and having a grandchild is derived from therapeutic conversations with older clients.

Emotional Changes in Later Life

As noted in the previous chapter, emotionality is thought to be more complex and probably less intense in later life. In general, my experience has been that sessions with older clients involve less expression of emotions than sessions with younger adults. Older people are less inclined to cry (especially to sob), to shout in anger, or to bounce up and down for joy. They often describe complex mixes of emotional reactions to the events of their lives. An argument between an older client and her middle-aged daughter may be described as arousing a mixture of anger, sadness, guilt, and pride; the same incident in a younger client may well be associated with only one of these emotions.

With regard to the expression of these complex emotions in older faces, I have not personally had much problem in reading emotional expressions in older clients' faces, but I grew up around older people and may have learned this skill without trying. I have noticed that some of the therapists I have consulted with or trained do not perceive an older client to be sad or angry when I feel that it is clearly expressed in their nonverbal behavior. Obviously, one needs to be able to recognize what clients are feeling, often before they do. It is also important to be ready for the potentially complex array of reactions to an event and not to accept clients' first affective description as the complete version of how they feel.

Personality Change and Stability
Across Adulthood and Into Old Age

Correlational stability of the Five Factors of Personality is well established into later life, especially for men. That is, people will keep the same rank in the population on extroversion, agreeableness, openness to experience, dependability, and neuroticism at least into the young-old period and probably later. The Oakland study suggests that women may experience a transition and some reorganization of personality at the end of middle age and the beginning of the young-old period. Mean-level changes may accumulate enough to become significant; this is still controversial. There is nothing in this picture of personality development to suggest that therapy will be more difficult in later life. If the androgyny concept holds up, it may suggest that older men will be more open to therapy than younger men (see Brody & Semel, 1993).

Many psychodynamic therapists have assumed that there is a natural increase in dependency in people as they enter old age—a return to a second childhood. Clinical reports by persons working with the aged vary. Some (e.g., Hammer, 1972) report more dependency than for younger clients. On the other hand, Rosenthal (1959) wrote of clients using age to excuse neurotic behavior and supposed dependency as a manipulative style. It seems likely that any increased dependency is the result of prolonged frailty rather than of developmental aging in the form of a "second childhood" and that the varied reports are the results of the all-too-common failure to consider whether certain attributes of older clients are the result of age or illness. Increased dependency is a common reaction to being ill at any age.

In a classic review of personality development in the later years, Neugarten (1977) concluded that there is an increase in interiority in old age. Interiority is an intrapsychic tendency to become more introspective and more concerned with the meaning of one's life. Interiority is not related to social interaction or other activity level and thus is distinct from introversion, which is stable. Increased interiority ought to make the therapist's job easier in that introspection and a search for meaning in one's life are important ingredients in psychotherapy. This change may account for the greater openness of elderly clients to interpretation remarked on by Rechtschaffen (1959), which I have experienced in therapy as a generally lower level of resistance to therapeutic work. Increased interiority may offset the within-session slowness noted above and account for equivalent lengths of therapy between young and old clients.

ADAPTATIONS THAT ARE COHORT BASED

As discussed in the previous chapter, there are many sources of differences between younger and older adults that are due to cohort dissimilarities rather than to developmental changes. These differences include variations across cohorts in cognitive abilities, educational levels, word usage preferences, normative life trajectories, and the sociohistorical context within which the individual's life story unfolds. These differences hold implications for the adaptation of therapy with older clients, who in this context are better described as *earlier born clients*. This phrasing emphasizes that it is the era into which one is born, rather than one's current position in the life cycle, that is the basis of the adaptation.

Older clients may have differing cognitive capabilities as a function of cohort. Not all of these differences favor the later born cohorts, although some do. These differences suggest that earlier born cohorts are likely to be disadvantaged on spatial abilities and on reasoning (e.g., see Schaie,

1990). These differences could require changes in the use of visual imagery in therapy and require more of the "thinking through" of therapy to be done by the therapist.

The lower levels of education in earlier cohorts will suggest less reliance on abstraction, less complex terminology, and less ability to assume that the client will share a psychological worldview. Older adults may require simpler language to describe therapeutic processes and more explanation of the nature of therapy. These changes would be similar to changes used when doing therapy with clients of lower socioeconomic status (Goldstein, 1973; Lorion, 1978). The focus on cohort differences and on education as the causes of these changes reminds us that more highly educated cohorts will be getting older in the near future and that not all older clients require this adaptation, but only the ones who have less education.

Word usage changes across cohort can be more subtle and introduce a need to be aware of differences in the meaning of words that is similar to the attention given to word use in work with clients who are from a different cultural background but who are fluent in English. That is, client and therapist use the same language but do not always mean the same things. Early in my career, I was emphasizing the use of the word *dementia* over the word *senility*. Many older clients clearly had a negative reaction to the term that I preferred. When I questioned what was being understood, I learned that in their younger days *dementia* was used to signify what we would now call psychosis. I find that older female clients resist using the word *anger* and that it is better strategy to use their words (often terms such as *irritated* or *frustrated*) than to insist that they use my words.

Life patterns change across cohorts and then (sometimes) change back. Knowing what is normative for a client depends a great deal on understanding these cohort differences. Therapists working with older clients may overinterpret a late age for first marriage if they are unaware that many people postponed marriage in the 1930s. In the early 1940s couples often married after what by 1990s standards would be a very brief acquaintanceship. On the other hand, a late marriage or a choice not to marry may be an important cue to as yet unrevealed life history information if the client matured earlier or later in the 20th century. The later born therapist can miss such cues by interpreting a 1920s (or 1940s) young adult life by 1990s standards.

Values about life events change from cohort to cohort. One client questioned whether her group therapists from two different later born cohorts would understand the impact that her parents' divorce and being the child of divorce had on her, because we had been raised in a time when divorce was more common statistically and more accepted socially. We were able to assure her that we were alert to the differences. (Because both of us had divorced parents and one of us was raising a child after a divorce, it was not always easy to hear her views on how awful divorce was.) One of the more consistent and dramatic changes I have noted is that clients who married in the early part of the 20th century do not have the same expectation for happiness in marriage that those of us born in later cohorts have. They evaluate relationships quite differently and without expectations of personal fulfillment or personal happiness. It is not that they expect to be unhappy; they simply do not evaluate marriage in terms of happiness.

To understand the client's life history, it is helpful to be able to place him or her in the flow of historical time. That is, to some extent, working with earlier born clients implies a need to understand in outline the history of the 20th century and especially the events that often have great personal or familial significance: World War I, World War II, the Great Depression, the waves of immigration from Europe in the 1920s, the Jazz Age, the ebb and flow of progressive and conservative politics and moral thinking, and so on. In understanding clients, I find myself constantly doing mental arithmetic to construct a sense of the client's life cycle and how it fits into historical time. That is, I transform statements about "I changed jobs 12 years after I married" into "That means he was 34 then, so it was 1944. Why wasn't he in military service during World War II?" The life course paradigm in sociological conceptions of aging describes this process as using "multiple time clocks" to track where the individual is in the life cycle and to place him or her in the flow of historical time (as well as within the changing roles of the family context over time; see Bengtson & Allen, 1993).

These latter changes may be some of the more significant changes confronting the therapist working with clients who are earlier born and whose lives are shaped by events that the therapist does not recall from personal experience. It implies some need to have an understanding of history, not always common among psychotherapists. Much of what one needs to know can be learned from the client, especially because the real issue in all cases is what the client understood the impact of these historical events to be. The questions must be asked, however, and I often find that younger therapists do not want to ask such questions for fear of displaying ignorance or of calling attention to the age difference between them and the older client. On the whole, I find that clients appreciate being asked such questions and feel more clearly understood when they explain events of which they know the therapist is ignorant.

Cohort differences provide one basis for thinking of older adults as a "special population." As mentioned earlier, older adults present problems similar to those of clients who are fluent in English but raised in a different culture: Not only are the same words used in different ways, but the client's experiences are rooted in a social context with which we are not familiar and may be influenced by values that are not similar to our own. The same answers apply: sensitivity to cues that words are used in different ways, awareness of not sharing a similar background, and willingness to use one's ignorance constructively to learn from the client about the client's experience. In work with earlier born cohorts, the client is from a different time rather than a different place.

ADAPTATIONS BASED ON THE
SOCIAL CONTEXT OF OLDER ADULTS

To the extent that older clients inhabit the specific social world of older adults in American society (and not all older people do), they must be understood in relation to the external social environment. This concept, and especially interventions derived from it, has its roots in social learning theory, which emphasizes the interrelatedness of person and environment and the need to understand both to plan appropriate interventions (Bandura, 1977; Rotter, 1954). In this sense, the "older American" is created by social policy and by stereotypical thinking of others in our society. Older people are usually retired and therefore living on a fixed income. Their health care decisions are dictated by Medicare regulations. They often (although not as often as is thought) live in age-segregated areas. The men are mainly married, the women are mainly alone; the discrepancy creates pressures on both men and women in later life. Stereotypical thinking about aging means that many older people find their relationships with others, including other older people, conditioned by such misconceptions as "All older people get Alzheimer's disease," "All elderly people are isolated and lonely," "Older people are (or ought to be) asexual," or "Older people are 'greedy geezers.' "

Therapists have three interests in the subculture of the elderly. One is to understand the various ways in which our society makes life difficult for the elderly and so creates some of the emotional problems that the therapist is trying to ameliorate. Without some exploration of the subculture and our formal and informal social policy, the therapist will often be perplexed as to when the client is being realistic about being insulted or discriminated against and when there is some psychologically important level of suspiciousness indicating anxiety or paranoia. The second interest is that the therapist needs to understand the social context in which the client lives to be able to understand the client and work effectively with him or her. The social ecology of the organizations in which older adults live, seek health care, spend leisure time, and so on affects the individual's self-concept and shapes options for behavior. The third interest, to which we return in a later section of this chapter, is the need to understand the social context well enough to be of active assistance to the older client when this is needed.

Residential Settings
as Examples of Contexts

One large component of the elderly's lifestyle is the various residential settings in which older people live. In addition to the physical character of these settings and their stated goals, there is virtually always a specific social ecology of that setting that must be understood so as to comprehend the client accurately and know whether the source of the problem is in the client or in the residential setting itself. Research on psychological interventions in nursing homes has often emphasized the way in which nursing homes as organizations create excess dependency in residents and deprive them of control over day-to-day decisions (e.g., Baltes & Reisenzein, 1986; Rodin, 1986; Schulz & Hanusa, 1978). Interventions that provide more independence or more control often have effects on cognitive functioning and mortality as well as emotional state. These effects may be reversed if interventions are discontinued (see Schulz & Hanusa, 1978). An important aspect of these interventions is that it is the environment that is analyzed and modified rather than the elderly resident. The locus of the problems of later life is often the social context rather than the older adult.

In another type of residence, life in segregated housing for independent, well elderly also has special characteristics. This category includes apartment dwellers, residents of mobile home parks, and residents of single-family dwellings where these types of housing happen to be age segregated. Segregated settings bring together people who have nothing in common but age (and the age range may be 30 years or more) in a fairly intimate setting. There is often little privacy, in that neighbors watch everyone who come and goes. On the other hand, there is also often very little socializing.

In one consultation experience, we discovered that large numbers of residents in a senior citizens' apartment building were quite lonely, especially in the evening. The building was enclosed and security locked, so there was no danger in residents' visiting one another at any hour of day or night. But there was no visiting, nor was there really any interest in promoting it. Many residents simply did not like one another or were fearful of having too many demands put upon them if they developed friendships within the building. At first the consultants were surprised and perplexed, but further reflection and discussion with residents brought forth two factors that took the phenomenon out of the realm of "Isn't it odd that the elderly are like this?" One factor was the realization that in our area, socializing with neighbors, especially neighbors in apartment buildings, was not done by people of any age. The second factor was the realization (pointed out by one of the residents) that most of the people in the building had never lived in an apartment before or been in such close contact with people with whom there was no family relationship. These cohorts had always lived in detached housing units with family members and had become apartment dwellers only in later life. What socializing was done was mostly with people from outside the building. For the therapist working with older people, it is important to realize that complaints of loneliness and isolation in congregate housing may be quite normal, that asking clients to initiate friendships with apartment neighbors may be quite unrealistic, and that recommending that seniors move into age-segregated buildings so as to be less socially isolated (not an uncommon recommendation among novices working with the elderly) may not be wise.

Residential settings are only one of many special characteristics of the older adult lifestyle. Programs funded by the Older Americans' Act and other social programs for senior citizens have created a variety of social settings with special characteristics, including congregate meal sites, senior recreation centers, senior volunteer programs, and various advisory and advocacy councils. For many seniors, doctors' waiting rooms, hospital emergency rooms, and other health care settings also function as major social outlets. Those readers who have tried to make social chitchat with a busy physician can understand the likelihood of frustration for both doctor and patient. For the therapist to function effectively and to understand what clients are talking about, some exposure to each of these settings is very useful. Preferably, visits should take place when the therapist (or therapist in training) can be somewhat out of the professional role and more of a "participant observer" in the anthropological sense.

Active Assistance for the Older Client

As noted earlier, the third reason to acquire knowledge of the context of the older client is to understand the network of aging services well enough to provide active assistance when necessary. Most discussions of psychotherapy with the elderly emphasize—and correctly so—the complex nature of the problems faced by elderly persons and the need for intervention in nonpsychological areas of their lives (e.g., Knight, 1989; Sherman, 1981; Zarit, 1980). Depending on the particular focus of the author, there is discussion of the need to do casework for older clients, the need to work within a biopsychosocial model, or the need to take a more interdisciplinary focus. As noted throughout this book, biological-medical and social problems may be more prominent for older clients than for younger ones. It is not clear, however, that the need to be concerned with the whole person is unique to working with older clients. The need to combine casework and psychotherapy has often been advocated for other clients who may present with complex needs, including children, minorities, and lower-SES clients.

The term *casework services,* which can be used to refer to a wide variety of activities, is used here to refer to two types of activities on the part of the therapist working with older clients. One is providing accurate information on available services for problems the client has that do not fall within the scope of the problems that therapy is likely to resolve; the other is actually providing or setting up services for the client.

Referrals. In providing information about services to clients, the emphasis must be on accurate information. Service systems for the aging are often complex, with various rules about eligibility, and not infrequently are misleading to some degree about what services are provided. For example, transportation services for the elderly usually advertise that they are available for any type of transport services the elder needs to remain in independent living. In practice, there are often limitations about where they will go (geography), what kind of trips they will make (medical visits only), and what days specific services are available. It clearly does a client no good to be told to call a transport service to be able to go to the store to buy groceries and then to discover that he or she lives in the wrong area to get service. Caution must also be exercised in that some services provide different information to professionals than to clients.

Each community will have a somewhat different network of services. Important services to look for in any local context are as follows:

1. Physicians who are knowledgeable about and comfortable with the elderly
2. Various types of residences available to older adults, including independent living, assisted living, residential care, and skilled nursing facilities
3. Specialized services for dementing elderly
4. Congregate meal sites and home-delivered meal programs
5. Senior recreation centers
6. Day care centers for the elderly
7. Income assistance programs
8. Transportation services
9. Hospital-based programs
10. Legal services, including regulations and agencies that cover guardianship of dependent adults or elderly
11. Home health services
12. Emergency services that provide monetary loans or food or that pay utility bills in bad weather
13. Elder abuse laws and hot lines

To get a start on locating supportive services, the local Area Agency on Aging, the aging service section of public social services, ombudsman programs, adult protective services, self-help groups, and hospital discharge planners are good initial sources. Remember that both public and private resources must be considered.

At times the decision to refer is quite clear-cut. The client needs a given service that is available, and providing the information is the easiest way to resolve the issue. In other cases, there is a judgment to be made about whether clients would do better to resolve the problem on their own. In one instance, a client who was quite delusional and disorganized in her thinking was facing eviction from an apartment where the rent had been raised beyond her fixed retirement income. As therapy proceeded, there was an active attempt to secure a placement in public housing. This was not an easy task, as the supply was far smaller than the demand. While the

housing bureaucracy was being dealt with, the client recovered sufficiently to implement her own plan: the recruitment of three roommates to
share expenses. The arrangement lasted for 2 years.

The outcome of the preceding example points to a potential conflict
between the values of psychotherapy and those of case management.
Therapy is generally oriented toward increasing client independence and
having clients do things for themselves and solve problems for themselves. Casework is often about solving problems for people by providing
concrete service solutions. As the preceding example indicated, it is not
always easy to know when an impaired client can still solve a problem
independently. The other end of this conflict is illustrated by considering
whether it makes more sense to pursue therapy with clients who are so
depressed that they have not eaten well in weeks or to refer them immediately to home-delivered meal services and to start therapy after a few
days of good meals.

The Therapist as Caseworker. The second major type of caseworker
activity arises when clients need more than referral. The referral may
have to be made on their behalf, eligibility forms may have to filled out,
and one may need to argue with other agencies about whether someone
who is, or seems to be, mentally ill deserves that agency's services.
Clients may need rides to doctors or other services, repairs for eye-
glasses, or a variety of other practical services. As before, the therapist
needs to question whether someone else could do them and whether an
appropriate referral source exists. Also, the effect on the therapeutic
relationship needs to be assessed: Will dependency be increased in a
nonhelpful way? Finally, one must ask what the client needs and what
the least costly solution to the problem is. There may not be anyone else
to do the job, or it may take 10 times as much time and effort to make
the referral as to do the task.

A major difficulty that becomes most obvious in the context of doing
things for clients is the need to keep the therapeutic relationship and the
nature of therapy clear in the minds of both client and therapist. With the
client, it is generally easy to be clear that certain activities are unusual for
the therapist and not part of the therapy but are not a problem given the
circumstances. With repeated requests, the therapist needs to explore the
meaning of the request and the client's view of the therapist in the same
manner as one would explore repeated questions about the therapist's
marital status. Some requests will, of course, need to be refused with
explanation and possibly with suggested alternatives. There are situations

in which refusals are in themselves therapeutic affirmations of the client's ability and worth as a person.

Lela

Lela was seen for the first time after discharge from the psychiatric unit of a local hospital. She had a long history of paranoid psychosis but had managed to stay in the community and work for 25 years. More recently, she had suffered several strokes that had impaired her speech and her ability to walk so that she spoke slowly and unclearly and walked slowly with great effort. She had become upset with her psychiatrist and refused to see him again. She was also refusing to see her physician despite having a large ulcerous sore on one leg. The home health agency involved with her was very distressed over this noncompliance and over the condition of her apartment. The apartment was cluttered and unclean and smelled from a seldom-emptied cat box.

Gradually, a trusting relationship was built up, and Lela consented to regular visits. She responded well to having someone to communicate with and appreciated the therapist's patience with slow communication, part of which often involved her writing out answers when the therapist could not understand her speech.

Two casework type problems arose very early. The first involved requests from the home health agency that Lela "be placed" in a more healthy environment. The therapist explained the agency's concern to Lela and respected her desire to remain in the apartment. He then explained to the home health agency that under local laws, Lela would stay where she was until she decided to move. Over a period of weeks, the health agency eased up their pressure on her to move. Not surprisingly, this casework intervention helped to build rapport with Lela.

The second intervention involved her need for coverage under Medicaid for health visits. Part of her noncompliance was due to the cost of care. Contact with the eligibility worker revealed that she had been denied in the past but was probably eligible now. However, she had a reputation for being dangerous, based mainly on verbal threats and angry outbursts when being asked personal questions during eligibility interviews. After some discussion, the therapist was cleared to take the application himself and did so.

After a few months of visits, and with the external pressure removed, Lela decided on her own that she needed to live in a retirement home. Arrangements were made for the move, and the question arose between the therapist and a social service caseworker as to who would help her move. The therapist felt that this level of personal interaction would destroy the somewhat formal nature of the therapeutic relationship that was essential to maintaining Lela's trust and comfort with the therapist. The caseworker felt that because the therapist had started the process of moving Lela, he should pitch in with the "dirty work." The impasse was resolved by Lela, who, when asked how she was going to move her belongings to the rest home, slowly wrote out the name of a local moving company that she had contacted on her own. Once again, the resourcefulness of the frail older client had been underestimated.

In the new setting, Lela's paranoia continued to improve. A few weeks later, she agreed to resume her psychotropic medication and returned to her usual level of functioning for the next 2 years.

One potential problem in referring psychotherapy clients is violation of confidentiality. There are several ways to avoid having to break confidentiality. One is to give the referral to the client and have the client make calls. When the client cannot make the calls, having an involved family member or friend make the contact is another possible solution. When it seems advisable for the therapist to take action, the client can be made aware of whatever risks there might be, and consent can be obtained. A useful protection for one's clients is to develop an identity as someone who makes referrals of elders in trouble who may or may not be clients in therapy. In several years of practice, I have found that I am usually more worried about breaking confidentiality than the client is; however, I have also observed pervasive disregard of the rights of older clients to preserve confidentiality and to refuse service. These issues are far more complex when the client is becoming demented (see Grisso, 1994); this discussion has assumed that the older adult is cognitively intact.

A greater problem is often the impact of these activities on the therapist's sense of identity and worth. When these activities are not a usual part of the therapist's role, some therapists feel diminished or insulted by taking part in such "menial" tasks. One must be cautious, however, about investing too much of one's self-esteem in what is not done rather than in what is done. The more common problem in work with elderly clients is that therapists become seduced into doing too much for the elderly and cease doing therapy in favor of doing casework only. The complex needs of the elderly seem to exaggerate therapists' conflicts about the value of psychotherapeutic work and to elicit feelings of therapeutic impotence. Either or both of these feelings can find expression in abandoning real therapy in favor of doing things for older people.

Summary:
A Framework for Optimism

To review, we have considered and rejected the presumed pessimism about the therapeutic work with older adults. The discussion of possible adaptations of therapy with the elderly has considered the following three possible perspectives on why modification might be needed:

1. The developmental perspective suggests that modification could be needed because of developmental changes in the adult as he or she ages. The conclusion so far is that such changes primarily mean a possible need to slow down the therapeutic conversation.

2. Cohort differences point to differences between groups born at different times. There is a need to comprehend the historical background and the values of the generational groups that are now older and to be aware that these differences are specific to persons of a given cohort. Future generations of elders will, of course, be different from the current ones.

3. The contextual view points to differences due to socially created and modifiable differences in lifestyle between the young and the old. These differences are specific to those elderly who are in given social contexts: who are retired, live in segregated environments, become senior advocates, and so forth.

The discussion of these sources of change has laid the groundwork for arguing that the major adaptations to therapy with the elderly will arise from cohort effects and social context effects rather than from developmental changes. This perspective makes the therapist's task in approaching work with the older client easier in that comprehending persons of different backgrounds is easier than comprehending stages of life that one has not yet experienced. It also brings the work of understanding the elderly within the range of familiar skills: Most therapists have had exposure to different cohorts and to persons of different social backgrounds. In addition, reflection on therapeutic experience suggests positive characteristics of older clients that may make them very well suited to the work of therapy: the broader range of experience that older people bring to therapy, their richer psychological histories, and the opportunities to experiment that are characteristic of the postretirement lifestyle.

Perhaps the most obvious thing that can be said about the potential for change in older adults is that older adults have lived longer than younger ones. This fact implies a broader range of experience and more time to have learned about oneself and others. Whether the implications are negative or positive for the therapeutic process depends in large part on one's model of the nature of the life cycle and what experience does to or for human beings. The more traditional, largely pessimistic view has been that adult development and increased experience make people rigid and set in their ways. Some clinicians working with the elderly have felt that the effect is quite the reverse: that growth and experience teach adults to be more flexible, less dogmatic, and more aware that there are different ways of looking at life. This may not be continuous change through the life span; it is quite possible that many middle-aged adults may become rigid for a time as they find themselves in relatively powerful positions, but besieged from all sides by parents and children at home and by bosses and underlings at work.

A closely related reason for optimism about therapeutic change with the elderly is that older adults have a much richer psychological history with which to work. Although there is seldom time to work through all of it, exploration of any given theme in life can produce multiple examples that provide the therapist with much richer data to build a conceptualization of the person's approach to that special aspect of her or his life. If, for example, the client is concerned about some quality of the relationships in her or his life, the older client can relate the rich experience of a lifetime of diverse relationships with friends, lovers, spouse(s), children, coworkers in various job settings, grandchildren, and others. If the issue has been of concern for some time, then there are probably examples of many different ways that the client has approached the problem in the past, with various patterns of success and failure. The therapeutic challenge is to be able to absorb as much information as possible and to interpret and reinterpret the data of the client's life in new and helpful ways that are relevant to current issues.

Therapy involves more than simply understanding oneself and learning new ways of looking at things. Once the understanding is reached, there is usually a need to do some things differently. For making these changes, some of the very factors that are traditionally considered losses in old age remove significant barriers to change. When a younger adult reaches a new understanding in therapy and wants to follow up with changes in life outside the therapy room, there is often considerable pressure to remain the same from coworkers, spouse, and family. In addition to actual pressure from others, the energy drain of working, raising a family, and so on may seriously reduce the ability to devote time and energy to making the change. The postretirement older adult with more leisure time and relatively little involvement in stable and stabilizing social environments such as work and family is in an excellent position to explore various alternative ways of acting and being. Virtually any change that clients desire to make can be experimented with in the context of the options open with enhanced leisure time and decreased social pressure.

This spirit of optimism about the possibility for change in late life runs counter to much of both common folk wisdom about aging and clinical lore about older adults. It is, however, based on an understanding of aging gathered from gerontological knowledge and clinical experience with a large number of older adults in various community settings. In the absence of ill health, not only is there no block to normal therapeutic work with the elderly, but positive factors can make working with the elderly a very rewarding experience for the therapist.

Having introduced some basic concepts of gerontology so as to stimulate a new perspective on aging and on older people, and having described the broad context for adapting therapy to working with older people, we turn to a consideration of the work of therapy. One task of the initial interview is to begin building a therapeutic rapport with the client. Inasmuch as older people find it difficult to seek out therapy and may be less prepared for the work of therapy, special strategies are needed to help the older client feel comfortable in therapy. These strategies are the topic for the next chapter.

3

Building Rapport
With the Older Client

Up to this point, the discussion has focused on the therapist's side of the encounter between therapist and older client. Basic findings from gerontology have been described, and some general adaptations of therapy to work with older adults have been explored. As our story in Chapter 1 of the encounter between Dr. Q and Mrs. G. illustrates, the older client may come into therapy with more inaccurate expectations about the nature of therapy than younger adult clients may have. In fact, these misperceptions may be major barriers to the elderly seeking therapy or establishing a relationship with the therapist. This chapter will present and discuss the need to educate older people to identify psychological problems, the need to educate the potential older client about the process of therapy, and some applications of gerontological concepts to building rapport with the older client.

The Decision to Seek Therapy

Gurin, Veroff, and Feld (1960) described a three-stage process that people go through before seeing a professional psychotherapist (see

Figure 3.1). The first stage identifies the problem as psychological rather than physical (e.g., "I am anxious in stressful situations" versus "My heart beats fast at times") or moral ("I am depressed in response to major stressors" rather than "I am too weak to handle life on my own"). Some people do not classify the problem at all but simply try not to think about it. In the Gurin et al. study, this stage of the decision process was the stage affected by age: That is, older people were less likely than younger adults to label problems as psychological. The second stage is deciding to seek help. Having defined a problem as psychological, many people decide to work it out themselves or to wait for the problem to go away. The third stage is the decision to seek professional psychological help. Having decided to seek help, many people will go to a physician, pastoral counseling, a self-help group, or a self-help book rather than see a psychotherapist. To reiterate, the first decision was the one that age affected in the Gurin et al. study: Having decided that a problem was psychological in nature, the old were as likely as younger adults to seek help and to seek professional psychological help.

In general, more recent research has tended to confirm that older adults are not so much reluctant to use mental health services as unable to identify problems as psychological or simply unaware that appropriate mental health services exist (Lasoki & Thelen, 1987; Powers & Powers, 1991; Waxman, Carner, & Klein, 1984). Evidence from a follow-up of the Gurin et al. (1960) study by Veroff, Kulka, and Douvan (1981) suggested that the underutilization is likely to be a cohort phenomenon rather than an age effect. This view was also supported by Koenig, George, and Schneider (1994).

The implication is that a major task of mental health professionals working with the elderly is to educate them to identify correctly problems that are psychological in nature. Education can take place in the community, by addressing groups of elderly people on mental health-related subjects, and also in therapy. Unlike younger adults who often come to therapy with a problem clearly defined in their minds as psychological, many elderly may be brought for help with the problem still largely conceptualized as physical or moral. Some examples of this difference in perspective were discussed in the previous chapter as requiring adaptations in the therapist's approach to certain phases of therapy. Here the issue is addressed as a potential barrier to older people establishing contact with a therapist.

For the client in the therapy room, the educational process is one of explaining the diagnosis and the therapeutic rationale in a step-by-step

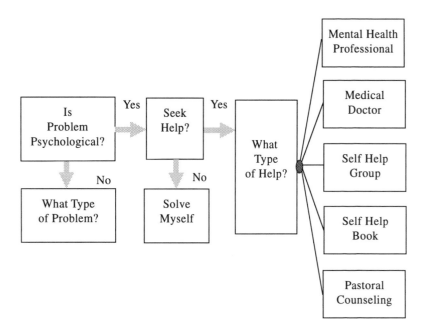

Figure 3.1. Process of Deciding Whether to See a Professional Psychologist

manner. The client may come in complaining of sleeping problems, weight loss, a very low energy level, irritability with friends, loss of interest in pastimes that have been pleasurable for decades, chest pains, and concerns about not being able to concentrate. The therapist will probably see the chest pains as needing to be checked out by the client's physician and the other complaints as signs of depression. (Assessment is covered in Chapter 5.) The therapist will also have some theory-based notion of the appropriate way to conduct therapy for depression and may be inclined to launch immediately into that treatment strategy. For many elderly, however, it will be necessary to describe which group of symptoms is due to depression, how depression begins and is maintained, and how the proposed treatment is expected to eliminate the depression, as the dialogue below illustrates:

Therapist: [toward the end of the first session] I think you're depressed.
Client: Well, I've been kind of sad the last few months, but does that explain being tired and not wanting to see my daughter?

Therapist: Yes, being tired or fatigued is a common sign of depression. So is not sleeping well and not eating, and the chances are good that not being able to follow the plot of the TV shows that you watch is due to not being able to concentrate, which also goes with being depressed. I do want you to have those chest pains checked out.

Client: I saw my doctor about that. She says it's nerves. So you think all of this is depression?

Therapist: Yes, you've been through a lot this year, and it would be normal to feel depressed about it. All of the things you've told me fit with depression. I think some therapy could be of help to you. [Here the therapist explains her therapeutic approach.]

Client: You think that would help me? Right now I don't feel like anything could help.

Therapist: Well, this is what I do. I've worked with other depressed people and seen it help them. Some of your feeling that it won't help is your depression talking: Nothing looks hopeful to you now because you're depressed. And some of it is because this is new to you. It's your decision whether to give this a try, but I hope you'll try it and see what happens.

With some clients, it may be necessary to repeat the educational process at intervals throughout the therapy.

To reach greater numbers of older people and to provide one form of outreach to the elderly as a group, talks to community groups can help explain psychological interpretations of familiar problems. For these community education talks, the best strategy is to start with those aspects of mental health that are least threatening and gradually move into more psychological areas. One may begin with talks on sleeping problems, getting along with neighbors, coping with stress, or communicating with family (see Knight, 1989, for more detail). As the presenter becomes more familiar to the group being taught and the group becomes more comfortable discussing these topics, the discussion can move naturally and easily to topics such as depression, memory disorders, anxiety, and what talking therapies can offer older people. It is usually good to point out that you do not believe that all older people have these problems and that you are interested in helping the ones who do to remain independent. There are still older adults who equate mental health services with inpatient hospitalization for long periods of time.

Educating Clients About Therapy

The concept that clients need to be educated about psychotherapy was first developed in the early 1960s with the spread of the community mental health movement, which made psychotherapy available to low-income people for the first time on a wide scale. It became obvious that these new groups of clients had ideas about what therapy was like that were different from those of the therapists who saw them; many of them dropped out of therapy after a session or two, and many of the ones who remained did not act like "good clients." Orne and Wender (1968) developed an antici-patory socialization for therapy model. Their assumption was that all therapy patients need some training to be clients but that some get their training implicitly in their environment. Middle-class clients were likely to have read books, taken classes, or known someone who had talked to them about their therapy. For working-class and lower-income people, the social milieu was unlikely to include much information about therapy, so the therapist was encouraged to educate the potential client actively about the therapeutic process. These efforts have been quite successful with prepa-ration of low-income clients for therapy (see Garfield, 1978, for a review).

The same strategy can be adopted for preparing older clients for therapy. As pointed out in connection with the example of Mrs. G., older people are also generally naive about therapy and tend to think of mental health in terms of inpatient care of psychotic individuals. In my experi-ence, this is not so much an active prejudice against therapy as a simple lack of information about it. In any case, orientation to therapy by the anticipatory socialization model is very helpful in resolving incorrect expectations about the therapeutic process.

The major points to be covered are as follows:

1. You do not have to be crazy or mentally ill to benefit from therapy; therapy helps with problems in living.
2. You and your therapist will work together to set goals for your therapy.
3. Although the length of therapy depends on many individualized factors, it will usually take more than one or two visits to see any benefit. (Where possible, it is a good idea to include here some estimate of when some relief of symptoms might be expected.)
4. Talking about your problems to a trained listener can be helpful.
5. Expressing your feelings can bring relief.
6. Outpatient therapy means meeting for about an hour per week (or other schedule by local practice) to work together on your problem.

7. What is talked about here is confidential. (Describe any limitations on that confidentiality: child abuse, elder abuse, suicidal threats, threats to harm others, etc.)

8. The fees are _____. (Describe any copayment, sliding scales, limited number of sessions, etc.)

The preceding outline defines therapy as useful for the client, explains the structure of the sessions, describes some of the major premises about why therapy works, and establishes whether the client can afford it. Even if one works in a clinic setting with reduced or sliding-scale fees, it should not be assumed that the older client is aware of the reduced charge or of insurance coverages. To make certain that the client understands and to establish good rapport, the therapist needs to take responsibility for discussing the fees regardless of the setting.

The anticipatory socialization for therapy can take place in a variety of settings. Some clinics have used a separate pretherapy interview to cover these topics. In other settings, incorporating these points into the first therapy interview may be most appropriate. Other clinics have used film, audiotapes, or slide presentations to cover these points; these media may also include excerpts from therapy sessions. Regardless of the medium, the method can be used to dispel misconceptions about therapy held by potential clients. My experience has been that once therapy is explained in jargon-free language, many older people who are depressed or anxious see the value of it for themselves.

It can also be important to educate referral sources in the use of these educational points so that they can make a good referral and make it more comfortably. My impression has been that workers in the aging network are much more reluctant to discuss therapy with the elderly than the elderly are to discuss or seek therapy. In several instances, once the senior service worker became confident enough to refer an older person, that potential client was pleased, if not actually relieved, to have someone to talk to about his or her problems.

The family member as a potential referral source poses additional problems. The same strategies can be useful, but the fact that the suggestion of counseling comes from a family member puts it into the context of decades-long family relationship dynamics and makes compliance less likely. When the recommendation from a family member has been tried and has met with resistance, two strategies increase the likelihood of success. One is to continue making the referral at intervals and to view this repetition as a process that may take weeks or months to work. The other is to enlist someone outside the family who can make the referral (family physician, nurse, caseworker, family friend, etc.). In any case, it is important to be clear about the reason for the referral and why counseling would help and to use the anticipatory socialization points.

Establishing Rapport
With the Older Client

Once the client has identified a problem as psychological, has sought help or been referred, and has been oriented to the psychotherapeutic process, the therapist is still faced with the task of establishing rapport. Every school of therapy advocates putting clients at ease, understanding their point of view, and showing empathy for the client's feelings. However, therapists often express doubt about their ability to understand older clients or to be empathic with them. A review of concepts of age and aging will help to build a framework for understanding the older client in a manner that facilitates the growth of a therapeutic relationship.

DEVELOPMENTAL INFLUENCES

As was noted in the preceding chapters, the major developmental changes are slowing of cognitive processes and the reduction of working-memory capacity. These may affect within-session speed of talking and require a more paced teaching of new material with repetitions and the use of simpler language. Slowing is offset by increased interiority, openness to interpretations, and the accumulation of life experience and expertise. Clearly, the therapist will need to adjust the pace accordingly to ensure that the client feels comfortable in therapy.

The stability of adult personality into later life implies continuity with earlier life stages and so provides a basis for increased confidence on the therapist's part in his or her ability to work with and understand the older adult. However, one needs to explore the client's self-perceived development. Schaie and Parham (1976) showed that even though objective measures of personality did not change over time, people tended to change their perception of their earlier selves in a manner that supported their concept of developmental change. In their review of the literature on self-concept, Bengtson et al. (1985) noted that subjective change was consistently larger than objective change in the self. These perceived changes need to be explored as part of understanding the client. We will return to this point and explore it in more detail in the chapter on life review therapy. In this context, the emphasis is on using knowledge about normal aging to build rapport and correct the client's misperceptions about aging.

When the perceived change is part of the problem (e.g., perceived decline leading to low self-esteem and depressed mood), the perception may need to be challenged at an appropriate time in the therapy. Other notions about development simply need to be understood as a part of the client's self-concept. The following example will help to illustrate exploration of a client's concepts of personal development in the adult years.

Client: [tone is quite sad] Things just haven't been the same since I've gotten older. . . .

Therapist: Tell me about getting older. What changes have you experienced?

Client: What do you mean?

Therapist: Well, you feel differently now; are you a different person than when you were middle-aged?

Client: Things were easier then. I had more energy. I seemed to have more interest in life. Of course, there was more going on too. It's harder to make friends now. The neighbors have moved away, and the younger people that moved in all have their own lives. . . .

Therapist: Are there any positive changes, changes you feel good about?

Client: [looks puzzled, warms up as speech progresses] Well, the children always took up a lot of time, especially when they were teenagers and rebellious; it's nice to have time alone with my husband. We have more perspective on life now, more wisdom, I guess [laughs]. It's not all bad, but I do wish I felt better.

Therapist: Well, many of the changes we go through in life have both positive and negative features. As we find out what's really important to you, you may be able to make more of the positive features.

Note: The therapist is well aware that many of the developmental changes seen by the client are the result of age-graded changes in social roles and that others are likely to be due to the influence of depressed mood on her perception of her life. At this point in therapy, however, there is nothing to be gained by challenging these perspectives. The therapist challenges only the implicit assumption that all aging-related changes are negative.

Taking the greater life experience and expertise of older adults seriously helps therapists avoid the trap of assuming that older adults are being irrelevant or rambling in their conversation due to dementing illnesses. Many therapists (and other younger adults) do experience the elderly as digressive and repetitious in conversation. There are several reasons that the elderly repeat themselves. First, because many younger people assume that older adults are rambling or have nothing useful to say, older adults frequently are not listened to. Second, younger people sometimes do not really comprehend the message behind a particular story, so the older person tells it again and again. For both of these reasons, it is often appropriate to point out that one has heard the story before and to inquire politely why it is being retold. In general, the response will be an expression of pleasure that the therapist is listening enough to recognize repetition along with an explanation of the meaning of the story.

The greater number of experiences means that one event reminds the older client of another, so the point of the story may be lost in the details or may be lost in the chain of digressive memory associations themselves. When this happens, the therapist needs to use active listening skills to inquire about the principal point of the story or needs to think at a process level and abstract the common elements of the related memories so as to grasp the point. All of these techniques imply the need to interrupt the client politely and to keep therapy sessions on task; these skills are commonly used with younger clients, but it can feel socially awkward to interrupt one's elders.

Other reasons for repetition are more pathological. Anxious clients, especially obsessive-compulsive ones, are repetitious and overly detailed in conversation. Because of stereotypes of this behavior as normal for older adults, the clinical significance of it is often missed for older clients. Psychosis also leads to loose associations and long, pressured, rambling monologues. Although it should not be assumed on the basis of age alone, the existence of memory-impairing disease in older clients is quite possible and requires careful assessment and a different response. This topic is discussed later as an illness-related influence on communication with older clients.

COHORT INFLUENCES

As part of understanding the client, the therapist needs to explore the client's base of experience as a member of a particular cohort. The client's perceptions of what historical events influenced his or her life, what values were and are more important to members of that cohort than to people born earlier or later, and how such events and values are influencing current relationships with family, friends, and neighbors are rich sources of material for understanding the client's ideas about self and others. Some ability to show comprehension of events that happened before the therapist was born can be important in building rapport. Authentic appreciation of values of other cohorts is also a good method for establishing that the therapist understands what is being said. It is quite helpful to know enough history to know which major events have influenced earlier born cohorts and when they occurred (e.g., the World Wars, the Great Depression, major waves of immigration, the Jazz Age). Local history can also be very helpful in establishing rapport (e.g., knowing that a client's house was in the country when they bought it and has been absorbed by an expanding town). Some appreciation or recognition of old movies, old music, and so on can help build relationships. (I've "made points" with clients by knowing who Glenn Miller and Billie Holliday were and being able to name some of their songs.) If the events are new to the therapist and the values are not consistent with the therapist's own values, then a genuine willingness to learn and a display of comprehending the importance of these events and values to the client help to bridge the gap between cohorts.

The differences between cohorts have been most salient in understanding the elderly. However, in principle, whenever the therapist and client are of different birth-year groups, there is some intercohort understanding taking place. When the client is a young adult and the therapist is middle-aged (or vice versa), there are issues similar to those discussed here for the young therapist-older client dyad. The following example shows how a therapist can use knowledge of another cohort's life experience to build rapport and to understand the client better.

Therapist: [responding to the client's earlier statement about a child] It sounds as if you and your daughter have really different attitudes about money, saving, and planning and as if that really causes a lot of conflict between you two.

Client: Yeah, she never really learned the value of money. She never had it rough the way we did when we were kids.

Therapist: I would guess that you grew up in the Great Depression, and I know that a lot of people learned really hard lessons from that time.

Client: [surprised] You're not old enough to remember that!

Therapist: No, that's a little before my time, but I've heard about it from other clients and other older people I've talked to.

Client: Yes, we really had to work hard for everything we got, and then sometimes we did without a lot when Dad couldn't get work. I promised myself my children would never have to go through that.

Therapist: That's a normal reaction to such adversity: to want your children to have a better experience than you did. Of course, your daughter didn't have those experiences, so she probably does have different values than you.

Client: [after a pause] Yeah, she's different because I protected her and gave her so much. [laughs] I still think she's wrong, but I understand better why we disagree.

Note: The therapist is able to gain some credibility by showing an understanding that the client would not have expected. As an aside, the example also illustrates the not uncommon happening that although the therapist was born 20 years after the Depression, the client is not acutely aware of this fact.

SOCIAL CONTEXT INFLUENCES

One aspect of their social role is that many older people are not listened to and may not be allowed to speak for themselves. In many clinical interviews, an older client brought in by spouse or family is spoken for by the others. It is essential that the therapist not fall into the trap of allowing someone else to speak for a supposedly incompetent older adult but that he or she instead continue to use good listening skills and focus attention on the client. As the client becomes aware of being listened to and responded to in a normal human way, two things are likely to happen. One is a rush of warmth and rapport, which in addition to being satisfying for the therapist serves to drive home the point that the elderly are very infrequently listened to. The second is that some elders who are vague, repetitive, or digressive in their speech will "clear up" and begin speaking quite logically and coherently when doing so is rewarded by active listening.

The therapist can also use an understanding of the special social context of the older client to build an accurate picture of the client as an individual in a special social world. Where does the client live? What organized groups is she or he involved with? Is the residential setting of these social groups age integrated or age segregated? Does the client experience age prejudice as a problem in living or as a negative influence on self-esteem? How does the client feel about other older people? Although the Harris poll (1975) found that many older people saw their own experience of aging as positive, they also endorsed the same stereotypes of other old people as did younger Americans. Comprehending the social world of older people is an important part of understanding the older client. Butler's *Why Survive?* (1975) and Frankfather's *The Aged in the Community* (1977) provide excellent pictures of the social settings of older people. The next case illustration also shows the impact of a specific subgroup setting and the therapist's awareness of the importance of an older person's perceptions of other older people on the individual client's self-concept.

Therapist: What kind of place do you live in?

Client: I'm in one of those senior citizen apartment houses, the ones where HUD pays some of the rent [names the building].

Therapist: I've been over there a few times. That's a good deal for you, helps with the budget.

Client: Yeah, but I don't like it there. The people in the building aren't that friendly. There's three or four that sit in the lobby and watch everybody come and go and gossip all day. Besides, it makes me feel old to live there.

Therapist: The people in your building are quite a bit older than you are on the average. Is that part of why you feel old living there?

Client: Yes, before I moved there I lived in a neighborhood with a lot of younger couples and the groups we were involved in had a lot of different types of people in them. But this makes me feel old. . . . I mean, I am old, I guess, but the people in the building seem to have given up on life. Some of them are as old as my mother, and they're ill. Getting down to check the mail is the high point of their day. I don't want to be old like that.

Therapist: How would you like to be?

Client: More like before, I'd like to associate with younger people, people my age and younger. . . .

Therapist: You could do that, couldn't you?

Client: [thoughtfully] You know, I guess I could. It's just that the move and my husband's death took a lot out of me, and I just felt that this

was the way life is going to be now. But I could look around and find
new activities in my area, look for people with the same interests.
[Session continues.]

Age-Graded Social Roles

Much of moving through the adult life span can be described as moving
through socially defined age-graded roles. As noted by Hagestad and
Neugarten (1985), many social roles of adult life are age linked in an
approximate way, and people often have a sense of being "on time" or "off
time" in their movement through these roles. For example, career development is often roughly related to a person's age. A person may be seen
as too young to be a middle management executive or too old to be a
newsboy. Family roles such as child, parent, or grandparent are roughly
age related and change as the persons in the roles become older: That is,
one is a child as long as parents are living, but the role of the adult child
is different than that of the young child.

Retirement is an excellent example of a socially defined role that has
often been arbitrarily set at a given chronological age. Although not age
related per se, widowhood is often seen as a role that is more appropriate
to older years. Exploring which of these roles the client occupies and the
meaning of these roles for him or her is a rich source for developing an
understanding of the client. An important aspect of exploration is learning
whether clients feel they are "on time" versus late or early in experiencing
their particular stage of life. The following case shows the impact of
retirement in making a client feel "really old."

Client: I just never thought I'd get to be this old.

Therapist: How old is "this old"?

Client: Well, look at me, I'm an old man now. You don't know what that
means: You're still young.

Therapist: I don't know from personal experience, but the truth is, you're
younger than most of the clients I see. So what does being old mean
to you?

Client: I don't know. . . . I feel useless ever since I retired.

Therapist: You didn't plan for retirement, I guess.

Client: No, I saw other people retiring and I went to the talks, but I didn't
really think it would happen to me.

Therapist: Did you have other interests outside of work?

Client: No, no hobbies or anything. Even my family—I was interested, you understand, but I never had time for them. Now I have time, and they've moved away or have jobs of their own to keep them busy.

Therapist: So when you say you didn't expect to get old, you really mean you didn't expect to retire and you don't quite know what to do now that it's happened.

Client: Yeah, that's right, I have so much time on my hands, and there's nothing worthwhile to do.

Note: This session continues with further exploration of feelings about retirement and other aspects of the client's current life (e.g., life with his wife). In future sessions, the client will be guided to rediscover personal interests that have been "on hold" while he worked, and ways to make his present life more interesting, although he still grieves for the loss of his job and sense of identity that depended on that job.

ILLNESS OR DISABILITY-RELATED INFLUENCES

Older adults in general and older psychotherapy clients in particular are likely to have some degree of chronic illness or physical/sensory disability. These physical changes are not part of normal development per se, but they occur sufficiently frequently in later life that handling them well is an important element of building rapport with older clients.

Sensory loss does occur frequently in older clients and requires adaptation by the therapist. The adaptations are the same as would be necessary in dealing with a younger client with sensory loss. About 30% of older people have significant hearing loss, and 20% suffer from severely impaired vision (Butler & Lewis, 1991). For the hearing-impaired client, one must speak clearly, face the client, and give an unobstructed view of the mouth; less often, one may need to speak more loudly. When an older client does not appear to understand or gives inappropriate responses, it is always wise to vary volume or pitch or to resort to written communication to see if the difficulty is due to hearing loss. In some persons, the slowness of the progression of the hearing loss or personal vanity may prevent recognition or admission of hearing impairment. For this reason, one cannot count on the client to volunteer information about hearing loss.

Those who are aware of it are excellent sources of information on how best to maximize communication.

Visual deficits present other kinds of problems, mainly in nonverbal areas of communication, which are quite important in therapy. Visually impaired clients do not recognize you on sight, do not see nodding or shaking of heads, and miss nonverbal signs of affect. The therapist must learn to verbalize these communications to build adequate rapport.

As noted earlier in the chapter, the existence of memory-impairing disease may lead to repetition of questions and stories by the client. In this instance, one may have to repeat information or answers to questions over and over, simply because they are not remembered. Repetition requires considerable patience on the part of the speaker and may require the occasional ventilation of anger and frustration out of the client's presence. It is important not to blame the client for being memory impaired or to expect him or her to remember things. Memory-impaired clients will need simpler sentences and will need to have points covered one at a time. A calm and unhurried demeanor does much to facilitate communication with the memory-impaired person.

Comfort with physical frailty is an important component of building rapport with the frail older client. Adjusting to the slower walking pace of clients with impaired ambulation and some comfort in helping maneuver wheelchairs can be quite useful. Talking to a client who is using portable oxygen for COPD can be anxiety arousing to the novice therapist. In general, the ability to discuss physical symptoms, illnesses, treatments, relationships with physicians and support staff, and insurance problems in an open and intelligent manner is an important component of building rapport with clients for whom these are essential aspects of their day-to-day lives.

Handling physical frailty appropriately primarily requires common sense and some experience with frail people and their equipment. The process by which people become psychotherapists may tend to select for individuals who are more comfortable with thoughts and feelings than with physical symptoms and the limitations of the body. Supported experience with frail clients and exposure to hospitals, nursing homes, and clinics can help orient the psychotherapist to the realities of illness, as can open conversation with clients who are ill and disabled. Colleagues in biomedical disciplines (medicine, nursing, rehabilitation therapies) can also offer useful information and insight. As therapy progresses, one must judge when physical symptoms are an appropriate focus and when they are distractions from the real work of therapy; however, rapport building requires an active and appropriate level of interest in the client's physical illnesses and frailties.

Home Visits and Rapport Building

Some elderly clients are homebound by illness or disability, and others live in areas where public transportation is poor or nonexistent. If these clients are to receive therapy, the therapist will have to leave the office and enter the client's home. The environment of the therapeutic relationship changes when the site of that relationship is moved from the therapist's office to the client's home. The education of the client to the task of therapy becomes more important because without the usual environmental cues that therapy is a special kind of relationship with a specific purpose, the client may be likely to relate to therapist as to a visiting nurse, a pastor, or "just a friend."

In addition to direct education, the formal character of the session can be reinforced by adhering to scheduled visits and the therapeutic hour and by creating verbal markers to clearly delineate the boundary between therapeutic work and whatever social chitchat occurs in getting in and out of the client's home. For example, beginning statements can include "Let's get started with the therapy" or "Let's pick up where we stopped last week." Near the end of the hour, the therapist should note that only 10 minutes remain and inquire what else needs to be discussed in this visit. The therapist may need to initiate leave taking nonverbally (e.g., standing up, moving toward the door) and should go over the time and date of the next visit. There is also a special need to assure the client of confidentiality and to point out factors that can limit that confidentiality (the spouse sitting in the next room, a neighbor gardening near an open window, etc.). The essential process and character of psychotherapy can be maintained in the home of the client.

The notion of providing therapy in the client's home setting, or any setting other than the therapy office, arouses mixed feelings in many professional therapists. The majority of us are trained exclusively in the clinic office setting and find that leaving the office arouses anxiety. The change to the client's home takes the therapist out of his or her own office, where the sense of authority and control is relatively high, and into other environments where real or imagined control is reduced, where interruptions may be more common, and where there is more burden on the therapist to define the work of therapy, the specialness of the therapeutic hour, and the limits of the relationship. For those therapists whose professional identity is not usually associated with home visits, doing therapy in the field may also lead to a loss of felt status: That is, the therapist may feel like "only" a visiting nurse, caseworker, or door-to-door salesperson.

Although one may well wonder if it is really appropriate for any therapist to have a high need for control or social status or to have the sense that his or her therapeutic powers function in only one setting, clearly the therapist working in client's homes will have to work through these issues. If the therapist stays calm and acts in the same therapeutic manner as in the office, the therapy will proceed in essentially the same manner as in the office. In return for the extra work, the therapist will gain exposure to clients who cannot come to the office, will gain much information about the client by seeing him or her in the home setting, and will gain a different awareness of the essential nature of therapy by doing it in different settings.

The home visit situation does impose the need to be scrupulous about allotting appropriate time and not imposing visits on "clients" who are not really interested. Obviously, careful thought must be given to seeing in their own homes clients who are paranoid, histrionic, or likely to form an erotic transference. This is a statement of caution and not a recommendation to avoid home visits with these clients. Especially with paranoid clients, it may be easier to form a therapeutic relationship when the client has the security of being on home ground. With some effort, home visit therapy can be very much like office therapy and at least as effective with a population of clients that otherwise will not be reached.

Professional Competency and
the Age Difference Issue

An important issue in establishing rapport with any client is the issue of professional competence. With younger clients, the question may be settled in formal or less direct ways such as confidence in the referring person, questions about one's degree, school of study, or licensure. The older client may take a more direct approach and often a more personal one. The therapist's age or years of experience may be questioned. This can cut either way: Some will feel that the younger therapist lacks personal or professional experience; others will feel that older therapists will be out of date or biased by their personal experience of aging. The client may question whether the therapist has ever worked with someone like him or her. In all cases, there may be a greater sense of being questioned, not only about one's professional qualifications, but also about one's personal maturity. The issues raised here are generally not so much about chronological age per se as about experience in the work world, experience in marriage or child raising, experience with illness, and so on. The answers must rely on expertise in therapeutic technique, as they do in work with younger adult clients whose life experience is different from the therapist's.

Although the experience of being evaluated in this manner may be unsettling for the therapist, the value for the client is obvious. There are not many professionals who are well trained to work with the elderly, and the elderly take many steps to protect themselves as much as possible. The therapist is well advised to answer questions about skills and experience in a nondefensive way and to provide a realistic degree of hope for positive change. In general, the questioning of competence is most at issue when the therapist is uncertain of his or her competence. A confident explanation of one's professional competence generally allays concerns about personal maturity as well.

With some understanding of how to build rapport with the client and understand him or her as a person, the next question to be addressed is the more complex level of the therapeutic relationship: transference and countertransference as they appear in work with older clients.

4

Transference and Countertransference With Older Clients

Regardless of the age of the therapist, there are likely to be differences in the therapist-client relationship when the client is older. Whether or not the relationship is a primary focus of the therapeutic method, these changes will alter the context of therapy and the therapist's experience of the therapeutic work. How does the "feel" of therapeutic work change with an older client? For several decades, it has been recognized that a primary source of the felt difference in working with older clients is the changed nature of transference and countertransference when the client is older (Genevay & Katz, 1990; Rechtschaffen, 1959). The feeling that therapeutic work is impossible with particular elderly clients may also have its roots in the therapist's countertransference (Hinze, 1987; Semel, 1993).

Transference and *countertransference* are terms most often associated with and defined by the psychoanalytic school of therapy. These terms have, however, developed different meanings and have been adopted in other schools of therapy, including psychodynamic therapy (Weiner,

1975) and behavior therapy (see Goldfried & Davison, 1994). In these more general terms, transference is the development of a relationship with the therapist by the client that is not based on the reality of the therapeutic relationship or on the therapist's real characteristics as a human being. Similarly, countertransference represents the therapist's perception of a relationship with the client that is not based on the reality of the relationship or the client's actual characteristics.

Transference

There are two levels of the therapeutic relationship. The first is the professional relationship between therapist and client working together to solve the client's presenting problems. The first level is itself affected by actual social factors such as age differences, gender of therapist and client, and personality characteristics of therapist and client. It is usually safe to assume that these factors are operative in brief therapy that is problem oriented (say, 8 to 12 sessions or less). In longer term therapies (and in psychoanalysis, which deliberately creates transference of a more intense nature as the major tool of analysis), the therapist may become aware of a relationship developing that is not typical of the first level.

In the second level of the relationship, either therapist or client is bringing into the therapeutic relationship responses that were learned in the context of other relationships. When the client relates to the therapist as if to a significant other, it is generally a sign of unresolved difficulties concerning the earlier relationship, and it is likely that the older relationship script is also replayed outside the therapy room and causes problems for the client. When the therapist responds to the client as if to a family member, the same conclusions may be drawn, but the behavior is less appropriate because this is, after all, the client's therapy.

Understanding transference is much like interpreting the relationship as a projective test: The real characteristics of the relationship shape the response of transference but do not entirely determine it. In general, the less the transference resembles the first level of the relationship, the more emotionally important it is likely to be. One departure is made in the following discussion from usual understandings of transference: It is explicitly argued that with older adults the origin of the transference can come from any stage of adult life and especially from any of the family settings in which the older client has lived. More typically it is argued that transference has its roots in the family of origin setting (see

Nemiroff & Colarusso, 1985a, for a more psychoanalytic discussion of this possibility).

As therapy progresses and relationship distortions arise, the therapist must be alert to being identified with emotionally significant others, including family members and persons from the client's past. With the dearth of information available on transference with older clients, the therapist is largely on his or her own in uncharted territory. The guideposts are one's clinical understanding of the client, the real stimulus character of the situation (i.e., in general, one is more likely to be identified with a family member of similar age and sex), and gentle probing of "Who do I remind you of?" or "Have you felt this way about someone else?"

The discussion of relationship issues in psychotherapy with the elderly has had a varied history. Some of the earliest descriptions of therapy with the aged focused considerable discussion on transference as the aspect of therapy most altered in work with older clients. In a review of the literature on therapy with the aged, Rechtschaffen (1959) summarized that early literature. More recent discussions, with case examples, can be found in Myers (1984), Nemiroff and Colarusso (1985a), Genevay and Katz (1990), Knight (1992), and Semel (1993).

Examples from clinical experience can point the way to some possible forms of transference with older clients. The therapist can be identified as child, grandchild, parent, spouse at an early age, erotic object, or social authority figure. Institutional environments have special client groups and organizational characteristics that elicit special relationship distortions as well as intensifying some of the above.

THE THERAPIST AS THE CLIENT'S CHILD

Many of the early psychodynamic writers, reviewed by Rechtschaffen (1959), asserted that the transference with the older client is reversed in that the client relates to the therapist as a child and so provides an opportunity to work through relationships with one or another of the client's children.

In work with the aged, the term *child* takes on a different meaning than what is generally thought of. Depending on the age of the client, his or her children will be adult, middle-aged, or themselves older people. An early surprise in working with the older people—which resulted in reorganizing my view of the social world—came when a client of about 76 started explaining that some of her marital problems were due to her relationship with her mother, who lived nearby and took up much of her time. When one is working with the elderly, being seen as a child does not imply being immature. In fact, often the client's children will be as old as or older than the therapist. The child transference is more likely to arise between a middle-aged therapist and an older client or between an older therapist and an even older client. The particulars of the transference are unique to the specific parent-child relationship with which the client is working. A common theme, given our society, is a concern with whether the child will be there to help when help is needed or whether the therapist-as-child will take charge of the client without good cause. Often there are unresolved conflicts dating back to the child's struggle for independence as a teenager or young adult.

The power issue between parent and child can be resolved in many ways: with either party the winner, with a forced draw, or with mutual acceptance of one another as independent but friendly human beings. Given that the therapist recognizes the child transference, exploration of relationships with the client's children and interpretation of the transference in the usual manner can be of great benefit to the client.

Case Example. One client in her 60s was preoccupied with fear of increased dependency as she aged. At one point toward the middle of therapy, she questioned me several times about whether I had plans to take another job. At first, I responded on a straightforward level, as I had been out of town for conferences. With the repetition, I transferred the question to the transference level. First, I identified the principal concern: "You're worried that I won't be here when you really need me." After exploration of that issue, we moved to "Is there someone else in your life who may not be there when needed?" The answer, of course, was her adult son. Therapy shifted to consideration of their relationship as sometimes mirrored in our own. Toward the end of therapy, I discovered that she had also misperceived my age, thinking I was her son's age. (He was about 20 years older.)

THERAPIST AS GRANDCHILD

Given that at present many therapists are considerably younger than their clients, a frequent transference is to perceive the therapist as a grandchild. Because grandparent-grandchild relationships have only recently been studied, some references on the social psychology of grandparenting are included for further reading (Bengtson & Robertson, 1985; Troll, 1980). Much of our thinking about grandparenting is guided by social mythology, but in understanding and using the transference, the important thing is to understand the client's own thinking about his or her own grandchildren. Clinical experience suggests that frequently the grandchild is somewhat idealized, that the power struggle of the parent-child relationship is absent, and that often a fairly honest communication about emotional issues exists. There is also a habit of discussing the shared middle generation (parent for one and child for the other) in a candid, ally-to-ally manner. The elderly client may have less trouble accepting the expertise of a grandchild than of a child and show less resistance to the therapeutic interpretation. There are, of course, negative transferences in which the grandchild is perceived as emotionally distant, threateningly different, or competing for the middle generation's time and love. Working through a negative grandchild transference can relieve negative affect about family conflicts.

Case Example.　One client, although attending sessions regularly and generally showing progress, kept making negative comments about my youthfulness and (mostly incorrect) attributions about what I would like or understand because I belonged to a younger generation. I gently challenged some of these perceptions (e.g., "Why wouldn't I like classical music?") and moved into a discussion of why she believed these things about all young people. Once she had begun to question her stereotypes, I switched to consideration of "Who do you know well who is like this?" The answer was her grandchildren. Further exploration led to the discovery that there was a substantial conflict between her and the grandchildren, a topic she had not brought up directly. It developed that she was, without intending to be or fully realizing it, competing with the grandchildren for the limited time and emotional energy of her daughter. She needed her daughter's support to enable her to continue caring for her own husband. The children needed their mother. Mother was working, going to school, and trying to please everyone. The realization led to some major changes in family interaction that were initiated by the client.

THE THERAPIST AS PARENT

A more traditional transference in which the therapist is seen as the client's parent is not impossible, even given the reversed age difference between them. It seems more rare, and clinical experience suggests that it is more likely when the client is ill or disabled and is regressing emotionally in response to increased physical dependency or when the client's relationship to the parent was extremely difficult and remains unresolved (e.g., in cases of child abuse or incest). In the first case, the client's taking of the child role is seen as therapeutic transference, and the therapist takes the role of the new parent, both accepting the client as is and encouraging growth into emotional maturity and greatest possible mastery of the problem. In pursuing mastery, the therapist may be in opposition to others in the client's life who wish to encourage the client's childlikeness or dependency for reasons of their own.

In the latter case, the therapy may be very similar to cases with younger adults. The material is often quite dramatic and traumatic, given that it has not been worked through earlier in the client's life. Providing the client with an opportunity to talk about the events, express the emotions, and be reparented by the therapist is as valuable for the older client as for younger clients.

THERAPIST AS SPOUSE AT AN EARLIER AGE

In some instances, the transference can take the form of the therapist's being seen as similar to the spouse early in life, at a time roughly corresponding to the therapist's perceived age or to a difficult time in the marital relationship, The spousal transference can provide a means of working with such issues as whether the whole course of a relationship justifies the effort and sacrifices involved in caring for a frail spouse or for settling old and unresolved guilt feelings, jealousies, and so forth. The description of work with Nora in the case histories volume (Knight, 1992) provides an example of this type of spousal transference.

EROTIC TRANSFERENCE

Erotic transference is part of therapy with clients of any age but is rarely mentioned in discussions of therapy with the elderly (see Nemiroff & Colarusso, 1985a, for an important exception). The omission is probably due to the general difficulty that younger adults have in thinking of the elderly as sexual human beings, much less as having sexual feelings about the young themselves. The handling of erotic transference in therapy with the elderly may require more diplomacy, inasmuch as the client may feel that her or his feelings are abnormal. The important thing is that the therapist neither miss the transference nor act surprised or shocked when the erotic feelings are recognized. The fact is that therapists who deal competently with erotic transference in other age groups can be surprised and inhibited by the appearance of erotic transference in therapy with the elderly.

Case Example. Several months into a therapy for severe depression, the client expressed some concern over improper advances she feared from a much younger neighbor. After inquiries revealed no overt behavior by the neighbor and he was described as physically similar to the therapist and as "someone who really listens to me, even more than my husband did," the therapist suspected an erotic transference. Choosing not to challenge the displacement of these feelings onto the neighbor, the therapist gradually led the client to acknowledge that she was attracted to the neighbor and that these feelings were quite natural. Discussing her needs for understanding, sex, and affection more openly readily led to a decision to seek more appropriate outlets. Some weeks later, the neighbor was reported to be less amorous and simply friendly.

Also, see the example of Lana in the case histories volume (Knight, 1992).

THE THERAPIST AS AUTHORITY FIGURE
OR MAGICAL EXPERT

Some elderly persons are powerless, and many middle-aged and young people exert considerable power over their lives. Within this context, it is little wonder that the therapist can be seen as a quite powerful authority figure. Although the transference can be helpful in establishing rapport and gaining acceptance of therapeutic interpretations, even a positive transference can be very disruptive to the therapy. The client may expect the therapist to make major decisions, intervene on his or her behalf with others, and provide answers and direction rather than exploration and growth. In a negative transference, the client may remain fearful that the therapist is constantly evaluating him or her for institutionalization or is acting as an agent of the family or the community to deprive the client of independence.

Given that the therapist's role with the elderly often does include some case management activity and assessment of mental status, and given that many mental health workers do act as agents for the family or society rather than the older client, there is sufficient reality to these concerns to make the distinction difficult for both therapist and client. Therapists and other helping professionals may have few outlets for human needs for power and recognition and so may be especially vulnerable to being seduced into acting out the role of powerful authority figure. The therapist needs to be clear about the boundaries of appropriate and inappropriate use of status and to communicate clearly to the client the boundaries of his or her role in that particular relationship (see also the discussions of autonomy and fidelity in Chapter 9).

For example, in most instances, using professional connections to help a client secure needed services will be an appropriate use of status, whereas intervening in family arguments to tell a client's daughter to take better care of the client will usually not be appropriate. It can be quite important to have the client recognize that his or her power to do things begins where the therapist's limitations start. For example, it may be a crucial learning experience for the client to discover that she, as parent, has more authority over the daughter than does the therapist. The case history of Sophia in the case histories volume (Knight, 1992) illustrates the role of authority transference with a paranoid client.

ISSUES WITH THE INSTITUTIONALIZED ELDERLY

The institutionalized elderly are different from community-dwelling elderly in a number of ways and clearly are more often severely ill or impaired physically, intellectually, or in memory functioning. In addition, living within a total-institution environment creates special demands on patients, enforces a higher degree of control over residents, and may induce high levels of dependency on the part of residents. These same factors may also tend to attract to institutions older people who are more dependent than others. The argument here is simply that living in any 24-hour-care setting demands an adherence to a general schedule for meals, sleep or quiet times, and group activity and some need to check in and out with those in charge. Supervised group living can elicit a parent-child type of relationship between resident and institution and may also attract people who prefer care and supervision over more independent and less structured environments. Some reflection on other environments that provide food, shelter, and supervision helps to clarify some of the common problems: residential schools and colleges, dorm or barracks life, communes, and monasteries, to name a few.

An early pioneer in psychotherapeutic work with this population was A. I. Goldfarb, who saw the elderly resident as developing a transference to the therapist as a protective parent. He felt there was great potential for therapeutic gain by allowing the client to achieve mastery over the powerful, protective parent.

Intervention is possible in a number of ways and at several levels. At the individual-patient level, the therapist can use the dependency of some residents to encourage the very rapid development of therapeutic relationships, which can then be used to accomplish therapeutic goals with relatively brief visits per patient over a period of several weeks. As often happens in regular outpatient therapy, initial dependency can be used to lead the patient to greater independence consistent with her or his ability. The therapist, having accepted the patient's dependency, can then be a gently encouraging parent who works to help the patient attain independence, setting goals and offering approval for attaining those goals as well as acceptance of failure. Goldfarb's work in allowing the patient to achieve mastery over the powerful parent figure of the therapist can serve as a useful way to have the patient achieve early victories in the struggle for independence (see Goldfarb & Sheps, 1954).

In work with the staff, the therapist can help the staff understand the reasons for the patients' dependence, which is then resented (see Langer & Rodin, 1976). It can also be helpful to encourage staff to express their own feelings about constant exposure to the dependency needs of older, frail people. These feelings are likely to include helplessness, frustration, anger, tenderness, identification, and depression, among others. These feelings are an occupational hazard of work with the frail and disabled aged.

Countertransference

The therapist is also affected by changes in the therapy relationship that come in working with older clients. Why does the thought of working with older people make many therapists anxious? Much therapist anxiety is due to lack of training in work with the elderly and a professional recognition of the limits of one's competence. However, there are other reasons for their discomfort, and many of these involve the therapist's personal conflicts and anxieties about aging.

The therapeutic relationship is a two-way street, with the therapist building up a relationship with the client that is based on the client's real characteristics as a person, the therapist's professional understanding of the client based on those characteristics, the therapist's theoretical understanding of the client's problems and personality, and also the therapist's projection onto the client of the therapist's needs, fantasies, and store of stereotypical social knowledge. Presumably, professional training (especially clinical supervision), constant self-observation, and perhaps personal therapy counterbalance the last of these factors. However, the failure of most training programs to prepare psychotherapists to work with the elderly increases the likelihood that when faced with an older client, the therapist has less theoretical understanding of the client, less training in perceiving the client's problem and personality accurately, and less self-knowledge in those areas in which older clients tend to elicit anxiety. Into this vacuum will rush the therapist's stereotypes (negative or positive) of old age, projections of relationships with older significant others, and defensive fantasies designed to protect the therapist from anxiety over death, dependence, and helplessness. The following will highlight some of these issues, considering the impact on therapy of unresolved relationship issues with parents and grandparents; personal fears about dependency, aging, and dying; and the impact of these issues and fears on working with the elderly, with special attention to making placement decisions and the home visit.

PARENTAL COUNTERTRANSFERENCE

The actual stimulus situation of work with older clients can be quite evocative of countertransference reactions for the therapist. With enough contact with older people, the therapist is likely to find clients who are reminiscent of his or her father or mother. What happens next depends on the therapist's relationship with the parent, how conscious the identification is, and the valence of the countertransference. The therapist may become overly committed to seeing a client change, become irrationally angry with a client, or feel very wounded by the client's questioning of the therapist's expertise. In work with couples, the therapist may become more involved than the couple in keeping their relationship together. The variations are as individual as possible combinations of clients and therapists.

When countertransference reactions are conscious, the therapist can distance him- or herself from them, can discuss the feelings with colleagues or supervisors, and may occasionally need to consider transferring the client to another therapist. The appropriate decision depends on the nature of the reaction, the ability of the therapist to work it out, and the potential impact on the client's therapy. Recognizing less-than-conscious reactions is a necessary skill of the therapist that must be learned through supervision and self-observation. The key clues include (a) a conviction, not supported by accurate diagnosis and theoretical formulation, that the client cannot benefit from therapy; (b) preoccupation with the notion that a client has dementia, despite good diagnostic workups ruling out this diagnosis; (c) a desire, not based on sound clinical practice, to have the client treated medically (medication or ECT) *instead of by psychotherapy;* (d) a sense of boredom, fatigue, or helplessness in the client's presence; or (e) intense emotional reactions to clients or particular actions of clients, or reactions that are atypical for that therapist.

The experience of countertransference may be quite different in work with the elderly. Whereas in work with adolescents the adult therapist may be tempted to rework old conflicts with parents through clients, in work with older adults the therapist may confront current issues in her or his own life and may also confront issues that are now only fearful fantasies. The anxiety aroused by parental countertransference can be alleviated to some degree by adequate knowledge of the variety of paths that aging can take. However, the core difference remains that many of life's most difficult problems are represented in the aged population, and the fact of possibly having to face those problems oneself arouses a different level of fear. A common distinct dimension of countertransference with older clients is that the issues aroused by the older client are likely to lie in the future rather than in the past.

For example, a young adult therapist trying to distance herself from an overprotective mother may become angry with a client's complaint that her daughter does not call or write often enough. A therapist who fears the death of a parent may be overwhelmed with anxiety when confronted with a patient who has a terminal illness. In my own case, I could only dimly understand my difficulty in formulating a clear picture of therapy with an older man until I realized that his storytelling conversational style was similar to that of my father, whom I could not presume to psychologize. Other examples of parental countertransference are described in the case histories of John and of Nora in the case histories volume (Knight, 1992).

The middle-aged therapist may find him- or herself confronting issues in therapy that are also being dealt with in the therapist's own family or that the therapist anticipates having to cope with in the near future: the illness of parents, fears of coming physical or mental deterioration, and fear of death itself. Unless these problems are very clearly worked out, there is the danger that the therapist's problems and values will intrude into the client's therapy and that the therapist will become overwhelmed by facing the same emotionally charged issues at home and at work. For example, a middle-aged therapist had worked quite well for 2 years with a variety of elderly clients. Suddenly she found herself unable to concentrate on what clients were saying and in one interview was feeling very resentful of the demands of a frail elderly man on his wife, who actually seemed to enjoy taking care of him. In discussion with colleagues, she became consciously aware that her feelings about her parents were intruding into therapy. Her father, until recently very healthy, had suffered a stroke. The therapist resented the impact that caring for him was having on her mother but found it difficult to talk to either parent about the problem. Her reactions were complicated by the expectation that as a geriatric specialist, she should be of more help to her parents than they were willing to let her be. She also felt that her expertise should protect her from the feelings she had about her parents' problems. Having recognized the problem, it was quite easy for her to return to being a therapist with clients rather than a frustrated daughter trying to protect her mother.

GRANDPARENT COUNTERTRANSFERENCE

Although grandparent countertransference also depends on the individual circumstances of the therapist, there does appear to be a kind of modal countertransference that involves a basically positive feeling for a somewhat fuzzily perceived older person who must be protected from the middle generation's interference. In therapy, the middle generation is the therapist's parents and the client's children. The positive affect may be good for motivating the therapist to build a good therapeutic alliance, but the impact can be quite nontherapeutic when it prevents the perception of real client problems (e.g., dementia, psychosis, substance abuse, personality disorder) or when it leads the therapist into unnecessary and unprofessional conflict with the client's children.

In the case history of Mildred in the companion volume (Knight, 1992), I have discussed the way that this essentially positive countertransference hampered diagnosis and some aspects of therapy.

Grandparent fantasies can also be negative and may take the form of being overly ready to see the elder as senile, complaining, and making irrational demands on a good, kind, younger family that must be protected. The therapist has an obligation to be aware of his or her reactions and to reach an individual assessment of each client's situation. One can also wonder if much theorizing about work with the elderly is not based more on these types of fantasy images than on accurate perceptions of the real people who are old.

Case Example. A psychologist working with older people had a client who in appearance was the archetypal grandmother. Her children and several workers in social services for the elderly were angry with her and disparaged her but could not describe exactly what was wrong with her. The therapist became quite invested in saving this woman from her family, whom she accused of only wanting her money, and in providing her with real help for her "depression." After several weeks of working with her, he became concerned about her fluctuating mood and occasional bouts of confusion. When he asked permission to discuss these symptoms with her physician, she became quite upset and gave a lengthy but not very clear description of problems with various physicians that had resulted in her having to change doctors three times in the past year. With some coaxing, she showed him her medicine chest, which had a variety of tranquilizers, sleeping medications, and pain medications from seven different doctors. The archetypal grandmother had a serious addiction to prescription drugs. The discovery of her substance abuse changed the course of therapy and made sense of the confused picture painted by family and service providers, who had sensed something wrong but could not imagine the client as a drug user.

THERAPISTS' FEARS OF AGING, DEPENDENCY, AND DEATH

Rechtschaffen's (1959) review of the literature and Kastenbaum's (1964a) essay on "the reluctant therapist" both discussed the impact of the client's aging, imminent death, and increased dependency on the therapist's anxiety level. Much writing on therapy with the elderly supposes that many therapists avoid working with the elderly for just these reasons. Clearly, our society teaches us to avoid thinking about these aspects of life, therapists tend to share this avoidance, and therapeutic work with the elderly confronts the therapist with these issues in a very personal manner.

Working with clients from earlier born cohorts forces an appreciation of the finitude of life at the beginning as well as the end. Talking constantly about the time before we were born reminds us that we were not always here, just as talking about dying reminds us that we will not always be here. Older adults, being from earlier times, can often point out that firmly held "modern" beliefs and facts often change over time and that some new ideas and values are recycled ones from decades past. These reminders of sociohistorical change may be as unsettling as reminders of death and disability.

Even if one assumes a life span developmental sequence in which adjusting to one's mortality is a task of middle age and may be resolved by young old age, the problem remains because most therapists working with older clients are not themselves elderly. The young therapist may not yet have acknowledged the finitude of life, and the middle-aged therapist may be actively struggling with (or avoiding) these issues in a personal way. Thus, the therapist may be forced to confront the issue earlier in life than is normal or may have personal anxieties reinforced by close contact with those near death. Unfortunately, even older therapists often seem to feel a need to have clients cope with illness, aging, and the approach of death in the same way that they did: with or without traditional religious beliefs, existential philosophy, stoic acceptance, and so on.

Older therapists (including peer counselors) are open to the possibility of overidentification with the client. This countertransference can lead to attempts to have the client age in the same way as the therapist or to avoidance of issues that the therapist does not wish to face. For example, in co-leading a group with an older female cotherapist, who was quite skilled and experienced in therapy with older adults, I once observed her repeatedly refuse to let one client discuss the loss of physical attractiveness and attention from men as part of her depression. In later conversation, it became apparent that the therapist dealt with this aspect of her own aging by deciding that the change was simply unimportant. Although this may have been true for the therapist, it clearly was not true for the client.

Regardless of cause, therapist anxiety when faced with issues of mortality and dependency is quite real. Appropriate training and education about these issues are helpful. The anxiety is worsened if one mistakenly believes that everyone gets demented or develops a serious illness with aging. Some degree of desensitization about death comes with reading about it, discussing it openly, and being exposed to it in the course of one's work. Nonetheless, the fact remains that people working with the aged—and especially therapists, who will be discussing these things on a more intimate and intense level—are exposed to high levels of illness, dependency, and death.

The manner of coping with the death of clients will, of course, vary with the individual therapist. Being able to talk about it helps, and to that end forming mutually supportive relationships with others in the aging network and in the hospice movement can be a major source of support for the therapist. Discussing cases of recently deceased clients with colleagues to examine irrational expectations of oneself makes the work easier over time (e.g., "Is it possible that you felt that the therapy for anxiety would prevent the patient from dying of cardiac arrest?"). Recognizing grieving for clients and expressing it openly, attending clients' funerals, and acknowledging mutual grief with family can all alleviate anxiety about death. One major effect of having clients die is that the therapist will develop a different view of life and death than is shared by others of similar age and vocation. On one hand, it is not possible to work with older people and fail to recognize that everyone dies, that death is generally unexpected, and that death is part of life. On the other hand, even very frail and sickly older people may live for years. The awareness of life after frailty makes it difficult to write off older people who are sickly as not needing help because of their presumed nearness to death. The awareness of how long frailty can continue can severely challenge the usual young adult attitudes toward life as valuable only when it is independent and unconstrained by bodily limitations.

Exposure to illness and dependency raises other, possibly even more anxiety-arousing, topics. The fact of chronic physical disability, the recognition of problems for which clients are not responsible, and the sight of clients forced into dependency against their will all pose major threats to the younger adult worldview that effort is rewarded and we get what we deserve. In addition, the therapist's need for control and his or her narcissism may be injured in the constant confrontation with physical factors in the client's life that are beyond the reach of therapy. One must constantly acknowledge that there are factors beyond the psychological in the client's life and also that some of these are beyond the control of patient, therapist, or physician. This view of life is no doubt more realistic and more valid than that held by some psychotherapists, but it needs to be carefully prepared for in training and supervision. The student therapist must be taught to recognize the value of improvements in terrible situations and the importance of the psychological factors in undeniably physical disabilities (see Chapter 7 on working with illness and disability).

Without appropriate preparation, therapists can be expected to react as others with less training do: with denial, adoption of unrealistic worldviews, avoidance of difficult patients, or the cynical helpless fatigue of therapeutic burnout. There may be intrusion into therapy of interpretations based on the therapist's anxiety, which are urged without regard to feedback from the client. The work of therapy will become the therapist's therapy rather than the client's.

Case Example. One younger therapist faced with an older client referred for depression after his third major heart surgery was overwhelmed with the idea that the client was near death. She constantly led the client to discussing death and interpreted the client's reluctance to do so as proof of tremendous anxiety about dying. The client, in fact, not only was comfortable with the idea of dying but preferred death to continuing to live with his disabling condition and the constant threat of more complications and more surgery. It was the keen awareness that life was going to go on for years with choices limited by his degree of disability that was depressing to this individual. After several sessions, the client requested another therapist and calmly informed the next therapist that the prior one seemed to have a lot of anxiety about death.

COUNTERTRANSFERENCE
AND PLACEMENT DECISIONS

One common distortion of clinical judgment that can be considered a form of countertransference occurs when the clinician has a strong need to see other families work out the decision to place or not to place an elderly family member in long-term care in a particular manner. The decision is a highly emotional one for any family, including those that contain mental health professionals or children who grow up to become mental health professionals. The emotional impact of the decision may linger on for years after the event itself and after the death of the relative. The mixture of uncertainty, guilt, frustration, and anger that often surrounds these decisions can take the form of either a need to justify the action taken by one's own family by advocating similar resolutions to others or a need to expiate guilt by helping others to avoid what is now viewed as a mistake made by the family.

Advocating either home care or institutional care for all frail elders will be a disservice to many. The decision to seek long-term care versus making the necessary sacrifices to maintain an elderly relative in home care is one of the most difficult decisions that any family faces. Any adequate decision requires a careful assessment of the elderly patient, the family's needs and resources, the actual alternatives available in the community, and the impact of the decision on everyone in the family. This decision process will lead to different answers for different families.

Clinicians who have strong personal needs to see their own decision backed up by the decisions of others may influence other families overtly, by recommending one or another course of action, or more covertly, by giving or withholding verbal or nonverbal cues of approval as the client discusses the various options. The therapist who is aware of strong feelings that one decision or another is the correct one in all cases should seek consultation or supervision to work through this blind spot and be able to deal with families as individualized systems.

TERMINATION

Psychotherapy does eventually come to an end, whether the therapy was brief or lasted months or years. The ideal ending is by mutual agreement between therapist and client that the goals of therapy have been reached, with a chance to review the therapy, share impressions of the various stages of therapy, and achieve some closure of relationship issues and feelings for both parties (Menninger & Holzman, 1973; Weiner, 1975). In practice, it is perhaps more common for clients simply to stop coming or to terminate for financial or other reasons, but the ideal model is an important component of the structure of therapy. Psychotherapy is perhaps the only intimate relationship that is intended from the beginning to have an end.

Experience in clinical supervision and in consulting with other therapists shows that terminating with an elderly client is often anticipated and sometimes experienced as the most difficult part of therapy with the elderly. It is virtually always the therapist rather than the client who experiences termination as very difficult. If explained clearly and in advance, clients often see termination as reassuring (i.e., that therapy will not go on indefinitely) and experience actual termination as a sign of having accomplished something. Older clients have, after all, had considerable experience with endings and may be more used to accepting them.

Therapists, however, often hate to say goodbye to older people. They express fears that the older person will be lonely, will feel deserted, or is too frail to survive without support. There may also be veiled expressions of concern as to whether the therapy was really of any value to the older client in the face of their real problems. These feelings may indicate a tendency to experience therapy with older people on a different level than therapy with younger adults. Many therapists appear to be more personally affected by contact with elderly clients and more tempted to cross the subtle boundaries between being a therapist and being a friend. In most instances, these problems with terminating suggest a need to examine one's fantasies about the elderly in general and the countertransference with the individual elderly client in particular.

Termination often calls attention to the sense of impotence felt by many therapists in working with the elderly. Older people, and especially older clients, are frequently dealing with illness, disability, grief over death of close loved ones, ageist prejudice, complex relationship problems within the older family, and living on a fixed income. If the therapist has any question about the value or the power of therapy or about his or her own competence as a therapist, it seems that working with clients facing these types of problems brings those self-doubts to the surface. The therapist working with aged clients must find a realistic view of the contribution of therapy to enabling elderly clients to resolve their problems more easily, free from anxiety, depression, relationship difficulties, and so on. The best source of that awareness of the value of therapy is the summing-up statements of older clients in termination interviews.

Having discussed the adaptation of psychotherapy to older adults and changes in the psychotherapeutic relationship in this and the previous chapters, we turn in the next chapter to a discussion of assessment with the older client.

5

Guidelines for Assessment in the
Context of the Practice of
Psychotherapy

The first session or two with any client is devoted to understanding the presenting problem and to understanding the client as a person (see Weiner, 1975). In work with elderly clients, assessment is likely to be the most difficult phase of therapy. The range of possible problems affecting the elderly client is great, and there are likely to be interactions among areas that we are inclined to consider separately with younger adults. Our understanding of many psychological problems facing the elderly is new and changing quite rapidly. For example, until the relatively recent past it was widely believed that the most prevalent mental disorder in late life was senile dementia (now more commonly called Alzheimer's disease). In more recent years, increased attention has been given to depression, anxiety, alcohol abuse, and psychotic disorders (Anthony & Aboraya, 1992; Atkinson, Ganzini, & Bernstein, 1992; Light & Lebowitz, 1991; Myers et al., 1984; Sadavoy & Fogel, 1992). Good assessment interviews and psychological tests for use with the aged are being developed but are still limited.

In any assessment with any client, the starting point is to understand the purpose of the assessment: What question is to be answered? In the past, the elderly have often been seen for assessment only, with the implication that treatment would be useless. In these instances, the assessment question was most often related to decisions about placement or to legal competency hearings. All too often, the question was actually answered prior to the assessment, which served as an official approval of decisions reached by others. The professional has an ethical duty to take responsibility for the results of the assessment. At times, this may mean challenging the proposed question. In practical terms, the referral may take the form of "Mom is senile, and we wonder if it is time to seek legal guardianship." The answer may be that the client is depressed and needs active treatment of depression to restore her to normal functioning.

The discussion of assessment that follows is intended to address assessment issues within the context of the practice of psychotherapy. The focus is on understanding the problem that has brought the older client to the psychotherapist's attention. This chapter is not intended to cover psychopathology in older adults in detail, nor is it a guide to psychological testing or to neuropsychological assessment. Resources for further reading in these areas are presented at the end of this chapter. Rather, the purpose is to help the therapist understand whether the client is in the right place and then what sort of psychological problem the client has.

As has been discussed in Chapter 3, older adults do not readily identify psychological problems in themselves and also often have coexisting medical and social service problems. More often than with younger clients, the therapist is faced with the task of deciding whether the older client has a psychological problem and, if so, whether the psychological problem is the only need of this particular older client.

Thinking of the assessment of older clients within a decision-model framework can serve as a helpful guide to this discussion of assessment. The framework used here (see Figure 5.1) is based on the Bayesian model for decision making under conditions of uncertainty. In fact, the first principle in assessment with older adults is to be aware of the essential uncertainty of the process: Sorting out a mix of biomedical, psychological, and social problems is not easy for any professional, for the older client, or for his or her family.

Base ——→ Assessment ——→ Treatment ——→ Outcome ———→ Value
Rate   (of outcomes)

Figure 5.1. Decision-Model Framework for the Assessment of Older Clients

Base Rates of Presenting Problems

The first portion of the model points to the context of the therapist's practice. Base rates for any one person's practice (this also holds true for hospital, nursing home, and agency services) are determined by the typical incoming referral flow. Either by design or by accident, most clinicians tend to see fairly large numbers of certain types of clients. For example, a person working in a dementia assessment center is likely to see many older clients who have dementing illnesses or who fear that they do. In contrast, a therapist working in an outpatient psychological service or in private practice is more likely to see clients with depression, anxiety, personality disorders, and so forth. In general, therapists tend to expect to see what they have usually seen. In the two examples given here, the therapist working in the dementia assessment center may miss people who are depressed or (even more likely) fail to recognize personality disorders in an older client. The person who is used to working with depressed or anxious clients may not recognize a dementing illness in an older client. Perhaps neither will recognize an acute paranoid state in the elderly client.

Base rates also provide helpful information and affect the likelihood of detecting problems. In general, rare conditions are hard to detect; in fact, the likelihood of being right is maximized by never diagnosing rare conditions. However, the circumstances of a particular practice can change these chances dramatically. Mental health problems, in general, are rare in the total population. However, in psychological practice they are less rare because of the ways that people come to talk to a psychotherapist in the first place. Certainly, depression, dementia, suicide, anxiety, and substance abuse will all be much more common in the professional experience of the clinician than in the population at large. Knowing who usually comes to see you and, more specifically, knowing what types of clients are referred by different referral sources is itself a guide to the kinds of decisions that will usually need to be made. A major challenge to the psychotherapist is staying alert to exceptions: What is usually true is not always true, and the aim of assessment is the accurate understanding of each individual person.

Assessment

DECIDING AMONG DOMAINS OF INTERVENTION

Once clients arrive at the therapist's office, the therapist must decide whether they are in the right place and what kind of problem they have. The assumption of the following discussion of assessment is that the clinician must understand the variety of possible competing explanations for the set of behaviors that has resulted in the elderly person's referral for assessment. The context of the referral must be taken into account: Is the client self-referred because of unpleasant feelings? Is he or she seen in a hospital after admission for somatic complaints that have been judged to have psychological components? Does the family bring the client in because of their exasperation with attempted caring strategies? Does a landlord want the person evicted? The list can go on and on. The context of the assessment must influence the clinician's perception of the client. A second assumption is that the assessment will include more than the client's verbal responses within the interview—for example, a reliable history of symptoms, the client's nonverbal behavior, and consideration of the conversational style of various types of disorders.

In work with the elderly, there is a widespread recognition that older people have multiple and complex problems that often cut across the usual disciplinary and service system boundaries.

This awareness is captured by statements that the elderly are best described by "biopsychosocial models" and by a constantly repeated call for interdisciplinary cooperation in service provision. Presumably, all human beings are best described in biopsychosocial terms and would benefit from collaboration among the professionals whom they utilize; but the elderly do seem to have medical, psychological, and social problems at the same time more frequently than do younger adults. The therapist is often confronted with a mix of medical, psychological, and social casework problems and may have to define for the client or the client's family which mode or modes of treatment and problem resolution are most appropriate. The question of domain is represented in Figure 5.2 as the first level of assessment in decision making.

Psychological Versus Physical

Considering the biological side of the integrated model, the therapist working with the elderly cannot rely on self-screening by the client to

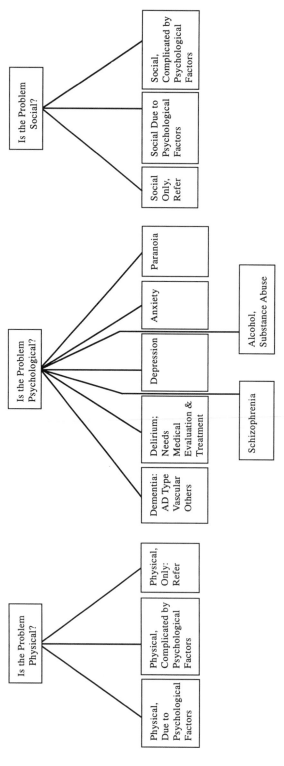

Figure 5.2. Decision Tree for Assessment

distinguish between medical and psychological problems. Although great advances have been and are being made in geriatric medicine and in continuing medical education for all physicians about geriatric medicine, it is still not safe to assume that elderly clients have been accurately diagnosed simply because they have an ongoing relationship with a physician or were referred by a physician. Furthermore, medical problems can cause psychological ones, psychological problems can cause or mimic medical ones, and medical and psychological problems can co-occur by chance. All of these relationships make assessment and treatment of older adults in psychotherapy an intellectual and professional challenge.

The signs and symptoms of both physical and psychological disorders change with age, and distinctions between real memory loss and complaints of memory loss, or between tiredness due to disease and the energy drain of depression, become essential. Most medications can affect the cognitive status or the emotional status of older adults. The psychotherapist should not practice medicine, but it is impossible to function adequately as a therapist with the elderly without some working knowledge of neuropsychology, psychopharmacology, and health psychology (see Frazer, 1995; Haley, in press; LaRue, 1995; Smyer & Downs, 1995). At a minimum, the therapist must (a) understand diffuse organic brain syndromes, (b) understand the interrelationship of common psychological and physical disorders, (c) know the psychological side effects of common psychotropic and general medications, and (d) be able to collaborate with physicians and nurses for the good of the client.

To form a clear picture of an older client, one must ask all elderly clients about their medical status, chronic diseases, and current acute diseases. Medications (all medicines, not just the psychotropic ones) need to be written out, preferably directly from the labels on the bottles rather than the patient's report. Assessment of eating habits and weight gained or lost is needed. If the client does not see a doctor regularly or has not seen his or her physician recently, a visit should be urged. If the presenting psychological problem is likely to have a physical basis, the therapist must have some standard for knowing whether the physical exam was sufficient to rule out the physical cause. The therapist needs to have access to a physician who can evaluate the adequacy of the diagnostic procedures that were performed.

The therapist must also have a particularly well-developed sense of what psychological disorders are and are not. When a presenting problem does not really fit the usual picture of a psychological disorder, physical explanations should be considered or reconsidered. Although more of the elderly tend to somaticize psychological problems, the reverse does also happen. I have seen several older clients who were self-referred for depression but did not have the full picture of depressive symptoms. On referral to their physicians, the medical problems discovered were as diverse as potassium deficiency, which causes tiredness; Parkinson's disease, which can cause psychomotor slowing and a rigid facial expression that may appear sad before causing tremors; and previously unrecognized chronic heart problems that can cause extreme fatigue and be experienced as severely depressed mood. In some instances, these clients were being referred back to unusually psychologically minded physicians who had perceived the clients as being depressed and were surprised to be told that they did not appear truly depressed. In this way, good psychological assessment can lead to further medical workups and an accurate diagnosis.

The psychotherapist should have some rudimentary ability to notice physical and behavioral signs of poor health. Fluctuating cognitive status often indicates a disease process or negative side effects to medication and needs to be reported to the attending physician. Unusual sleepiness or fatigue, grey or otherwise unhealthy skin color, lack of muscular coordination or presence of tremors, and swelling of ankles are signs of common physical problems in older adults. It is also important to be able to recognize extrapyramidal symptoms and tardive dyskinesia in older adults on psychotropic medications. The psychotherapist's role is not to make physical diagnosis based on such signs but rather to recognize common danger signals and urge the client to tell his or her physician or (with the client's permission) communicate the symptoms directly to the physician.

With some degree of comfort in discussing physical problems with the client and with the physician, the psychotherapist will have a more complete view of the client's problems. In some instances, the therapist may play a role in ensuring an accurate diagnosis by recognizing important psychological problems and by detecting the inaccurate attribution of symptoms to psychological causes. The interplay of physical and psychological factors in determining physical and mental health is an important and fascinating area of study, and working with older adults provides ample experience in confronting these issues in clinical practice.

Psychological Versus Social

As has been discussed in previous chapters, despite the existence of information and referral services for the elderly, the therapist is likely to see some elderly who are looking for help and who need home-delivered meals, help with housecleaning, or a friend more than they need psychotherapy. At other times, one may need an assessment interview to be certain what the problem is. Clearly, if a person needs a referral to another service or needs friendship, he or she should be informed of and directed to appropriate resources. On the other hand, the elder with such complaints should not be dismissed too rapidly because not all psychological problems are presented directly. The therapist should explore previous attempts to resolve practical problems and why they failed and should evaluate these attempts for signs of depression, anxiety, agoraphobia, substance abuse, or personality disorder.

Some older adults have not made use of congregate meals or senior recreation centers because they do not know they exist, others may be looking for a different type of social interaction, and still others may not go because of severe depression or a social phobia. In making the decision, the therapist does not want to take advantage of the lonely elderly by offering them the purchased friendship of supportive therapy (see the classic Schofield, 1964) instead of a more lasting and probably less expensive solution. When human contact is what is needed, friendly visitor programs, peer counseling, or socialization programs and clubs are more appropriate. On the other hand, the depressed or phobic elder should not be frustrated in an attempt to seek help for a serious and treatable psychological problem by having that problem incorrectly normalized.

In deciding between casework and therapy, the therapist should keep in mind that the network of aging services is not well known for being tolerant of odd behavior (see Frankfather, 1977), and clinical experience verifies that even people with personality disorders or neurotic-level dysfunctions may have difficulty either in being enrolled for various services or in being accepted by other elderly at the service site. Those who are more severely eccentric or actually psychotic may be excluded from needed services by caseworkers who are made anxious by the client's unusual behavior or thought processes. In one instance, the only way that a client could get an eligibility interview was for the therapist to be present to "protect" the eligibility worker. The client, who was quite paranoid, had made verbal threats and had waved her cane around in a threatening way but had no history of actual violent behavior. She was so physically impaired that it took her several minutes to get out of her chair, and then she walked only very slowly. Her threat value was difficult to understand from a mental health worker's point of view, but the eligibility worker was actually quite frightened of her. Older adults with social service needs who end up in a therapist's office may very well be there because of psychological problems that have gotten them rejected from aging service network services.

The other side of the coin is that mental health professionals become very accustomed to unusual behavior. For this reason, they may perceive someone who has been excluded from the social service network of the elderly for correctable eccentric behavior as needing only social support services. Depending on the severity of the problems that the therapist treats, psychotherapists may perceive a potential client as relatively well adjusted who would be perceived to be eccentric or deviant in a senior meal site.

In deciding that a client needs a social service referral rather than psychotherapy, it is imperative to check out the client's previous attempts to seek help and to evaluate these attempts for signs of acute psychological distress, character disorder, or other behavioral problems. With the client's permission, it can be very helpful to contact aging services workers that the client has seen so as to get their perception of the client's behavior and rationale for referring them to you. These observations can be used as additional data to build a complete psychological assessment of the potential client.

Summary:
Deciding Among Domains of Care

Currently, services tend to be divided into broad realms of health, mental health, and social services. The disciplines involved tend to include physicians, psychologists, social workers, rehabilitation therapists, and nurses, along with the paraprofessionals associated with each of these disciplines. The preferred model of service is an interdisciplinary team that includes as many of these disciplines as possible. (An example of an outreach team in community mental health is described in Knight, 1989.) An ideal model would combine the separate realms of health, mental health, and social service into one gerontological service, although typically government regulations and insurance provisions prohibit the ideal mix.

Where preferred and ideal models are not possible, the professional will have to attempt to approximate them with good referral contacts so as to provide adequate services to elderly clients. Once the decision is made as to whether therapy is an appropriate mode of service for the aged client asking for help—either alone or in combination with medicine or casework—then the therapist begins to ask what type of psychological problem the client has. Making an appropriate diagnosis can be especially important with the elderly client, as distinctions among diffuse organic brain syndrome, depression, anxiety, and psychosis can be difficult to make and have important implications for the therapy.

The foregoing discussion portrays the psychotherapist as caught between medicine and social work, and one may well wonder what ground is left for the therapist to cover. Inasmuch as psychology is a recent arrival to aging services (nursing and social work precede it by decades; more recently medicine has entered the field), the therapist's new colleagues in the aging network may also raise this question. The answer is quite straightforward: The elderly do have psychological problems, including depression, anxiety, phobias, paranoia, psychosis, marital disorder, and disturbed family relationships. Clearly, these are the sorts of things that psychotherapists treat. Equally clearly, the present state of affairs is such that neither physicians, social workers, aging-network service providers, nor even many psychotherapists are very likely to recognize psychological problems in the elderly or to feel that such problems are treatable. The decision process will be discussed next in terms of distinguishing among psychological disorders.

DECIDING AMONG PSYCHOLOGICAL DISORDERS

Distinguishing among psychological disorders is important with any client and becomes an even more salient issue among older adults, primarily because of the prevalence of dementing illnesses and acute delirium states in older people. It is not possible to see large numbers of older adults without being asked to assess whether memory lapses are signs of early stages of Alzheimer's disease. Moreover, because memory complaints are more common in later life (Zelinski, Gilewski, & Thompson, 1980) and because clients often forget (or "forget") homework assignments and therapeutic insights, the therapist will often wonder about the memory functioning of older clients, even when the client does not initiate the question.

Having decided that a client is cognitively intact does not end the assessment: Older clients (like younger ones) have a variety of problems. The tendency to see all or most older adults with psychological problems as depressed is only slightly more enlightened than the belief that all older adults with problems are demented. A common problem such as social withdrawal and self-isolation can be due to depression, dementia, anxiety, agoraphobia, alcoholism, paranoia, or schizophrenia, to name a few common possibilities. This section of the discussion moves to the second level of the middle section of Figure 5.2.

The level of expertise needed to assess older adults accurately is a question that is unresolved and somewhat controversial (see Gallagher-Thompson & Thompson, 1995; Niederehe, Gatz, Taylor, & Teri, 1995). Most older adults in psychotherapy practices can be screened accurately by a responsible clinician who has a reasonably broad range of exposure to older adults who have had these problems and who can accurately assess these problems in younger adults. Some cases will need expert assessment by a clinical geropsychologist or neurogeropsychologist. A key question in the controversy is whether the less expert therapist can recognize the limits of his or her expertise and know when to refer to a specialist.

The following discussion provides a summary description of various disorders, guidelines for diagnosis, and short case portraits. The disorders covered include dementia, delirium, depression, paranoia, anxiety states, and schizophrenia. The organic disorders are covered first not because they are more important or more prevalent but rather because their identification with later life is so strong that one must understand what can and cannot be explained by organic pathology before the others can be presented. Readers who want more comprehensive coverage of the disorders themselves are referred to the reading list at the end of this chapter.

Normal Aging Versus Dementia

A key question in assessment with the elderly is whether some degree of diffuse organic brain disease is present. Although differentiation of psychological from neurological disorders is important with any age of client, the prevalence of organic brain syndrome does increase with age. In addition, the slowness of onset and the diffuse nature of the disease with dementia of the Alzheimer's type make differential diagnosis more difficult. A further complication is that the slowing of intellectual processing with aging and the decrease in memory performance characteristic of normal aging that were discussed in Chapter 1 can be misinterpreted by the inexperienced clinician as signs of organic brain syndrome. These normal changes become more pronounced in advanced age, and other cognitive abilities probably show some decline after the age of 75 or 80 (see Schaie, 1990).

Another source of confusion is an unintentional negative consequence of an otherwise positive social change. Since 1980, there has been growing public education about Alzheimer's disease and related dementing disorders, a change that is positive for demented elderly and their families and that one hopes will lead to greater public understanding and sympathy and a more rational public policy for the victims of dementing illness. However, the growing popular awareness of the dementias leads to greater self-diagnosis and to diagnosis by families, and to diagnosis by professionals with little experience of the disorder. When the diagnosis is accurate, this is positive, but when it is inaccurate, it is tragic. The greater awareness and concern about the disease must be balanced by concern for good diagnosis.

The changes of dementing illnesses eventually are more dramatic in quality and quantity than those of normal aging. The slowing of reaction time is greater in the demented elderly. For example, Klingner et al. (1976) found an average difference of 0.1 second between old and young volunteers, with the difference between the demented elderly and normal elderly three times greater than that. The normal elderly frequently complain of decreased ability to remember names of new acquaintances and forgetting where they put things. The moderately to severely demented elderly forget names of family members, their own past history, where they live, and important activities in recent time. These differences become more pronounced as the dementing illness progresses. In the beginning of the disease process, dementing elderly will be indistinguishable from normally aging persons, and they will gradually become moderately to severely demented. The difficulty of accurate assessment therefore gradually moves from impossible to easy over the course of progressive dementias.

The assessment batteries typically used to detect organic disorders in younger adults (e.g., the Halstead-Reitan, the Wechsler Memory Scale-Revised, and the WAIS-R) now have norms that extend into the young-old years, with some norms available for the old-old on some tests (see, for example, LaRue, 1992; Storandt & VandenBos, 1994). These batteries are typically better with the assessment of acute, focal lesions than with chronic, diffuse disorder (see Matarazzo, 1972). The best available tests tend to be the dementia screening inventories such as the Folstein Mini-Mental Status Examination (MMSE; Folstein, Folstein, & McHugh, 1975; Folstein, Anthony, Parhad, Duffy, & Gruenberg, 1985). These screening devices are limited and have fairly high error rates, especially with low-education older adults, very intelligent older adults, and people with psychological disorders (see Folstein et al., 1985). A meta-analysis by Christensen, Hadzi-Pavlovic, and Jacomb (1991) confirms the value of these screening inventories (MMSE; also the Mattis Dementia Rating Scale [Mattis, 1976], the Blessed Dementia Scale [Blessed, Tomlinson, & Roth, 1968], and the Short Portable Mental Status Questionnaire). The Buschke Selective Reminding Procedure (Buschke & Fuld, 1974), the total score and selected subtests of the Wechsler Memory Scale, and the Boston Naming Test (Kaplan, Goodglass, & Weintraub, 1983) all show promise in detecting dementia, including mild dementias (Christensen et al., 1991). Of course, the difference in scores between normal and dementing older adults increases with the certainty and severity of the diagnosis (Storandt & Hill, 1988).

Medical screening is likewise not conclusive in evaluating intellectual decline in the elderly. There is no positive medical screening for dementia short of autopsy. The medical screening for dementia (including most imaging techniques) is designed primarily to rule out possible treatable causes of the observed symptoms (see McKhann et al., 1984, and the *Diagnostic and Statistical Manual of Mental Disorders,* fourth edition [DSM-IV]; American Psychiatric Association, 1994). The diagnosis, given the ruling out of other causes, is based on mental status examination, behavioral observation, and history. Thus, the diagnosis is currently an essentially psychological one, regardless of who makes it.

A key problem in distinguishing normal aging from dementia is that the two clearly must overlap in the early phases of dementing illness. That is, there is a period of time when the dementing individual experiences relatively minor (and quite possibly not yet testable) cognitive changes that will, in time, become major cognitive decline. Other older adults may take equal notice of and experience equal anxiety about cognitive changes that will not become the disabling changes of dementing illness but that result in a level of functioning different from that of earlier adult life. At present, only repeated testing will distinguish the two.

The psychotherapist is then placed in the position of making a very difficult distinction with few guidelines and, to date, very little truly definitive information concerning either the defining symptoms of dementia or the developmental course of normal age changes. The decision is of sufficient importance that it is imperative that the clinician know as much as possible about current findings and have experience with demented, normal, and otherwise impaired elderly. Without this level of expertise, it is too easy to adopt a decision rule such as "All old people are demented,"

"All old people who act different are dementing," or "Only those older adults with very severe impairment have Alzheimer's disease."

With appropriate clinical experience, the clinician can feel comfortable with the range of differences among the normal elderly, learn to document real changes in memory complaints, track stability or change in memory, and relate memory changes to the client's ability to handle day-to-day tasks of living. This ability depends on the use of dementia screening inventories described below in the section on dementia, on the client's knowledge of his or her own past, and on the clinician's knowing a variety of older people with and without significant memory loss. An important part of this learning process is learning when to refer a particularly difficult case for more expert evaluation. These decisions also depend on knowledge of the various psychological disorders themselves.

Age-Associated Memory Impairment

In recent years, there has been a move to identify a new category of memory impairment that is intermediate between normal aging and dementing illness. In part, the idea is that some older adults experience memory impairments that are functionally limiting to them but that do not develop into progressive and severe dementing illnesses. The diagnosis is somewhat controversial and is listed in the *DSM-IV* among "other conditions that may be a focus of clinical attention" (age-related cognitive decline, 780.9). Those not in favor of it feel that there is confusion with either normal aging changes or common anxiety about such changes or that these changes represent nonprogressive brain illnesses or injuries or slowly progressive ones (Crook et al., 1986; Reisberg, Ferris, Franssen, & Kluger, 1986; Rosen, 1990; Smith, Ivnik, Petersen, & Malec, 1991). Research is needed to clarify the importance of this proposed distinction. At present, its primary value may well be as a reminder that not all memory impairment is progressive, even among those whose memory impairment has necessitated changes in work or in complex social behavior.

Dementia

The term *dementia* refers to cognitive impairments that represent a change from an earlier and higher level of functioning. Dementias are presumed to result from diseases of the brain or physical disorders that affect brain functioning. It is important in the assessment of older adults to remember that there are nonacquired cognitive deficits: Some older adults have been developmentally disabled (or have had a low-normal IQ) all of their lives, and some people will score in the cognitively impaired range on questionnaires due to low education or language difficulties.

It is generally estimated that about 5% of persons over 65 suffer from moderate to severe degrees of dementia, with another 5% to 10% suffering from mild impairment. It can appear as early as the age decade of the forties, and it increases in prevalence with each decade to reach about 15% to 25% for octogenarians (see Anthony & Aboraya, 1992; LaRue, Dessonville, & Jarvik, 1985). There are higher estimates, but these use tests that may confuse normal cognitive changes in the 80+ group with mild dementia. It is not true that everyone will get "senile" if he or she lives long enough. Also, it must be noted that prevalence figures should be taken with a grain of salt, as there are obvious problems in estimating the prevalence of a disorder that is difficult to diagnose and that is often misdiagnosed. Due to the problems in distinguishing normal aging changes from dementia, it is likely that misdiagnosis increases with age.

Behaviorally, the principal marks of dementia are decreased intellectual functioning, usually first noticeable as decreased memory functioning. First symptoms may include difficulty remembering important appointments, the names of people who are known well, and an increase in losing important items. The disease can impair the ability to calculate, to comprehend the visual environment, and to follow a conversation for any length of time. In the latter stages it can disrupt bodily functions. Most of these changes take place in a state of clear consciousness. That is, the individual remains clear in the present moment and can hold a coherent conversation until language itself becomes impaired. In general, demented people retain the ability to hold a social conversation far into the progression of the disease as long as the conversational partner does not introduce topics that require memory or as long as the other person does not know the correct answer to the question asked. Even in conversation with clinicians, the impression is often left that the client has a good recall of remote past events; however, in most cases, the clinician does not know whether the recalled events occurred or not.

Usually, the demented patient is not terribly emotionally distressed. In the early stages of the disorder, some will be depressed by the dementing process in much the same way that others react to the losses entailed by heart disease or cancer (see Newton, Brauer, Gutmann, & Grunes, 1986). As memory worsens, however, emotional troubles tend to be transitory because the cause of the upset is easily forgotten. These factors, which are strengths for the patient, can make the diagnosis easier to miss, especially in people with relatively little impairment or very specific intellectual losses. A brief contact that does not include probing for memory loss reveals a very charming older person who may have a convincing explanation for whatever occurrence has led to the interview. This strength can lead to problems for the principal caregiver, whose testimony about problem behavior at home may be discounted by professionals and by other family members who have brief contacts with the patient. Thus, coherence in conversation, likability, and freedom from emotional distress are not a basis for excluding the possibility of dementia.

Indicators for considering dementia are various. The demented older person may complain of losing things or of things being stolen. He or she may get in trouble for not paying bills. Getting lost from time to time may result in a referral. There is often a withdrawal from social contact as social rules and the identities of friends are forgotten. Withdrawal is a two-way street: As the disability becomes obvious, others will tend to shun the demented person. Sometimes withdrawal is seen by referral sources as evidence of possible depression. Once some rapport is developed, the question "Do you have any trouble with your memory?" can yield a good deal of good information from the patient and serve as a transition to the use of mental status tests to explore further the kinds of losses and the degree of impairment. This probe does not work if the assessment takes place in a context in which the client fears that the evaluation will lead to institutional care.

Alzheimer's Disease. Dementia is always due to a specific disease. The most common causes are Alzheimer's disease (AD) and vascular dementias. AD is a progressive disease with gradual onset that is characterized by a rapid loss of brain mass and the spread of plaques and neurofibrillary tangles throughout the brain. The brain pathology is also characterized by depleted neurotransmitters and the buildup of amyloid proteins. Present medical treatments for AD focus on increasing usable acetylcholine and controlling behavioral symptoms with psychotropic drugs. On the average, 10 to 15 years elapse between recognition of the disorder and the death of the patient. Classically, about 50% to 65% of accurately diagnosed cognitive impairment in the elderly was attributed to AD (estimates vary; see Zarit, 1980, and Reisberg, 1981); however, recent studies in other countries have suggested that vascular dementias may be more common (e.g., Rorsman, Hagnell, & Lanke, 1986; Shibayama, Kasahara, & Kobayashi, 1986).

The diagnosis is difficult and basically is a matter of the accurate assessment of the cognitive impairment followed by elimination of all other possible causes of the dementia. The elimination process is important and is largely based on medical assessment. In many areas of the United States, there has been substantial improvement in the diagnosis of AD in the past decade or so, due to the spread of geriatric medicine, AD research centers, improved medical education (including continuing education), and public education through the media. A good medical assessment would include a physical workup to screen for other possible causes. This workup should generally include blood chemistry panels, brain imaging (to assess for tumors and lesions as well as to estimate global cerebral atrophy), and an evaluation of medications, medication interactions, and alcohol use (McKhann et al., 1984; see also the *DSM-IV*). Although medical diagnostic practice has generally improved, there are still practitioners who have simply replaced older terms such as *senility* and *senile dementia* with *Alzheimer's disease* without changing their practice. The psychotherapist working with older adults needs to be able to roughly assess the adequacy of the diagnostic workup and to refer clients for good workups when needed.

At the level of general psychotherapeutic practice, the assessment of cognitive abilities may depend mainly on the use of screening questionnaires such as the Folstein MMSE. Clear cases are either those in which there is no evidence of cognitive impairment from the tests and no complaints of memory loss or reports of functional impairment or those in which there is clear indication of cognitive impairment from testing, no evidence from the medical examination of other causes of dementia, and a history of intellectual loss and functional impairment. When the tests and the reported history disagree or when there is evidence of medical illness, multiple medications, severe emotional distress, focal neurological signs, or symptoms of psychosis, a more expert assessment with more sophisticated psychological and neuropsychological testing is called for.

Although the general process of intellectual deterioration in AD is progressive, there is no clear and reliable pattern to the progression of symptoms, nor is the speed of decline predictable. Gradual onset is not always easy to determine because families may recognize the disorder all at once (in a crisis in which the client is unable to cope with increased stress or on a vacation where new surroundings produce a panic reaction), even if there has been gradual decline. Most texts report a steady decline in patients, whereas most families describe good days and bad days and report that the decline is faster sometimes than at other times. These discrepancies may very well reflect the family's struggle with recognizing the disorder in that denial often breaks down in response to specific incidents even when the dysfunction has been present for some time. The deterioration can have positive effects on caring for the patient in that troublesome behaviors such as suspiciousness or aggressiveness usually disappear with increasing memory loss (see Haley & Pardo, 1989, for a discussion of the course of dementia and its impact on caregivers). The reader interested in more information on AD is directed to readings listed at the end of this chapter.

Vascular Disorders. Vascular dementias are the intellectual impairment syndromes related to what are commonly called strokes when the infarct is large or transient ischemic attacks (TIAs) when the lesions are small. More rarely, vascular dementias can be due to white body disease or occluded arteries. The intellectual deficits are often more specific in nature than those of AD and classically have been described as having a rapid onset linked to the occurrence of the stroke. If there is a series of strokes, the pattern tends to be stepwise, with marked decline after each stroke and some recovery of functioning over the weeks or months following. The recovery often does not reach prestroke levels. If, however, there is a series of TIAs, the pattern of decline may be very much like that of AD. Multi-infarct dementia has been thought to account for about 10% to 20% of accurately diagnosed cognitive impairment in older adults, with a roughly equal proportion due to mixed cases of AD and vascular dementia (LaRue, 1992; Zarit, 1980). Not all strokes, of course, result in intellectual impairment; some affect primarily movement or vision or other brain-governed functions. Some stroke patients are handled entirely within the context of the medical care/nursing home system, whereas others are seen in psychiatric hospitals. The basis for this decision is not always clear for particular patients.

In addition to the more focal nature of the cognitive deficits and the stepwise progression, the medical history obtained from the client is often helpful in indicating the possibility of vascular causes of dementia. If the client has any history of cardiovascular diseases (e.g., hypertension, heart disease, arteriosclerosis), the psychotherapist should consider the possibility of vascular dementia if cognitive impairment is detected. This suspicion should be discussed with the attending physician, who may need to hear from the therapist about the basis for the concern in the cognitive assessment, behavioral observations, or the client's report of functional disability. Clients may share more of their concerns about such issues with the therapist, with whom they talk for an hour a week and have a good rapport, than with the physician, whom they see less frequently and for shorter durations.

Other Causes. A variety of other causes of dementia are considerably less common but can often benefit from active medical intervention. Among these are Parkinson's disease, brain tumors, traumatic brain injury, normal-pressure hydrocephalus, and subdural hematomas. The variety of possible disorders dictates a need for medical screening even of persons who clearly have a dementing illness. In many instances, severe depression can produce cognitive impairment or apparent symptoms of dementia.

Delirium

Delirium is a different collection of intellectual and behavioral deficits that are generally associated with treatable conditions. If it is identified quickly and treated, the patient usually returns to normal levels of intellectual ability. If it is not treated, many of the underlying diseases will produce a permanent dementia. Mistaking delirium and other treatable syndromes for nontreatable disorders, including AD, has been all too common and is one of the great tragedies of care for the elderly. The differential diagnosis often depends on good behavioral and mental status assessment, so the mental health professional can play a major role in the correct identification of these disorders.

The major characteristic of delirium states is the clouding of consciousness of the patient. Unlike the demented patient, the delirious person is not "clear" in the present moment: That is, he or she is not in good contact with the immediate sensory environment. Conversation is confused and often impossible. The delirious person may change his or her line of thought within one sentence. There may be rather rapid changes in orientation, with the patient clearing for a few moments from time to time. (See *DSM-IV* criteria for further definition. Also, Trzepacz, Baker, and Greenhouse, 1988, have developed a delirium rating scale.)

The clinical "feel" of talking with a person in delirium is rather like that of talking to someone who is acutely intoxicated or in an acute psychotic episode. Whereas the demented patient may not remember the name of the place where she or he is, the delirious patient may believe it is a different sort of place altogether, perhaps mistaking a psychiatric ward for a used car lot. There are often changes in sleep pattern and psychomotor activity. Hallucinations, especially visual hallucinations, are common in delirium but are rarely seen in demented patients until the very late stages of the disease.

The most common causes of delirium states are (a) reaction to medications and to recreational drugs such as alcohol; (b) malnutrition; and (c) acute medical disorders, including infections, uncontrolled diabetes, thyroid dysfunction, uremia, tumors, encephalitis, electrolytic imbalance, heart disease, and many others. (Lists range up to 120 or more diseases.) Obviously, psychological assessment must be coordinated with medical assessment and care. As a closing note, it is important to recognize that delirious patients generally appear more disabled than demented patients. Professionals of all disciplines often fall into the trap of assuming that delirium, likely to be treatable, is less severe in presentation than the untreatable dementia.

The psychotherapist should be alert to the behavioral signs of delirium and know enough about the patient's medical history to suspect causes. The diagnosis and treatment will be medical but may depend in part on these observations of behavior and of changing cognitive functioning. Medical professionals not trained in geriatric medicine or dementia assessment do not always readily distinguish delirium from dementia. (See LaRue, 1992, for greater detail and for recommendations on assessment.)

Depression

Depression in older adults, like depression in younger ones, can take many forms. In diagnostic terms, the range goes from adjustment reaction with depressed mood (a more prolonged or severe emotional reaction to a stressful event) to major depressive disorder (a more intense depression accompanied by a sense of helplessness, guilt, loss of appetite, sleep disturbance, trouble concentrating, thoughts of death and suicide, and possibly even psychotic features such as delusions and hallucinations). Major depressive disorder may or may not be related to a stressful life event. In younger adults, depression is often accompanied by an unrealistic concern about bodily functions, sometimes becoming a delusional belief that one is ill. In older adults, the same process can lead to unrealistic concern about memory, cognitive impairment, and brain disease.

Depression is generally considered to be one of the more common mental health problems in the elderly (Anthony & Arboraya, 1992; LaRue et al., 1985; Myers et al., 1984). It often occurs after some major stressful event in the life of an older person. These stresses can include the loss of family and friends by death or by moving away. Many elderly people who are depressed have experienced three or more deaths of family or close friends in the 2 or 3 years prior to becoming depressed. Major illness and surgery may also be the precipitating factor for a depression (Phifer & Murrell, 1986). Other depressions may seem to arise with no apparent cause.

It is also commonly assumed that older adults suffer from depression more than younger adults. Several studies question this belief and in fact suggest that older adults may have lower rates of depression (Myers et al., 1984) and report less intense sadness on measures of depression (Gatz & Hurwicz, 1990) than younger adults. One paper argues that depression has increased in prevalence among later born cohorts, especially those born since World War II (Lewinsohn, Rohde, Seeley, & Fischer, 1993). It seems clear, however, that older adults with depression are still underserved. Moreover, the question of prevalence does not contradict individual need for psychotherapy. In fact, depression in older adults is often dismissed exactly because it is presumed to be normative. Recognizing depression as an uncommon response to later life should motivate the desire to understand it and correct it.

The older depressed person frequently withdraws from social activity, eats less and less, loses weight, and begins to appear very frail. She or he may complain of not being able to remember what is read or the plots of TV programs. In conversation, there may be complaints of not being able to remember as well as in the past and a preoccupation with the idea of growing old and life now being over. There may be veiled or open expression of such ideas as "Life is not really worth living" or "I would be better off if I could just die."

The people around the depressed elder may see him or her as senile or getting old and failing physically and mentally, "as older people do." They may inadvertently reinforce the depression by communicating these ideas to the depressed person and by doing things for him or her that he or she could do alone. It is even possible that the wishes to die or expressions of considering suicide will be reinforced by family, neighbors, and professionals who themselves feel helpless in the face of depression in old age and agree that there would be nothing worth living for at that age. In short, the social circumstances of the elderly and our ideas about old age often enhance depression.

In general, psychotherapists are well skilled in the recognition of depression and have little trouble recognizing it in older adults if they are free from ageist prejudice and therapeutic despair about older clients. There are factors that can complicate recognizing depression in older adults, however. First of all, as noted in Chapter 3, older adults may be less likely to recognize mental health problems, including depression. This means that older clients are less likely to do the work for us and come in and say, "I'm depressed, I need help." They may very well describe a full set of depressive symptoms but not reach the conclusion unaided.

Second, the coexistence of medical problems and prescribed medication can make the meaning of many common symptoms of depression unclear, especially the somatic ones. A healthy younger adult with somatic complaints, disturbances of sleep and appetite, low sexual desire, and so forth presents little ambiguity. But because older adults are seldom entirely free from disease or the treatment of disease, these symptoms are likely to be highly ambiguous and quite possibly due to either depression, a medical disorder, or medications prescribed to treat a medical problem.

Third, older adults with depression often complain about memory problems or worry about having Alzheimer's disease. It is quite difficult to sort out the true cause of such complaints. Older adults often accurately recognize memory changes, which may be normative for their age (Zelinski et al., 1980) or may be not yet testable signs of dementing illness. (For example, Reding, Haycox, and Blass, 1985, found that 57% of persons originally diagnosed depressed developed dementia on 3-year follow-up.) On the other hand, depression can lead to complaints about cognitive functioning (Niederehe, 1986) and also to changes in cognitive functioning in depressed patients (Kaszniak, 1990; LaRue, 1992). Depressed older adults frequently describe failures in concentration and attention, such as the inability to follow their TV programs or articles that they are reading. Sometimes they also report being unable to remember what others have said to them in conversation or have asked them to do. In most cases, these failures can be understood as failures to process information and register it in memory, due to competition from depressive thinking (Hartlage, Alloy, Vazquez, & Dykman, 1993). All such complaints require assessment. Therapists new to working with older adults often are overly ready to see such memory complaints as evidence of dementing illness. On the other hand, a therapist with a positive rapport with an older client may ignore signs of true cognitive impairment.

Case Portraits

The following case portraits are chosen to illustrate differences in older adults with such complaints of cognitive impairment as may be presented in the initial interview. Not all depressed people show any cognitive impairment; some are just like younger depressed people, only with more gray hair and wrinkles.

Mary

Mary was in her early 60s, and her daughter had asked that she be seen by a therapist because she felt that Mary might be getting depressed. She had quit going to her bridge club meetings and had been making excuses not to see some friends that she used to enjoy seeing. She spent most of her day at home and did not appear to be doing much more than looking out the window and sometimes watching television. Mary received the therapist graciously. After a few minutes of conversation in which the therapist learned that she had no acute or chronic medical problems and took only vitamins, the following exchange took place.

Therapist: You know, I'm here because Susan was concerned about you.

Client: Yes, I know she is, but she doesn't need to be. I'm really fine.

Therapist: Well, Susan seemed to feel that you might be a little depressed.

Client: Oh, no I'm not depressed or anything like that. Nothing to be depressed about. [In fact, she does not appear at all depressed.]

Therapist: You haven't been going out lately, not playing bridge like you used to.

Client: Who told you that?

Therapist: Susan did.

Client: [relaxing] It just doesn't seem the same as it used to.

Therapist: How doesn't it seem the same?

Client: Well, I used to be really good at bridge. Quick, you know, but lately I get kind of confused about the rules. The others get impatient with me. So I just stay home. [Tone is matter of fact, almost unconcerned.]

Therapist: You have trouble remembering the rules?

Client: Yes, when you get old you get more forgetful, I guess.

Therapist: Do you forget other things, too?

Client: People's names, I forget names a lot. I don't remember yours right now. [smiles graciously]

Therapist: Do you just have trouble with names of people you've just met or people you've known a while?

Client: Oh, people I've known. [She tells a story about not recognizing a friend she's known for 10 years.]

After asking Mary's permission to ask some questions to check her memory, the therapist proceeded to establish that she knew the current year and her birthdate but could not get her age correctly. She knew her address but could not explain where her children lived. She had difficulty describing some of her close family relationships and was not certain if Susan was her daughter or sister. Throughout the interview she was gracious and charming. She volunteered that she seldom went out because once or twice she had had trouble finding her way back home. She found these incidents frightening and embarrassing. Her house was neat and clean, and she cooked regular meals for herself. Toward the end of the interview she referred to a previous meeting with the therapist, who had never seen her before. Mary was not depressed but was mildly to moderately demented. She was still able to take care of herself. The intervention at this stage would be support for Susan, education about the disorder, and letting her know about available support groups and sources of advice on practical problems that might arise from day to day. Susan might need help to accept the disease and to learn to expect less of her mother.

John

John was also in his early 60s. His family, who did not see him often, reported that he had "developed Alzheimer's disease recently." It was difficult to get any real sense of why they thought this or whether this was a sudden change. When the therapist arrived at the apartment, John invited her in before she had a chance to identify herself. Early conversation suggested that he had mistaken her for someone who worked for the housing authority, but correction of this error did not affect him at all. As they talked, he got up from time to time and walked around the apartment.

Therapist: Have you lost something? [John looks puzzled by the question.] You look as though you're looking for something.

Client: They've stolen my keys again. I thought that's why you're here.

Therapist: Who stole your keys?

Client: I've had trouble ever since I've been in this hospital.

Therapist: [matter-of-fact tone] This is not a hospital. This is an apartment building.

Client: Yeah. [moves away, again looking around]

Therapist: Do you see your doctor often?

Client: Yes. I just saw him in [names month 8 months back]

Therapist: Do you take any medication?

Client: They keep coming in at night even when I lock the door.

Therapist: [interested] Who comes in at night?

John proceeded to describe some short people (about 3 feet tall) who came into the apartment at night and took things. The stealing had continued even after he had changed the locks and blocked the door with a heavy chair. To any other topic he gave confused and contradictory answers. At one point, he addressed the interviewer with what she experienced as great clarity and stated that things had been bad for him ever since his wife had died. He had no idea of when she had died or what she had died of. The therapist found several bottles of medicine in plain sight on the kitchen table. These included (from three different doctors) two minor tranquilizers, an antipsychotic, a medication advertised in medical journals as helping the senile elderly by increasing blood flow to the brain, two heart medications, and one she did not recognize. When he could not answer questions about what he ate, she asked permission to look in the refrigerator and found a frozen dinner and some moldy luncheon meat. As she got ready to leave, he handed her his savings passbook. As she handed it back, she repeated firmly three times that he should keep it. A quickly arranged family conference that included the team psychiatrist enlisted the family in clearing out nonessential medication and getting home-delivered meals started. The therapist visited weekly and saw major changes in 2 weeks. John was suffering from delirium resulting from medication interactions and lack of food.

Sara

Sara was referred by the manager of the apartment building in which she lived. She "had become senile lately," and the manager was concerned about how long she could manage to live alone in that building. She would soon be 80 years old. Sara was somewhat hesitant about letting the therapist in but agreed (gave in?) when the nature of the concern was expressed. She appeared very frail, moved slowly, and seemed unsteady on her feet. Her voice was soft, and she took a while to answer questions. She often stated that her memory was not as good as it once had been. She had diet-controlled diabetes and a heart condition for which she took the usual medications. The interviewer's comments and questions often had to be repeated, as she seemed to drift away at times. She apologized and explained that she was, after all, getting old.

Therapist: You seem worried about getting old and losing your memory. What kind of problems do you have with your memory?

Client: I just forget things more. People do at my age.

Therapist: What kind of things do you forget?

Client: Where I put things. People's names. Like that.

Therapist: People you just met or people you know well?

Client: [long pause] Acquaintances.

Therapist: What about people you've known a while, old friends?

Client: [irritated but without emphasis] At my age, old friends are dead. The ones left I know well enough.

Therapist: It must be depressing to have lost so many old friends.

Client: What can you expect when you're old? [Her voice is hostile, but for the first time she looks the therapist in the eye and there is a sense of real contact.]

Therapist: It can be pretty rough at times. Do you feel depressed a lot?

Client: Most mornings I wake up and wonder why I'm still here. I never thought I'd live this long; my parents died in their 50s. I don't know why I'm still here.

Therapist: Do you have trouble sleeping?

Client: I wake up early every morning, about 3:00 or 4:00.

Therapist: When do you go to sleep?

Client: There's so little to do I go to bed about 6:30.

Therapist: Do you eat well?

Client: I don't have any appetite. I eat a little, but it's hard to get it down. I can't have salt or sugar, nothing tastes right.

Therapist: Have you lost weight?

Client: I don't know. I look thinner in the mirror.

Therapist: Could I ask you some questions about your memory?

There was a long pause and then passive consent. Some questions were answered slowly, others more quickly and with short flashes of irritation. She was totally unable to do serial sevens and did not know her street address but gave the name of the building. Her perception of the passage of time was uneven, and she got questions wrong about how long ago things had happened. All other items were answered accurately. When told her memory is good, she was unimpressed. She cut the interview short, complaining of being very tired, and reluctantly agreed to have the therapist return the following week. Sara was depressed.

Combinations of Dementia, Delirium, and Depression

The three disorders of dementia, delirium, and depression are not mutually exclusive. Having any one of the three disorders does not make one immune to the other two. Demented elderly may become depressed about the loss of intellectual functioning or about being shunned by former friends. They may also forget to eat regularly and develop delirium from malnutrition. Depressed older adults may not eat or may neglect care for chronic medical conditions and thus may develop a delirium. Someone who is depressed can develop dementia for unrelated reasons. The possibilities are many, and the clinical picture becomes more complex with mixtures of two or three of these disorders. In all cases, the important thing is not to miss the treatable disorders. Active treatment of delirium and/or depression will increase the day-to-day functioning level of even a rather severely demented person.

Anxiety

The triad of depression, dementia, and delirium occupies much of the clinical literature on aging and does, in fact, comprise much of the clinical practice of the psychotherapist working with the older client. Older people do, however, suffer from the full range of psychological problems, and it is important to recognize these other problems in the older adult as well. In fact, phobias ranked in the top four most common mental health disorders in the NIMH Catchment Area Survey (Myers et al., 1984). Anxiety is a common focus of much therapeutic practice and is often part of other disorders, including major depressive disorder. It may also manifest itself discretely in generalized anxiety disorder or in various types of phobias. The clinical picture is basically the same in older adults as in younger ones, with reports of excessive worrying, muscular tension, autonomic nervous system stress reactions, and possibly panic attacks.

As was true with depressive clients, with the older client the changes in cognitive processing associated with intense anxiety (indecisiveness, inability to concentrate, disorganized thinking, a tendency to be concrete or circumstantial) may be attributed to "senility." In fact, the clinical presentation of rambling digressive and detailed speech that is characteristic of obsessive older clients with acute anxiety seems to be one of the most negative clinical presentations to younger therapists, who may insist that such clients must be cognitively impaired. It is only when they observe the great recovery of cognitive ability that takes place if sessions begin with a relaxation exercise that the new therapist seems really to accept that anxiety is the cause of the confusing speech pattern.

The somatic symptoms of anxiety (e.g., tachycardia, intestinal cramps) are even more likely to be interpreted as a real disease in older people than in younger clients. After retirement, it is relatively easier for people to withdraw and isolate themselves so as to avoid situations that arouse anxiety. Anthony and Aboraya (1992) noted that about 4.8% of older adults have phobic disorders (6.1% for women, 2.9% for men). Rates for panic disorder and for obsessive-compulsive disorder for older adults were both under 1%. Rates for generalized anxiety disorder were not reported. From our discussion of barriers to therapy in Chapter 3, it follows logically that many elderly people with symptoms of anxiety would seek medical treatment and tranquilizers rather than psychotherapy or relaxation training interventions. It is also quite likely that many elderly with symptoms of anxiety develop increased cognitive deficits as side effects of tranquilizing medications and go on to be labeled as confused and possibly suffering from Alzheimer's disease.

Paranoia

In the elderly, various manifestations of paranoid thinking need to be considered when diagnosing an elderly person with unrealistic suspicions of others. It is first necessary, of course, to be certain that the suspicions are not realistic. Elderly people often live in high-crime areas, have practical jokes played on them by young people, are victimized by unscrupulous business people, and are plotted against in various ways by family members. If the client is memory impaired or depressed, the story can become vague enough to make the reality difficult to ascertain. For example, one older woman in a psychiatric hospital was seen as paranoid partly because of "persistent delusions" about strange men who were trying to take her house away from her. She was mildly memory impaired and so was unable to give details. A long-time friend who visited her cleared up the supposed delusions by explaining that the woman owned a house in a very desirable and soon-to-be-redeveloped area of town. The strange men were real estate agents who dropped in unsolicited and tried to convince her to sell the house to them.

One type of paranoid thinking is brought about by sensory losses. Hearing is the sense modality of much social communication and many of us have entertained suspicious thoughts when something was said that we did not quite hear and people began to laugh. For the hearing-impaired elderly person, social interaction is further complicated by the fact that many younger people feel free to discuss older people as if they were not present and to make decisions about them without their input. Under such circumstances, it is no wonder that some hearing-impaired elders become very suspicious, even expressing delusional ideas of persecution or of threats. Visually impaired older adults are left in an unclear world and are often physically isolated as well. Poorly perceived images and loneliness can become the basis for experiences that sound substantially like psychotic delusions or even hallucinatory experiences. However, these delusions are often based on lack of complete information. In these cases, correcting the sensory loss (if possible), establishing communication with the impaired person, and showing significant others how to communicate usually eliminates these paranoid symptoms. Families are not always as willing to have the sensory loss corrected or to reestablish communication as the therapist may expect or hope. When unwillingness occurs, it suggests problems within the family system.

A second type of paranoid thinking in the elderly is that which occurs in memory-impaired older adults. In these individuals, the sense of threat and the emotional tension that are so much a part of paranoid psychosis tend to be absent. What is very much present is the belief component of paranoid delusions and the accusations against others. There may also be protective behavior based on those beliefs. A more accurate understanding of these "delusions," however, is that they are a direct consequence of the memory loss. The pattern is that the patient forgets that some item has been sold, given away, or used up. For the individual at that time, it is easier to believe that the item was stolen than to admit the forgetting to self or to others. Given the incorrect belief, most behavior can be understood in real terms. The items "stolen" may be of great value (thousands of dollars of savings) or of very little value (old shirts or cans of beans). The emotional reaction is often more like petulance than the righteous indignation or sense of violation that comes with real theft. The people around the patient often make the situation worse by arguing with him or her about the mistaken belief, becoming angry and aggrieved about being falsely accused, and acting out their anger without regard to the disability of the accuser. A better strategy is recognition of the memory-impaired person's sense of loss and fear, interventions to increase his or her sense of security, and nonargumentative, nonemphatic, but repeated confrontation of the fact of the memory loss. If the memory disorder is progressive, this phase is usually temporary.

A third instance of paranoid thinking in the elderly is true paranoid psychosis. Elderly people can be truly paranoid for the first time late in life, and paranoid individuals can grow old with or without contact with the mental health system. The symptom picture is essentially the same as in younger adults, with similar levels of intense anxiety and sense of threat. Unlike the pseudodelusions of the demented, the delusions of the truly paranoid tend to involve threats of being poisoned, being followed by the CIA, being monitored by complex electronic equipment, and so on. Treatment in terms of psychotherapy and medication is similar to that with younger adults and about equally difficult to initiate because of problems in establishing a trusting therapeutic relationship. As can be true with younger adults, the people around older paranoid individuals often do begin to talk about them behind their backs and to plot against them and try to sneak medicine into their food. With skill and experience, it is possible to build a relationship slowly with the paranoid older client, and it may be necessary to have such a relationship before one can initiate treatment with psychotropic medication. See the case history of Sophia in the companion volume (Knight, 1992) for an example of working with a paranoid older client.

To further complicate the diagnostic picture with the elderly client, it must be noted that some clients with affective disorders (mania or depression) also express paranoid-like ideas. In such instances, the best assessment strategy is to pick the diagnosis most congruent with the total clinical picture and to plan treatment accordingly, keeping the other possibilities in mind as alternatives. The response to treatment and information gained during therapy will usually clarify which alternative was correct. It may, however, point to an important reality of the role of the elderly within our society: They are often threatened, taken advantage of, and deprived of personal power and importance. The frustration of these basic human needs is the psychodynamic root of much paranoid-like thinking.

To summarize the varieties of paranoia among the elderly, the following guidelines can be noted. Sensory impairment and associated communication problems must be eliminated as a possible explanation. The content of the "delusions" and the intensity of the emotion can serve to indicate whether the suspiciousness is secondary to memory impairment or is primary paranoia. Ideas of persecution should not be taken as reason to diagnose paranoia over the mood disorder.

Schizophrenia

Schizophrenia in old age has recently begun to receive more attention (Light & Lebowitz, 1991; Miller & Cohen, 1987). Schizophrenics do grow old, and there is some evidence that some individuals may become schizophrenic for the first time in later life. This latter phenomenon has been recognized in Britain for some time (e.g., Roth, 1955), whereas in the United States the diagnostic criteria of the *Diagnostic and Statistical Manual of Mental Disorders,* third edition (*DSM-III;* American Psychiatric Association, 1980), expressly excluded a diagnosis of schizophrenia if onset was after age 45. This wording was changed in the *Diagnostic and Statistical Manual of Mental Disorders,* third edition, revised (*DSM-III-R;* American Psychiatric Association, 1987), and the *DSM-IV* described late-onset schizophrenia as being generally similar to the early-onset disorder.

Schizophrenia was once considered an early-onset dementia (*dementia praecox*), and dementia was thought to be a consequence of aging. It was once a common practice in some psychiatric hospitals to rediagnose persons with a long history of schizophrenia as demented when they reached their 60th birthday without any real change in their behavior. The deinstitutionalization movement of 1955 to 1975 moved many older schizophrenics from state hospitals to nursing homes or residential care homes and therefore out of view as psychiatric patients. It is often taught that schizophrenia "burns itself out" as the patient ages in the sense that symptoms become less intense and acute episodes are less frequent or nonexistent. In fact, however, fairly large numbers of long-term schizophrenics, many of whom spent major portions of their lives in psychiatric hospitals, live in nursing homes, board and care homes, and in single-room occupancy hotels. Some of them find their way into senior recreation centers, congregate meal sites, and other services for the elderly. Some continue to have acute episodes of their psychosis with hallucinations, delusions, and bizarre behavior. When not acutely disordered, they can fit well into settings that tolerate the degree of eccentricity of manner that tends to be characteristic of the residual phase, along with flat affect and detached social behavior.

Most long-term patients have rather good ideas, based on years of experience, of what kind of treatment approaches work best with them. Relatively few receive the treatment that they need because mental health services did not follow them from the state hospitals to their new homes. Many encounter prejudice from other senior citizens and people working in the senior services network, who regard them as "crazy" and ostracize them. Obviously, community-based treatment and community education are needed to increase awareness and acceptance of the older chronically mentally ill. Older schizophrenics are also a great oral history resource for understanding in a very personal way the history of mental health treatment in our nation. The young-old in this group represent the first cohort of older psychotics to have graduated from years of community-based care, with little to no experience of the state hospital era. They may well have different symptoms and treatment needs than earlier born cohorts with extensive histories of institutional care.

Alcohol and Other Substance Abuse

Alcohol and other substance abuse is a fairly common problem in older adults and one that has tended to be overlooked in discussions of therapy (including, for example, the first edition of this volume). Asking questions about alcohol use and prescription drug use should be part of any complete assessment. Inquiring about past and current problems with abusing such substances can be helpful in that it opens up discussions about the topic with those who are ready to admit problems with abuse. The problem with assessment in older adults is similar to that with younger adults: Clients are often motivated to cover up the problem and may be in denial about it within themselves. Clues for the assessment are often observational: the smell of alcohol, a glazed or unfocused expression in the eyes, unsteadiness of movements, unexplained falls, and prescription drugs that are obtained from several different physicians or different pharmacies. Unexplained changes in mood or cognitive ability from session to session can be a warning sign, as can frequent, unexplained changes of physicians.

Suicide

Suicide has long been recognized as a serious problem among older adults, especially white males, who are disproportionately represented among successful suicides in the United States and are the highest risk group for successful suicide by age and sex (McCall, 1991; McIntosh, Santos, Hubbard, & Overholser, 1994). Suicide rates for older adults declined from the 1930s to 1981 and have been increasing since then (McCall, 1991). The ratio of attempted suicide to completed suicide is much lower in older adults than in young adults (McIntosh et al., 1994).

Suicide is generally asserted to be tightly linked to depression, but there is evidence that alcohol abuse, psychosis, and organic brain syndromes can contribute to suicide, although these other factors are not much explored in the elderly (McIntosh et al., 1994). Knight (1994) reported that successful suicides have been noted in older adults with non-Alzheimer's dementias: vascular dementia and *dementia pugilistica*.

As far as is known, suicide assessment is similar with older adults and should involve evaluation of suicidal ideation, plan, lethality of the plan, and history of previous attempts. In my own experience, suicidal ideation should be evaluated by its precise definition. Many older adults talk of death without depressed mood or suicidal intent and scare younger adults by doing so. Depressed older adults, and some who are not depressed, may look forward to or even long for death without having any intention of killing themselves. Reasons for disavowing suicide often include religious convictions or an awareness of the emotional impact on surviving family members. An expressed intention to kill or harm oneself should be taken as seriously in older adults as in younger ones.

A further complication in assessing suicide in older adults is the possibility of a rational decision to take one's life due to painful and prolonged illness, progressive dementia, or other progressive and debilitating illness. The psychotherapist's role in such cases should be to assess for depression, cognitive impairment, family pressure for suicide, and other psychological factors that may impair the rationality of the decision. Active treatment in therapy should be offered in all such instances. On the whole, it seems unlikely that people who rationally decide to end their lives will feel a need to discuss it with a psychotherapist, so anyone who voluntarily seeks therapy should be presumed to want to find a reason to live. On the other hand, if older adults contemplating suicide are referred within a medical setting or (as seems likely under many states' proposed assisted-suicide laws) are legally compelled to see a psychotherapist, the desire for suicide, in and of itself, should not be taken as conclusive evidence of mental disorder. (Also see McIntosh et al., 1994, for a discussion of these issues.)

Other Disorders

It ought to be explicitly recognized that "other disorders" includes all of the possible psychological disorders of younger adults, including psychosexual problems, personality disorders, conduct disorders, and so on through the *DSM-IV.* The expression of certain symptoms of behaviors may be altered by the circumstances of late life, and the severity of longstanding disorders may be lessened or increased by the social circumstances of the postretirement lifestyle, but nothing is excluded by the fact of a chronological age greater than 60.

Finally, with regard to standardized assessment of emotional problems and personality style in the elderly, it should be noted that progress has been made in that domain over the last 9 years but that there is much less consensus on emotional assessment of older adults than on cognitive assessment. This lack is tragic in that most of the real problems facing therapists and older clients have more to do with the realm of emotional problems than with the question of whether there is cognitive impairment due to dementia. The newer versions of some personality assessment instruments (e.g., the MMPI-2) have norms on at least the young-old (people in their 60s to early 70s). Most clinicians and researchers working with older adults have argued for the use of brief inventories whenever possible. The Beck Depression Inventory (Beck, Ward, Mendelson, Mock, & Erbaugh, 1961), the CES-Depression Scale (Radloff, 1977), and the Geriatric Depression Scale (Yesavage et al., 1983) have all been widely used with older clients. The Spielberger State-Trait Anxiety Inventory (Spielberger, 1984) has been used in research with older adults, as have both the SCL-90 and its shorter Brief Symptom Inventory version (Derogatis & Spencer, 1985). All of these brief inventories have the disadvantage that they are quite face-obvious as to what is measured and can be manipulated by clients who are motivated to do so. There is also the potential problem that older clients who are reluctant to engage in therapy anyway will be put off by having a great deal of paperwork and assessment to complete in initial sessions. My own bias is to be sensitive to this problem and to begin talking with the client as soon as possible, saving written assessment until later in the first hour or until later sessions if feasible.

Any therapist who has felt blocked or confused in a given case can appreciate how useful fresh ideas from any source can be in resolving an impasse. Toward the middle of therapy and with selected clients, traditional testing with MMPI, Rorschach, and TAT can be acceptable and even exciting to the older client. With limited assistance from objective testing at present, the differential diagnosis of older clients in the emotional sphere will of necessity rely on the clinical interview and the diagnostic skills of the clinician.

Choosing Interventions

With the assessment completed and a provisional diagnosis in mind, the therapist now comes to the presumed purpose of assessment: choosing the treatment (see Figure 5.1). By this point, the therapist has formed an opinion about the cognitive status of the older client, the nature of the emotional distress, and also whether there are medical and social problems that need to be handled. In some cases, the result of assessment may indicate that the older potential client is a normal older adult with medical or social problems who simply needs referral. In other cases, the older adult may be too cognitively impaired to benefit from psychotherapy. In these cases, some consultation with a colleague who specializes in dementia may help locate assistance or interventions for the demented client, or it may be possible to work with the family to improve the overall situation.

More frequently, the assessment is the beginning of therapy and will guide the psychotherapist in focusing on appropriate problems. Perhaps even more often, the assessment will have led to the identification of multiple problems, some of which the therapist can handle and others of which will need coordination with physicians, caseworkers, and others in the aging services network. As can be seen in Figure 5.2, psychological problems may be an intrinsic part of these medical or social service problems. In such instances, coordination is even more necessary.

Although the mapping of assessment to intervention is not a one-to-one correspondence at present, broad categories of diagnosis do have implications for intervention. It is clearly important to know whether the client has a cognitive impairment, whether it is treatable, and whether it is progressive. These decisions will shape what type of treatment is needed, whether treatment should be pursued, and how one will respond to the client's forgetting treatment-related information (i.e., is it dementia or motivated forgetting?).

Knowing that the principal problem is depression or anxiety suggests a different course than knowing that it is psychosis, alcohol abuse, or personality disorder. These decisions, and what to do next, are part of the normal expertise of therapists. In the remainder of this volume, the focus is on what is more specific to therapy with older adults (working with chronically ill clients, grief work, and life review) rather than on elaboration of those aspects of therapy that are shared with younger clients. Given an accurate assessment, these shared aspects will come naturally to most therapists.

In some settings where older adults are seen, assessment seems not to lead anywhere but to be an end in itself. When this happens, one must wonder what the purpose of the assessment was. The next section explores how the values placed on assessment outcomes and the larger context of assessment affect their use and the decisions made from them.

Placing Values on Choices
Based on Assessments

The Bayesian decision model used here recognizes that decisions are made under conditions of uncertainty and that values placed on differing outcomes may appropriately affect the choice of recommended intervention. In a classic paper on psychometric theory and assessment, Rosen (1971) noted that there is always error in assessment decisions and that a choice must be made between tolerating high false-positives or high false-negatives. He noted that we tolerate high false-positive error rates when assessing suicide because the value of preventing suicide outweighs the costs of increased vigilance and active treatment with those who are incorrectly identified as suicidal. In assessing for early dementia, one can argue that false-negatives should be tolerated, given the importance of finding and correcting treatable causes of dementia and the likelihood that continued intervention will make the error clear (for progressive dementias) as time passes.

In some settings, psychological assessments can be used to achieve values that are not client centered. Psychological assessment may be used to justify the end of medical intervention in a managed-care setting without guaranteeing an effective psychotherapeutic intervention. Psychological assessment can also be used to remove residents from long-term care settings rather than to help them get treatment.

The same principles can be applied to decisions to refer or seek consultation. What is the value/cost of failing to call the client's physician about possible physical symptoms or medication side effects? What is the value/cost of reporting versus not reporting elder abuse? What is the value/cost of incorrectly identifying an alcoholic client as depressed? These questions permeate all clinical work and are more salient with the older client, who nearly always has the possibility of problems from different domains as well as needing differential psychological assessment. The potential safeguards for therapists are to think of psychotherapy as a clinical trial that tests the initial diagnostic formulation and to continue to assess throughout contact with the client.

Suggested Readings

General Background

Albert, M. S. (1988). *Geriatric neuropsychology.* New York: Guilford.

Blazer, D. (1990). *Emotional problems in later life.* New York: Springer.

Carstensen, L. L., & Edelstein, B. A. (Eds.). (1987). *Handbook of clinical gerontology.* New York: Pergamon.

Jarvik, L. F. (1988). *Essentials of geriatric psychiatry: A guide for health professionals.* New York: Springer.

LaRue, A. (1992). *Aging and neuropsychological assessment.* New York: Plenum.

Lewinsohn, P. M., & Teri, L. (1983). *Clinical geropsychology: New directions in assessment and treatment. New York: Pergamon.*

Lewinsohn, P. M., & Teri, L. (1986). *Geropsychological assessment and treatment: Selected topics.* New York: Springer.

Storandt, M., & VandenBos, G. R. (Eds.). (1994). *Neuropsychological assessment of older adults: Dementia and depression.* Washington, DC: American Psychological Association.

Anxiety

Salzman, C., & Lebowitz, B. D. (Eds.). *Anxiety in the elderly: Treatment and research.* New York: Springer.

Delirium

Lindsey, J., MacDonald, A., & Stube, I. (1990). *Delirium in the elderly.* Oxford, UK: Oxford University Press.

Dementia

Aronson, M. K. (Ed.). (1988). *Understanding Alzheimer's disease: What it is, how to cope with it, future directions.* New York: Scribner's.

Aronson, M. K. (Ed.). (1994). *Reshaping dementia care.* Thousand Oaks, CA: Sage.

Bergener, M., & Reisberg, B. (Eds.). (1989). *Diagnosis and treatment of senile dementia.* Berlin: Springer-Verlag.

Cummings, J. L., & Benson, D. F. (1992). *Dementia: A clinical approach* (2nd ed.). Boston: Butterworth-Heineman.

Hart, S., & Semple, J. M. (1990). *Neuropsychology and the dementias.* London: Lawrence Erlbaum.

Jarvik, L. F., & Winograd, C. H. (1988). *Treatments for the Alzheimer's patient: The long haul.* New York: Springer.

Mace, N. L. (Ed.). (1990). *Dementia care: Patient, family and community.* Baltimore: Johns Hopkins University Press.

Mace, N. L., & Rabins, P. V. (1991). *The 36 hour day.* (2nd ed). Baltimore: Johns Hopkins University Press.

Miller, E., & Morris, R. (1993). *The psychology of dementia.* Chichester, UK: John Wiley.

Reisberg, B. (1983). *A guide to Alzheimer's disease.* New York: Free Press.

Depression

Blazer, D. G. (1993). *Depression in late life* (2nd ed.). St. Louis: C. V. Mosby.

Schneider, L. S., Reynolds, C. F., Lebowitz, B. D., & Friedhoff, A. J. (Eds.). (1994). *Diagnosis and treatment of depression in late life: Results of the NIH Consensus Development Conference.* Washington, DC: American Psychiatric Press.

Schizophrenia

Light, E., & Lebowitz, B. D. (Eds.). (1991). *The elderly with chronic mental illness.* New York: Springer.

Miller, N. E., & Cohen, G. D. (Eds.). (1987). *Schizophrenia and aging.* New York: Guilford.

Suicide

McIntosh, J. L., Santos, J. F., Hubbard, R. W., & Overholser, J. C. (1994). *Elder suicide: Research, theory, and treatment.* Washington, DC: American Psychological Association.

Osgood, N. J. (1991). *Suicide among the elderly in long-term care facilities.* New York: Greenwood.

Osgood, N. J. (1992). *Suicide in later life: Recognizing the warning signs.* New York: Lexington.

6

Grief Work With Older Adults

Grief work is a common part of therapy with older adults, as the death of others is a common occurrence in later life. In general, it has been my experience that grieving for others is a more common theme in therapy with older adults than preparation for one's own death. Grief may enter psychotherapy with an older adult simply because a client in therapy for other reasons loses a loved one during the course of therapy. Grief may be a principal focus of therapy when there are multiple losses within a short period of time, when there is unresolved grief from losses that occurred earlier in life, or when the relationship with the deceased was problematic for some reason.

Is Depression During Bereavement Normal?

The question of when grieving is within normal bounds and when it becomes pathological and an appropriate focus for therapy has been discussed and debated ever since Freud wrote "Mourning and Melancholia." The American Psychiatric Association's Diagnostic and Statistical

Manuals have redefined the debate by requiring distinctions between uncomplicated bereavement and clinical diagnoses.

Wortman and Silver (1989) described several myths about the grieving process that are not supported by available scientific evidence. Distress during bereavement is generally thought to be both inevitable and necessary. In fact, on the basis of evidence in their review and a study of bereaved older adults by Gilewski, Farberow, Gallagher, and Thompson (1991), many bereaved people, including the elderly, do not experience depression after the loss, and the initial reaction tends to be fairly stable over the next few years. That is, those with initial psychological distress tend to remain relatively highly distressed. This evidence also bears on two other myths: the expectation of recovery and the attainment of a state of resolved feelings. In general, the evidence suggests that affective and cognitive effects of bereavement continue for at least 2 to 7 years after the loss (Thompson, Gallagher-Thompson, Futterman, Gilewski, & Peterson, 1991; Wortman & Silver, 1989).

The importance of "working through" the loss is perhaps more equivocal. Wortman and Silver (1989) argued that the existing evidence does not support a connection between active processing of the death and lower emotional distress from 18 months to 4 years after the death. Stroebe and Stroebe (1991) reported that among younger adult bereaved spouses, avoidance coping impaired adjustment for widowers but not for widows, whose depression was so stable over time (78% of variance in Time 2 scores predicted by Time 1 scores) that there was little additional variance to predict. One could also question, on the basis of psychodynamic concepts of defense strategies, whether people who report not thinking much about the death would not also be likely to fail to self-report emotional distress on research questionnaires; however, this line of thought needs further empirical study so as to avoid intellectual sophistry. The empirical evaluation of interventions based on different models of helping could clarify these issues.

The finding that the emotional response to the death of a loved one is stable but not universal challenges the concept of depression in response to grief as a normative reaction with a naturally occurring recovery. These observations could lead to more questioning about the severe depression reaction when it occurs. It is likely to be of clinical and scientific importance to understand why some bereaved persons become depressed and others do not. It is possible that depressed mourners were depressed prior to the death (Gilewski et al., 1991), had specific types of dependent or conflictual relationships with the deceased, or have long-standing difficulty in coping with stressful life events, perhaps due to character disorders or dysfunctional personality traits. In any case, it seems that there is reason to question the policy of both public and private insurers in the United States who disallow bereavement counseling on the grounds of the normality of bereavement and expected recovery from grieving without intervention.

In working with older adults, one cannot escape noticing that in some cases the death of a loved one brings an improvement in mood and functioning. In the case histories volume (Knight, 1992), I discuss Elaine's reaction to Warren's death as a specific instance. In numerous other instances, the death of a loved one has brought primarily relief and the chance at a new and less complicated life.

On the other hand, it is not uncommon to minimize the impact of grief on older adults. Probabilistically, death is more expectable in later life, and we seem to believe that the experience of it is easier for older adults than for younger ones. Clinical experience suggests that death, especially the death of others, is virtually always a surprise emotionally, even if it follows a prolonged illness with a known prognosis. The death of older adults does not always come so predictably. In fact, in my experience of the deaths of older clients, it has often been the apparently healthy and active ones who have died (from heart failure, respiratory failure, stroke, undiagnosed cancers), whereas the frail ones who seemed to be near death have lived for years. The timing of death for chronically ill clients can often be a surprise because they seem no more frail before death than they have been for months previously.

Aside from the issue of expectability, the emotional impact of deaths of loved ones on older adults can in some ways be more difficult because the relationships have endured longer. In later life there is also often the perception, not always accurate, that starting new relationships is not possible. Statistically speaking, of course, it is much more likely that a younger widow will remarry than that an older one will. For widowers, there may be little change in the likelihood of remarriage with age. Nonetheless, the question of a new life for oneself after the death of the loved one remains an important question that must be resolved for the older widow. As can be seen in the case history of Elaine and Warren, (Knight, 1992) anticipation of the social role of widowhood can be at least as distressing as anticipation of the coming death of the spouse.

Clinical Grief Work

The discussion that follows presents a fairly traditional approach to grief work that follows Worden (1992) and Rando (1984) especially. As this approach is presented, examples and comments will be shared that describe this approach with older adults. The elements of this work are taken to be expression of emotion, putting the loss in perspective, and adjusting to life without the deceased. The following section will describe problems that therapists seem to have in doing grief work with older adults. The concluding section discusses ways in which grief work is generalizable to other losses in later life and the limits of such generalizations.

THE EXPRESSION OF EMOTION

Grief work depends in large measure on catharsis for its presumed therapeutic impact. The assumption is that clients who need grief work have suppressed their emotions about the loss of the loved one and have been denied the opportunity to reach a normal resolution of feeling by expressing these feelings. In fact, older adults are often discouraged from expressing much feeling because family and friends are uncomfortable with the emotions expressed or seem to believe that they should have expected the loss or that the best thing for older adults to do is to act happy and be active. The negative feelings and expectations that many people have about aging may also inhibit them from encouraging older adults to express their feelings or to talk about future options out of the mistaken idea that the old do not have anything to look forward to.

The problem with encouraging the expression of suppressed emotion is that it is difficult, if not impossible, to distinguish between someone who is suppressing feelings about the death of a loved one and someone who actually is coping quite well. In practice, the distinction is made on the basis of who shows up in therapy. Older people often are brought in by family members, and it is not uncommon that family members who are themselves struggling with grief project the unresolved grief onto the older adult. I once had a middle-aged man in my office describing how his father was depressed because he had trouble grieving for "his wife." After hearing it phrased this way several times, I inquired if his father's wife was also his mother. When the son said yes, he also began to sob.

The answer often depends on the therapist's ability to perceive the suppressed emotion: People struggling not to express anger, sadness, anxiety, guilt, and so on often show some "leakage" of these feelings or else a characteristic sense of tension. In older adults, suppressed emotion may be a cause of fatigue or of social isolation. More debatable judgments may be made on the basis of the person's not moving the belongings of the deceased, maintaining a "shrine" in the house, or failing to establish a new life for him- or herself. The time lines for these are tricky: Moving too quickly (within days or weeks) may indicate problems, as may moving too slowly (5 years or more). There is a large grey area, however, and religious and cultural practices vary greatly.

The intervention itself is quite easy in terms of technique. Most of what is done utilizes basic listening skills of summary and reflection. Virtually any emotion is possible in response to a death, and it is typical that several emotions will be expressed during grief work. Often an initially suppressed emotion turns into something else once expressed. That is, people who fought against being angry express anger and then break down in tears and sob; people who fought crying start cursing the deceased for leaving them, for leaving the financial affairs a mess, and so on.

Encouraging the expression of emotion in grief work requires considerable confidence in the basic assumption that the feelings will eventually be completely emptied out and the client will feel better. Certainly in the short term, the impact is to make the client feel worse. Experience is helpful here; once you have seen the process work a few times, it is easier to enter into it with confidence and to sound confident when describing the process to the client. It seems to me that this experience has to be separately learned for older adults: That is, for reasons that remain unclear to me, many therapists do not seem to generalize success with younger clients to their older clients. To be fair, it does feel different, and somehow worse, to make older clients cry than to make younger ones cry. Perhaps it is simply a less common experience, or perhaps it arouses feelings associated with getting parents or grandparents upset.

The active part of the work involves bringing the issue up over and over again. One of the simpler ways to uncover the feelings is to encourage the client to talk about the death itself in detail in session after session until the work is done. As we will come back to in the discussion about therapists' issues, this may be emotionally difficult for the therapist. Kind persistence is everything in grief work: The material is repeated and the emotions are uncovered again and again until the catharsis is finished and the client has accepted the death and is capable of moving on to other feelings and issues. The case history of Rose in the companion volume (Knight, 1992) provides an example of this process.

Although the technique is repeated, the sessions are quite different: Both the story itself and more especially the emotions change. Again, clients may say the same words, "I'm all done with that," both when they are truly done and when they do not want to face painful issues. The difference is in the emotional inflection of the words and has to be learned by experience and through supervision.

Guilt

Guilt deserves some special mention in that it involves cognitive components and often requires more than simple catharsis to be resolved. The grieving client often feels guilty about various aspects of the death of the loved one. A wide range of actions may occasion guilt: not recognizing a symptom soon enough, not calling the ambulance sooner, not being present at the deathbed, unfinished business with the deceased, not having made the deceased change doctors or hospitals (the implicit belief is that another one could have done better), having been angry with the deceased at some time in the past several decades, not having lived the life that the deceased expected, not having been a better parent, and so on. Usually there are elements of irrational belief in the guilt, and making the irrationality explicit helps to resolve the grief: for example, "Would it really have made a difference if you changed physicians?" "Could you actually have done more to get your husband to stop smoking?"

Another approach to guilt is to explore the potential limits of it. Some clients are completely convinced that they did do something wrong and will not be shaken from this conviction. In such cases, it can often be helpful to discuss how long they should punish themselves and in what manner. The essential question is "How long is enough?"

Guilt can also involve unfinished business with the deceased. Some form of role-played conversation with the loved one can help resolve the feelings. Depending on the client's reaction to the various techniques, this can involve imagining the deceased is present in an empty chair in the therapy room; role-playing the conversation, with the therapist acting the part of the deceased; having the client talk to the loved one at graveside; or writing a letter to the deceased.

Religious resolutions of guilt should also be considered when the client has a religious affiliation that includes some ritual for forgiveness. Many, though not all, churches or temples have some procedure for seeking forgiveness, and clients from such traditions can get considerable relief from the ritual of their belief (e.g., confession, day of atonement, symbolic restitution).

PUTTING THE LOSS IN PERSPECTIVE

Putting the loss in perspective has several meanings. The first and simplest is an instance of the rational-emotive therapy principle that the loss of a loved one is a terrible event but is not a catastrophe and does not signify that one's own life is over. Although this comes naturally to most therapists when they are working with younger adult clients, it is a measure of our pessimism about late life that it is more difficult for most therapists to say this with a sense of conviction to an older client.

Nonetheless, it is true that the client's life is going on and that he or she will benefit from taking an active role in shaping that life. Believing that one's life is ruined and acting on that belief is a certain recipe for depression. The cognitive change of putting the loss in perspective can be effected only in the later stages of the release of emotion described in the previous section. The example of Rena in the case histories volume (Knight, 1992) demonstrates the potential for finding new purpose in life after the death of two disabled sons for whom she had cared for several decades.

As discussed by Worden (1992) in some detail, another issue is the exaggeration of positive qualities of the deceased. In the early phases of grief work, the deceased may be presented as perfect in virtually every way. Many widows in therapy describe the deceased husband as having been ideal in every way and assert that they never fought in 40 years or more of married life. After rapport is established and some catharsis is achieved, one can begin to question this perception gently (e.g., "If that's true, you had a highly unusual marriage. Most people have some slight flaws, and most couples disagree from time to time"). As the grief work progresses, the client starts to "recall" that there may have been a disagreement or two and that the husband had some minor irritating habits. The case of Joann in the companion volume (Knight, 1992) demonstrates how recalling conflict with the deceased can be a key issue in the resolution of grief.

Key issues in recovery from grief are "letting go" and "moving on." Older clients often hear these phrases as exhortations to forget the deceased and will reply with some heat that they could never forget someone who occupied such a large part of their lives. The response, of course, is that forgetting the deceased is not a therapeutic goal. The memories and the fondness will always be part of the client's life. Rather, the goal is to achieve enough emotional healing to be able to handle the remainder of life.

Another part of putting the loss in perspective is often a spontaneous life review process. In the context of grief work, the relationship with the deceased is reviewed in all its ups and downs (both Helen and Rose in the casebook, Knight, 1992, provide examples of this process). The therapist's role in this process is often that of active listener: keeping the client on task, making encouraging noises, occasionally offering summaries, and even more occasionally offering interpretive comments. Within the therapy, the point of the review is not so much its content as the fact of its completion. This part of the client's life has now come to a conclusion and can be summarized. That summary can lead naturally to deciding what to do with the remainder of the client's life.

DESIGNING A NEW LIFE

Once the work of grieving for the deceased is done, the question arises of what the remainder of one's life will be like. Some aspects of this question involve instrumental tasks; there are jobs that the deceased performed that still need to be done. Often the early part of grief-oriented work in therapy will include some discussion of how to solve these practical problems: who balances the checkbook, mows the lawn, fixes plumbing, cooks, mends clothes, drives the car, and so forth. In many cases, active problem solving and advice giving on the part of the therapist will be in order here. The client may need to know how to find someone to mow the lawn, to know that there are frozen and canned meals available, or to know that many banks will balance a customer's checkbook for a minimal fee. Sometimes these issues will also lead to discussions of how to use support that is available: Which family members and which friends could assist with particular tasks?

The bulk of this task is one of choosing life goals. If it is the spouse who died, one issue that needs some exploration is the client's feelings about remarriage. The feelings are important to clarify regardless of the actuarial likelihood or perceived chances (i.e., as all gerontologists and most other people know, older men are very likely to remarry and older women are not, simply due to availability of eligible partners). Many people are so aware of what is likely that they have not thought of what they want. Many women do not desire another husband. Quite a few men are not interested in remarriage, and certainly not in a quick remarriage.

Where one wants to live is often an issue. The client's children may push for the client's making a rapid move to live with or near one of them. Major, irreversible changes in one's life are usually not recommended after the death of a loved one unless the cognitive or physical frailty of the surviving partner demands it. My general observation has been that the decision to move at such a time is based on overestimating the importance of living near family and underestimating the importance of friendships and familiarity of place during the time of bereavement. The decision is often made by an adult child who may be acting out needs to protect the surviving parent from death, without regard to the parent's wishes or welfare.

Picking up old activities, including activities that may have been set aside because of the loved one, is an important part of the readjustment. Most relationships involve some accommodation, and especially if there was a period of illness before the death, the client has probably set aside activities and goals that used to be important and sustaining. Rediscovering and renewing these pursuits can be an important part of starting a new life.

Throughout this discussion, it is imperative to be alert to the client's complaints about the advice offered by others. The emphasis here is on finding the client's own individual desires, goals, and enjoyable activities. Our society places a great value on activity for its own sake, and the widowed and other bereaved get a great deal of nonspecific advice along this line. Part of helping the client find his or her individual path is offering sympathy and support for the rejection of bad advice from others, while perhaps exploring why the client found the suggestions unhelpful. The therapist needs to avoid offering advice or endorsing rejected ideas and should instead reinforce the client's right to choose. Older people are often told what to do to start a new life; affirming clients' independence involves supporting their right to reject advice as well as the right to choose their own path.

Some Observations on
Grief Work as a Process

The activities described above (expressing emotion, putting the death in perspective, designing a new life) do not necessarily occur in that order and may, in fact, overlap in messy ways in any given therapy. Expressing emotion may be intertwined with practical problem solving early in therapy and may require more work during the life review. As noted in the case histories volume (Knight, 1992), there are few therapies in which grief work is the primary and only focus (JoAnn is the closest example in that book). Grief work can arise in therapy as deaths occur (see the cases of Helen and Rena) or may be discovered in cases in which unresolved grief was not suspected (e.g., Rose).

Grief work is itself more specific to the person lost than is discussed here. For older adults as well as for younger ones, it matters whether the person who dies is a parent, a child, a sibling, a spouse, or a friend. As is remarked on often in writing on grieving, losing a child seems the cruelest and most unnatural loss; this remains true when the child is 60 or 70 years old.

Grief work with older adults is often complicated by the multiplicity of deaths. The older adult may lose a spouse, a friend, and a sibling within a couple of years. The emotions about multiple deaths are often inter-twined, and the therapeutic work may move from one to another and back quite rapidly. There is the additional complexity that one grief tends to remind us of others, so older adults, with so much life history, often are reworking losses from the remote past as well as those of the recent past (see the stories of Rena, Rose, and Elaine).

It seems to me that unresolved grief stays unresolved and can do so for years or decades. If this is true, the all-too-common practice of discount-ing the impact of a loss on the current emotional functioning of an older client because the death occurred months or even a few years prior to the beginning of therapy seems entirely wrong-headed. This practice is even more peculiar given the widely known difficulties that older adults have in getting connected with therapy: That is, the gap between the death and the start of therapy may have more to do with reluctance to refer older adults to therapy than to any aspect of the natural course of emotional reactions to death.

For both older and younger adults, we need to know more about the connection between grief and depression. Clearly not all who grieve become depressed; as noted earlier in this chapter, recent evidence seems to suggest that those who do become depressed are not at all likely to recover without intervention.

Therapist-Centered Issues in Grief Work

Given that the techniques used in grief work are fairly basic listening skills, the difficulty of grief work must lie in its impact on the therapist rather than in any intrinsic complexity of the process itself. There are, in fact, a variety of reasons why therapists may find grief work, and especially grief work with older adults, difficult. One such reason, of course, is countertransference (see Chapter 4); therapists with unresolved grief of their own are likely to find working with grieving clients emotionally painful or not to notice that grief work needs to be done because of their own denial. The reasons discussed in this section are more generalized and reflect the difficulties that grief presents for many people in the present era of our culture.

Death is, of course, a highly emotionally charged issue for all of us, and one that is often ignored in our society. Psychotherapists are not always trained either didactically or experientially to work with death and dying issues. Without specific preparation, the therapist is left to his or her own devices and stage of development to understand and react to death and dying issues. As a trainer of new therapists, my observation is that grief and other death-related issues are most often simply not perceived. For example, when one group of supervisees were asked to do case presentations, there was ample reason to explore death and dying issues in virtually every case: One client had started therapy because his mother had died, two others had reported recent deaths in the family, one's mother was thought to be dying, and one had had a mastectomy within the 6 months preceding therapy. In every case, the therapist had focused on other aspects of the client's life and failed to see the possible relevance of death to the client's depression or other emotional disturbance.

Once the therapist is made aware of the relevance of death to the client's distress, another quite common objection to raising the issue in therapy is the presumed fragility of the client, often expressed in terms of concern about breaking down the client's denial. As reported by Lehman, Ellard, and Wortman (1986), what most people coping with grief want is a chance to talk about it and express their negative feelings. It is a major failure of psychotherapy if the therapy room cannot be a place where this can happen. Clients are seldom truly in denial about grief or about terminal illness; their daily experience of it makes denial difficult to maintain. Denial is a strong coping process and virtually never breaks down simply because it is questioned. In virtually all such cases, it is the therapist rather than the client who is fragile. Once the therapist shows a willingness and ability to talk about death, the client is ready and relieved to be able to do so.

There are reasons beyond the therapist's death anxiety for being reluctant to listen to people talk about grief and death. Some of the stories that you hear are actually quite gruesome: I have a fairly high tolerance, and I have finished sessions feeling somewhat nauseated. You learn how many different ways there are to die, some of which are more pleasant than others. You hear a lot of unsettling stories about the ineptitude and callousness of paramedics, emergency room staff, nurses, physicians, and so on. These lessons tend to dispel whatever sense of security you may have taken from the existence of emergency medical care.

The expression of emotion in grief work is fairly intense. Clients may cry, sob, curse the deceased, yell at the therapist, lapse into depressed silences, have anxiety attacks in the session, and so on. One of my first clinical supervisors observed that emotion is for psychotherapy what blood is for surgery, his point being that it is inevitable and that ability to tolerate emotion may determine who can be a therapist. My observation is that new therapists tend to prefer to talk about the client's emotion rather than to observe it. There may also be a tendency to avoid probing for emotional expression that is specific to older clients. Making older people cry may be difficult for everyone, perhaps especially for those who like older adults enough to specialize in working with them. This tendency would be especially troubling for grief work.

A commonly expressed concern in supervision and in consultation with practicing therapists is whether the older person who is grieving really does have anything to look forward to. Grief is the quintessential example of a loss that simply must be accepted. The client has the choice of working it through and feeling better or continuing to feel depressed. Therapists, out of pessimism, may make this choice for the client by implicitly choosing to withhold therapy.

Some degree of comfort and life experience with death may be an implicit factor in how people choose to work with older adults. In my experience as a supervisor, it seems that those students who have not chosen to pursue a career with older adults have to be actively encouraged to talk about death and grief, whereas those who have chosen a career in aging sometimes have to be restrained from plunging into difficult material with the client too quickly.

Working with older adults will, in any case, expose the therapist to the realities of death, both vicariously through clients' experiences and directly as clients die. In addition to grieving for clients (missing them, getting angry that they did not complete their work in therapy, putting off writing the discharge notes on their cases, semiconsciously expecting them to come in at the regular hour, and so on), the fairly regular exposure to clients and other elderly acquaintances who die teaches lessons about death above and beyond, and earlier than, one's own life experiences. Death is final, unpredictable, often sudden. Our own emotional reactions are not always what we would hope for and do not always fit within the schedule of professional life. It hurts to lose people whom we feel close to (such as clients), and it can be difficult to keep on getting close to clients if we do not deal with the hurts as they arise.

These are all issues that need to be more thoroughly addressed in training: in the classroom and in clinical practice and supervision. One can also note that scheduled lectures on death and grief work are often characterized by high levels of absenteeism.

Is Grief Work a Model for
All Therapy With the Elderly?

Grief work is different in form and feeling from much else that goes on in therapy. Much of therapeutic work with younger adults consists of encouraging clients to try out new behaviors and explore options, while helping them contain their anxiety. Grief work is about expressing feelings and letting go of lost loved ones. This can feel more depressing than helping young people explore potentials. The belief system that supports a negative evaluation of working with older adults in this way overlooks positive aspects of later life and negative aspects of younger adult life.

People routinely underestimate the number of years that older adults have ahead of them and the potential positive experiences that those years may bring. The prognosis for grief work is positive, and older adults have years of experience and strength to draw upon, know themselves well, and often have coping styles and find solutions that the therapist has not imagined. Young adults sometimes have problems with bad prognoses (e.g., serious character disorders), do not know themselves and their capabilities well, and do not always succeed when exploring their potential. My point is simply that the sense of pessimism with older adults as contrasted to younger ones is not founded in realistic comparisons but may have more to do with the therapist's reaction to the form of the therapeutic work.

It is tempting to generalize grief work to other losses faced in later life. There is a sense in which one grieves for lost physical functioning, which will be covered in the chapter on coping with physical illness and disability. The process of expressing negative emotion is similar with regard to the techniques used with the client. In rehabilitation counseling, the phase of accepting the loss of ability may be superficially similar to putting death in perspective and designing a new life. However, the processes and goals are quite different, and describing both as adjusting to loss obscures more than it clarifies. In brief, lost functioning is often recovered or compensated, but deceased people stay deceased.

Summary

The distinctive nature of grief work, which has as its goal the acceptance of truly unchangeable loss and moving on into the rest of life, may color our reaction to doing psychotherapy with older adults in general. The emotional salience of the work for the therapist and the superficial similarity in form to some other therapeutic issues that arise in later life (e.g., loss of physical functioning) may account for the overgeneralization that therapy with the elderly is about coping with loss. Though grief work is an important topic in therapy in later life, it is far from being the only topic. Older adults also seek therapy for the same reasons that younger adults do, including depression, anxiety, self-understanding, and problems with friends, family, and lovers. Younger adults have loved ones die and need grief work. The identification of grief and death as issues for older people may be a basic misperception on the part of therapists who have not yet accepted death as a personally relevant reality.

Suggested Readings

Fitzgerald, H. (1994). *The mourning handbook: A complete guide for the bereaved.* New York: Simon & Schuster.

Kubler-Ross, E. (1991). *On death and dying* (2nd ed.). New York: Macmillan.

Rando, J. (1984). *Grief, dying and death.* Champaign, IL: Research Press.

Rando, J. (1993). *Treatment of complicated mourning.* Champaign, IL: Research Press.

Worden, W. (1992). *Grief counseling and grief therapy* (2nd ed.). New York: Springer.

7

Chronic Illness in Later Life

This chapter addresses issues and techniques in working with older adults who are experiencing emotional distress related to chronic illness or disability in later life. The purpose of the chapter is twofold: to explore working with chronic illness and disability and to explain the use of various therapy techniques, primarily those developed by cognitive-behavioral therapists. The joining of chronic illness and cognitive-behavioral techniques is not meant to imply that these approaches are the only ones used for chronic illness or that this is the only problem with which they should be used. However, these are commonly used and effective strategies in dealing with a common problem that is faced by older adults.

Emotional Consequences of Illness and Disability

Chronic illness and at least mild levels of disability are common in late life. About 80% of older adults have at least one chronic condition (LaRue, 1992). Estimates of functional disability are quite variable, but 12% is a commonly accepted figure (Weissert, 1983). Depression is considerably more common among medical inpatients than in the population as a whole (Rapp, Parisi, Walsh, & Wallace, 1988), affecting about one fifth of patients. Illness is a good predictor of subsequent depression in community samples of older adults (Phifer & Murrell, 1986). In short, chronic illness is common among the elderly and is likely to be even more prevalent among older adults in psychotherapy.

Even normal emotional reactions may be cause for referrals to therapy. Physicians are often not trained to deal with high levels of emotionality and may be too busy to handle patients who are atypically upset or more dependent than average. Psychotherapists can often be of assistance to both physician and patient and can reduce unnecessary physician visits or calls by providing basic listening, support, and a place to vent emotions for patients whose sadness or anxiety may seem a natural consequence of their medical diagnosis.

Medical treatment brings its own emotional consequences in addition to those brought by the illness. In earlier phases of life, when one is dealing with acute medical problems and those only rarely, the patient role is temporary and the emotional reaction to it passes as the role is ended. In later life, chronic illness or disability may necessitate long durations of treatment with more frequent physician visits, hospital stays, long-term medication regimes, and long-term alterations in life patterns due to the limitations of the illness or its treatment. Treatment adherence, the patient role, and one's relationship with the physician and his or her office staff take on much more emotional importance when "being sick" becomes a matter of years rather than of days.

What, then, is the role of the psychotherapist with the older physically ill or disabled client? In the remainder of the chapter, this question will be answered first in terms of the therapist's role in helping clients understand the illness and its necessary impact on their lives and then in terms of what therapists can do to improve clients' emotional functioning and thus their overall level of functioning. The chapter concludes with observations on what therapists need to know to do this work and on common emotional reactions of the therapist to working with physical illness.

Understanding Illness and Its Consequences

The focus of this section is on helping the client to understand illness and its effect on daily functioning. The section describes first the common problems of overestimating or underestimating the effect of chronic illness on functional ability and then the importance of attributing the symptoms of illness to the specific disease rather than to the aging process.

BETWEEN A ROCK AND A HARD PLACE: HOW MUCH INDEPENDENT BEHAVIOR IS HEALTHY?

A central question and therefore an ongoing assessment issue in working with chronically ill older adults is establishing the optimum level of independent functioning. People can, and usually do, err in one or both of two ways. The more commonly discussed error is often described as "excess disability." In excess disability, psychological factors (e.g., anxiety, depression, dependent personality style) are presumed to cause the patient to act more disabled than he or she physically is. People with chronic obstructive pulmonary disease (COPD), for example, may become homebound due to their fear of becoming short of breath. People who are severely visually impaired may be too depressed to try out alternate ways to read (e.g., use of large-print books or books on tape). In some cases, the dependent patient role is more enjoyable than the person's previous life. For lonely patients, a chance to talk with nurses and office staff may be a highlight of their social life. In some family systems, being ill may improve the way the person is treated by other family members.

In the case histories volume (Knight, 1992), John, Harold, Lana, and Nora all illustrate the possibility of functional limitations that are partly psychological and partly physical. John and Harold provide interesting contrasts for one another in that John, who was much more physically disabled, was more capable of finding ways to enjoy his life and continue to engage in meaningful activities than was Harold, whose incapacity was largely due to characterological traits of dependency and inferiority. Nora's anxiety both created symptoms for which she sought medical treatment and interfered with ongoing medical treatment for the physical problems she did have. Lana pursued medical treatment largely out of a need to play out relationship scripts with physicians. All had, in some sense, excess disabilities.

The opposite problem can also become an issue in therapy. Some people push too hard to get well and fail to accept real physical limitations. The consequences are often physical: accelerated progress of the disease, physical collapse due to overexertion, frequent readmission to hospital, and so forth. The case histories of Rose and of the couple Elaine and

Warren in the companion volume provide examples of people whose day-to-day functioning (and physical health) was harmed by trying to continue activities that were now out of range of their capability. In Rose's case, repeated attempts to return to work and to be the most responsible employee at work returned her to the hospital; for Elaine and Warren, continuing to paint the house, mow the lawn, and work in the garden resulted in exhaustion and relapse.

Obviously, it is of critical importance to know whether the patient is trying too little or too much. This assessment can be done only with input from the attending physician(s), rehabilitation therapists, nurses, and other health care professionals who may be involved. Whenever possible, input from family members or others who observe the patient in action is helpful, as patients' motivations will also influence their self-assessments and self-reported functioning at home. Unfortunately, even with optimal communication among the health care team, the optimal assessment is often not clearly knowable and may well involve some trial-and-error experimentation. There simply is not a clear mapping from diagnosis to functional level, and there is sufficient individual variation so that usual courses of recovery may not hold true for a particular individual.

The principles remain that it is vitally important to form a complete physical and psychological picture of the patient, to revise this picture continually as new information develops, and to keep in mind that mistakes can go either way.

ACCURATE ATTRIBUTION
OF EXPERIENCED SYMPTOMS

At the most general level, a common and usually inaccurate attribution is to interpret the signs of illness as being related simply to growing older. There are several problems with misunderstanding illness in this way. First, one may miss out on the possibility of treating or compensating for symptoms of the illness or the illness itself, as aging is inevitable and must be accepted. For example, people who attribute failing sight or hearing to aging seem less inclined to use talking books or to learn lipreading and other compensating techniques than people who perceive the loss as due to specific pathological changes in eyes or ears.

Second, symptoms of illness usually are known and somewhat circumscribed; on the other hand, "symptoms of aging" are believed to be general and pervasive. If one knows that vision loss is due to cataracts, there is no expectation that deafness is coming on as well. If the loss in vision is attributed to aging, hearing loss and impaired mobility are also expected (inaccurately, of course).

Third, illnesses often have expected outcomes: We may get better, stay the same, or get worse over an approximately known period of time. Understanding the prognosis can be helpful in future planning. Aging is popularly and wrongly assumed to be an inevitable, global decline spread over an unknown period of time. Obviously, knowing that an illness may remit or even that it will stay about the same is better than the inaccurate assumption of decline. Even when the illness is progressive, most clients seem to feel better knowing that they have a specific disease process that can be studied. The knowledge acquired about the disease can then guide future planning.

Techniques for Working With
Older Chronically Ill Clients

The next few sections provide an introduction to techniques that are frequently helpful in working with older clients who have chronic illness or disability. The techniques covered are relaxation training, increasing pleasant events, cognitive restructuring, contingency analysis, and naming and expressing emotions. These techniques are drawn from cognitive-behavioral therapy and its applications in health psychology. Further readings on these topics are listed at the end of the chapter.

THE ROLE OF RELAXATION TRAINING

When anxiety complicates the illness, the symptoms, or the treatment, relaxation training can be a helpful component of treatment. Relaxation training has been studied in older populations and found to be effective (DeBerry, 1982; Rickard, Scogin, & Keith, 1994; Scogin, Rickard, Keith, Wilson, & McElreath, 1992). The primary modification of relaxation training in use with older adults is to instruct them *not* to tense muscle groups in areas where they have pain. A script for relaxation training follows:

> Settle back as comfortably as you can. . . . Let yourself relax to the best of your ability.
> Now close your eyes.

Take a few deep breaths. . . . Inhale. . . . Exhale. . . .Inhale—feel the tension building as you inhale. . . . Exhale—feel the tension leaving your body as you exhale. All the tensions of the day are going out of your body. Inhale once again. . . . Hold your breath. . . . Exhale.

I'm going to ask you to tense each muscle two times. The first time, tense quite hard; the second time, only half as much.

Now let us begin.

Tighten your foot muscles—hold it, relax. Experience the sensation of relaxation when you relax your feet. . . . As you feel the tension leaving your feet, allow this soothing feeling to move upward to your ankles. Repeat.

To relax your calf muscles, press your feet and toes downward, away from your face, so your calf muscles become tense. Hold for a few seconds, then relax. Repeat once again. . . . This time, bend your feet toward your face so that you feel tension along your shins. Bring your toes right up. . . . Relax again. . . . The second time, tense half as much.

Tighten the muscles in your thighs by pushing them against the chair. Hold. . . . Relax. . . . Once again.

Tighten your buttocks muscles. . . . Hold. . . . Release. . . . Again. . . . Hold. . . . Relax.

Pull the muscles of your stomach inward. . . . Try to visualize your navel pressing against your spine and organs inside. I seem to hold a lot of tension in my stomach; maybe you do, too. . . . I like to think of all my organs as rubber bands. . . . Hold. . . . Relax. . . . The second time only half as hard. . . . Tense. . . . Release.

Next you are going to relax your shoulders and upper back. You have two choices: Pull your shoulders back as though you were trying to touch your shoulder blades together, or you may want to try an alternate movement—raise your shoulders as though you were trying to touch your ears with the tops of your shoulders. Hold. . . . Release. . . . Repeat once again.

Hold your arms out and make a fist. . . . Hold. . . . Release. . . . Repeat, the second time half as hard. . . . Relax.

For the neck, there are two techniques to choose from. Pull your chin toward your chest, using the muscles in the front of your neck, or you may wish to pull your head back with the muscles pushing back toward the wall. Begin tensing your muscles. . . . Hold. . . . Relax. Experience the relaxation for a brief period of time, then repeat.

Clench your teeth and pull back the corners of your mouth. At the same time, press your tongue firmly against the roof of your mouth. Hold. . . . Release. Repeat once again.

Make a face—raise your eyebrows as high as they will go, wrinkle your brows and nose, shut your eyelids tightly together. . . . Hold for several seconds. . . . Relax. . . . Repeat again.

Now, as you sit in your chair, with eyes closed, explore each of the regions you have relaxed. Think about your feet, calves and shins, thighs, buttocks, stomach, upper back, shoulders, arms, neck, mouth, and face. Try to be aware of any tension left in these muscles. If you are now free from tension, just quietly savor the feelings of calmness and relaxation.

When following up on relaxation training in later sessions, it can be helpful to have the client do the exercise on his or her own initiative while the therapist watches. A very common reason for the failure of relaxation therapy in my experience is that the client rushes through the sequences in a couple of minutes.

In my experience, relaxation has proved helpful in anxiety with COPD, memory complaints, anxiety about falling (after the cause of falls have been eliminated or the person has adequate support from canes or a walker), anxiety about treatment procedures, and pain control.

Not all clients can use progressive relaxation. Some people find it too boring or find that it releases suppressed anxiety. In these cases, active relaxation that is suitable for the client's physical condition is likely to be better (e.g., walking, swimming, stationary bicycle). For clients with a poor response to either of these approaches, deep breathing, mild hypnotic induction, or attention-focusing approaches may be workable options.

PLEASANT EVENTS APPROACHES IN
IMPROVING EMOTION AFTER ILLNESS AND DISABILITY

This section borrows loosely from Lewinsohn's pleasant events approach to understanding depression. Lewinsohn (Lewinsohn, Munoz, Youngren, & Zeiss, 1978; Lewinsohn, Youngren, & Grosscup, 1979; Zeiss, in press) argued that people stay depressed because they often engage in fewer pleasant events and engage in or are exposed to more unpleasant events. As applied to rehabilitation from illness and disability, it is argued that either directly because of functional losses or through depression related to the illness, ill and disabled people share a similar pattern of experience.

As in the Lewinsohn model, the focus is on the highly individualized nature of these pleasant and unpleasant events, so the first step is to have clients identify what they do now that is pleasant and unpleasant and what they enjoyed prior to the illness. In my own clinical work, I have found it possible, and less intrusive, to gather this information in clinical interviews rather than requiring the use of the Pleasant Events Schedule (PES). The PES can be helpful as a guide to the therapist and certainly can be used with clients who do not find paperwork daunting or distasteful. (See Zeiss, in press, for a more positive view of the PES and its alternate forms.) Because depression is often neglected in chronically ill older adults, this may involve going back months or even years to recall the previously enjoyed activities. In this instance, the next stage of the intervention is to discuss which of these pleasant activities can be resumed, which ones there are potential substitutes for, and which must be given up due to the realistic circumstances of functional losses. A key assumption in this work is that *some* improvement in mood is virtually always possible, even though it is quite possible that a return to pre-illness levels of happiness may be unrealistic. People tend to assess happiness in all-or-nothing terms. The therapist will often need to teach the client explicitly that it may be impossible to return to life as it used to be but is that it is possible to be happier than the client is now. Drawing graphs of average happiness prior to illness and average happiness now and showing the goal as between these two levels can provide a helpful visual aid. This initial work may need to include some grieving for the activities that are irretrievably lost. (See previous chapter for discussion of grief work.) After this groundwork is laid, the contracting for change in behavior can begin.

The next stage is the relatively straightforward, though not usually quick, process of contracting for more pleasant events (and possibly for the cessation or reduction of unpleasant ones). For example, someone who enjoyed going out to listen to classical music may contract to listen to tapes or to a classical music station for an hour or so each day. For some clients, reduction of unpleasant events may involve contracting to stop watching the news several hours each day and to fill that time with comedies, reading, or looking out the window. As is true of all behavioral contracting, it is important to schedule change in small and clearly achievable steps. Much of the time in these sessions is spent negotiating the client down from goals that seem too ambitious. The client may enjoy the process and the creation of the resulting contract, and he or she is likely to end up more strongly committed to a goal that he or she is certain can be achieved. Examples in the case history volume (Knight, 1992) can be found in John's case history. Comparing John and Harold points to the fact that failures of this approach are more psychological than physical in origin.

COGNITIVE RESTRUCTURING

Cognitive restructuring can be of benefit in reducing the discomfort of symptoms and in changing health- and treatment-related behaviors. At a high level of abstraction, the point can be made that people tend to catastrophize about illness and disability. That is, many people take a bad situation and make it even worse by exaggerating the impact of the problem and by overgeneralizing its effects. For the chronically ill/disabled older person, reality is bad enough. Active cognitive work to keep the individual dealing with the reality can help to reduce "excess depression."

Seligman's concept of pessimistic explanatory style (Peterson, Seligman, & Vaillant, 1988; formerly, "learned helplessness") offers a useful guideline for analyzing and changing unhelpful attributions about illness or disability. Pessimistic explanatory style consists of attributions for negative events over which the individual in fact had no control that are global ("everything is bad"), stable ("things will always be—and/or have always been—bad"), and internal ("I was responsible for the bad events").

In counteracting global attributions, it is important to help the client focus on the exact nature of the disability rather than to see him- or herself as completely disabled. This process consists of the candid recognition of abilities that are lost combined with the encouragement to recall the abilities that remain (e.g., "I can no longer see well with or without glasses, but my hearing is intact and I can still walk").

The attribution of stability to disability is also important to consider and reframe if possible. Some clients will see their condition as stable even when the medical prognosis is positive. Achieving a realistically optimistic expectation for rehabilitation in therapy can be an important step toward adherence to medical treatment and/or rehabilitative therapy. In a less obvious way, stability attributions can also be helpful when the disability is going to be continuous or even progressive. In these instances, the limitation of stability is found in considering the past: It can be quite important emotionally to recall that one has not always been disabled and to relive memories from better times (but also see material below on emotional expression and the chapter on grief).

The third and final component of pessimistic explanatory style is the attribution of internal locus of control for events that were not controllable and are negative in their impact. People often look for ways in which they are responsible for the illness or disability. Usually the appropriate intervention is the more correct attribution of external locus of control: It just happened. In conversational terms, the question is often expressed as "Why me?" The answer in a sense is "Why not you?" In this view, bad things that are beyond control happen to people; there is no reason that any individual should be exempt. In clinical practice, this reframing is often not in "all-or-nothing terms." Some clients need to retain a sense of having contributed to the illness, but this is a more limited attribution than their feeling that the illness was completely under their control. It is also important in working with older adults to reestablish their place in history: We know *now* that many illnesses are related to poor health behaviors. However, for the current cohort of older adults, this information was discovered fairly late in their lives, and many of these same behaviors were considered health enhancing when they were young (e.g., cigarettes were once marketed as having positive effects on health, including improved thinking and breathing).

Before leaving the issue of control, it is important to recognize that this effort to deemphasize control is specific to attributions of control related to uncontrollable negative events. Control of current life events is, in general, positive in terms of health impact (Rodin, 1986; Rodin & Salovey, 1989). Health problems and their treatment often diminish both perceived and actual control. Enhanced control has been shown to have beneficial effects in pain control, in dialysis, and in nursing home care (see Langer & Rodin, 1976; Rodin, 1986; Schulz & Hanusa, 1978; Turk, Meichenbaum, & Genest, 1983). It may well be important to be certain that the level of control can be maintained. Schulz and Hanusa (1978) showed negative effects of increasing control and then decreasing it again by ending an intervention.

CONTINGENCY ANALYSIS AND PSYCHOLOGICAL INTERVENTION IN ILLNESS AND TREATMENT

Contingency analysis is the identification of chains of behaviors, thoughts, emotions, and sensations that precede and follow a target that one wishes either to increase or to decrease in frequency. In health-related interventions, the target may be behaviors (taking medications, showing up for appointments, calling the physician, screaming at family members), automatic thoughts that are enhancing depression or pain, emotions (anxiety, panic attacks, depressed moods), or sensations (most often pain). The chain of antecedents is constructed by asking "What happened before the target? What happened before that? Before that?" and so on. The chain of consequents is formed in the same way by asking what comes after the target.

The antecedents can help in one or both of two ways. Recognizing antecedents in the chain gives warning of what is to come. Helen in the case histories volume (Knight, 1992) learned to control her depression by recognizing such antecedents as the way her dog looked at her and her own bingeing on chocolate. Antecedents thus become a cue for changing the sequence early rather than late. To continue the example, Helen learned to use the dog's expression as a cue to take more antidepressants and to make telephone contact with friends. The second use of antecedents is that they often point to situations or behaviors that can be avoided (or increased). In Helen's case, the chocolate was not only a cue but also a likely contributor: Stopping the bingeing also ameliorated the depression. Social interactions are often part of the antecedents for emotions and behaviors. The analysis may point to a need to increase contact with some individuals and decrease contact with others. Excessive office visits or telephone calls to physicians often have emotional antecedents (anxiety, loneliness) that are more effectively handled in other ways (e.g., contact with friends or the therapist; see the Lana case example in Knight, 1992).

Consequents may be thought of as reinforcers if they maintain or increase the target and as punishers if they decrease the frequency of the target. This distinction is highly individual and needs to be determined by analysis of individual cases: One client's punishment may be another's reinforcer. Consequents are examined to determine their role in relation to the target and then can be used either to effect the desired change or to change the contingency between the target and the consequence itself. For example, excessive visits or calls to a physician or to an emergency medical service are often maintained by the attention provided by health professionals. A first step in the intervention is to substitute the therapist's attention and social reinforcement for that of the medical professionals. This is generally easy because therapists see this as a natural part of their role and because, by the time of the referral, the medical professional is exasperated and so is no longer as reinforcing. The next step is to find other, more natural sources for attention and social reinforcement. This step often involves work on the client's social skills or on solving problems in primary relationships.

Another type of problem is the client who perceives a treatment as punitive. Medications, special diets, or medical equipment are often seen as inherently unpleasant so that adherence to the medical treatment plan is self-punishing. At times, there are relatively immediate positive consequences that can be identified in the therapy interview or by the use of journal-keeping homework to track consequences of taking and not taking medication. Some medications and diets make the person feel better immediately or limit how bad the person will feel in the short term. Once this connection is made, adherence to the treatment is self-sustaining.

The more typical situation is that the beneficial effect is long term and the short-term effects are neutral or negative (e.g., unpleasant side effects). From a learning theory standpoint, behavior will be governed by the short-term effects. In these situations, the patient may need both external rewards (e.g., praise from therapist and family members) and self-reinforcement (pairing taking the medicine with some pleasant, healthy treat or an enjoyable experience such as good music). Although these may seem like simplistic solutions, the more common practice is to criticize the client for not complying with medication regimes, not to praise them for correct behavior.

Antecedents and consequences often form tight feedback loops in natural circumstances. For example, people with emphysema often become phobic about going outside or being in social situations. Shortness of breath makes people anxious, and anxiety makes people short of breath, setting up a rapidly escalating cycle that can lead to panic attacks and breathing crises. This anxiety in turn often generalizes to the situations in which it occurs. Teaching clients to recognize early antecedents of shortness-of-breath episodes can make it possible for them to begin calming themselves and to use relaxation early enough in the causal chain that it still has a chance to work. The control of anxiety makes the episodes less frequent and/or less severe. The increased mobility is virtually always self-reinforcing. In this way, a self-perpetuating negative cycle can be turned into a self-perpetuating positive cycle.

RECOGNIZING AND NAMING EMOTIONS

A common feature of many clients who have significant somatic symptoms is an inability to name their emotions (sometimes called *alexithymia*). In this cognitive interpretation, the failure to identify certain internal states as emotions may result in their being interpreted and reported as physical symptoms. It may also result in prolonged stress and the development of some stress-related disorders (see Rodin & Salovey, 1989).

The clinical presentation will usually involve a number of physical symptoms without an identified diagnosis or with an indication from the physician that the diagnoses do not explain the symptoms. There is also an inability to identify emotional reactions in situations that commonly produce an emotional response (e.g., argument with spouse or other family member). The range of interventions can include the use of feeling charts to teach the client emotional words and to help them to identify the internal feelings with these emotional words. While the client discusses emotionally laden topics, the therapist interrupts occasionally to ask that feelings be identified. The client will usually resist naming any feeling, then will be able to make crude distinctions such as "good versus bad" or "positive versus negative." Eventually it is possible to recognize basic feelings such as *happy, sad, fearful,* and so on.

Gendlin's (1978) focusing technique is also useful in identifying the physical and/or emotional sensations that may be present during discussion of stressful situations in therapy. Clients are instructed to relax, breathe naturally, and focus on an internal spot where feelings may occur for them. Sitting silently, they observe the feelings for a while, being instructed that these may change while being observed. After a few minutes, they are roused to alertness, and the experience is discussed. With this type of client, the exercise will often first yield somatic descriptions rather than affective ones. For example, Nora in the companion volume (Knight, 1992) identified a feeling of having something stuck in her throat. Various alternatives were suggested, including that it was words that were stuck in her throat. Eventually, this led to a recognition of a lifelong inability to express anger.

It may also be necessary to analyze the situations in which somatic symptoms appear and to suggest alternative emotional states that people often experience in those circumstances. In one instance, a male client was so emotionally inhibited that he was at first able to identify only what "someone else" would be feeling in stressful situations. Over a period of months, he was able to recognize that he might have some of those feelings. Learning to identify the emotions accurately leads to better understanding of current stressors, to some release of emotion, and to resolution of the somatic complaints.

Issues for the Therapist in Working
With Chronically Ill Older Adults

A variety of skills are needed when therapists begin working with chronically ill older adults. In my view, the need for these skills is based on the special characteristics of therapy with people who are chronically ill rather than special characteristics of older people per se. However, there is a strong correlation between age and the prevalence of chronic illness, and it is quite likely that many older adults who seek therapy will be chronically ill and that the illness will be directly related to the depression, anxiety, or other emotional distress that is the focus of the therapy. This probabilistic association between age and illness poses the dilemma for the professional psychotherapist that therapists who are attracted to work with older adults need to know about psychotherapy with clients who have physical illness. In the same way, therapists who are attracted to work with chronically ill patients (i.e., to hospital consultation, health psychology, behavioral medicine, medical social work, etc.) will find themselves needing to know about gerontology.

KNOWLEDGE ABOUT PHYSICAL ILLNESS
AND MEDICAL TREATMENT

Psychotherapists working with older adults will need to know about physical illnesses, their treatments, and the emotional consequences of both illnesses and their treatments. Frazer (1995) and Smyer and Downs (1995) have written about the level of knowledge needed about illnesses and about pharmacology and include potential reference sources. Therapists do not need to be as sophisticated about these issues as the treating physician, but they need to know as much as or more than the client. The therapist should be able to read a history and physical and to read other medical reports well enough to understand the prognosis, the effect on the patient's functioning, and the recommended course of treatment.

To work with clients who are ill, it is of course necessary to be able to discuss illness intelligently. In most cases, the level of information needed will be that obtainable by an intelligent layman. Frazer (1995) suggests several sources for such information, including popular books, medical texts and references, and voluntary health organizations (e.g., American Heart Association, American Cancer Society). The purpose of obtaining this information is to be able to discuss the illness intelligently with the client and with attending health care professionals and to be able to form reasonable working hypotheses about what is due to physical illness, what is due to psychological factors, and how the two interrelate. Quite possibly one of the most disastrous mistakes made by psychotherapists working with older adults is to avoid all discussion of physical complaints and to avoid contact with physicians working with the client.

Aside from the assessment of the case, being able to discuss physical problems intelligently helps in building rapport with older clients. People in general avoid listening to the physical complaints of others, and listening helps build trust and closeness. Although physical talk can be off the subject and can be used to avoid deeper emotional issues, with older adults, the physical complaints are most often the source or focus of the emotional issues. That is, clients may be depressed because of the illness or pains, or they may be talking about current pains as a way of bringing up concerns about future disability or their beliefs about aging.

COMMUNICATING WITH PHYSICIANS

For the client's sake, it is necessary to be able to communicate effectively with the attending physician. Effective communication generally includes defining who you are, why you are calling, what information you have to offer, and what information you need. Physicians can be territorial (with one another as well as with people of other disciplines) and sensitive to criticism. Not being a physician can be helpful in avoiding territorial issues. If you are offering information that may be relevant to medical treatment, it can be very helpful to be clear what your source of information is and to avoid appearing to draw a medical conclusion about it. For example, "When I was visiting Mrs. X, I noticed that she had several medications on the coffee table from several physicians. I know you're the primary care physician and wanted to make sure you are aware of this" is better than starting by saying that you believe Mrs. X is overmedicated.

Psychosocially trained therapists tend to have a discursive style of communication and to convey a sense of having plenty of time to discuss issues. We are often also trained to avoid stating conclusions clearly and unequivocally in favor of entertaining several possible hypotheses or case formulations. Biomedical professionals tend to convey a sense of being pressed for time and to communicate in clear, tightly worded assertions. These different styles can lead to physicians' becoming impatient and the therapists' feeling hurt. It is wise to learn how to communicate in the biomedical style so that messages can be heard (see Qualls & Czirr, 1988, for more on interdisciplinary communication).

As is true for interdisciplinary communication in general, it is helpful to remember what each discipline has to offer in understanding the patient. Physicians mostly understand and treat serious physical problems. Psychotherapists mostly work with emotion and behavior. Each side tends to be uncomfortable with the other domain and either to avoid it or to disparage it. Working together is easier if one recalls that the common ground is the client's well-being and if each works within a context of respect for the other.

UNDERSTANDING MEDICAL SETTINGS
AND THE PATIENT'S POINT OF VIEW

As has been argued elsewhere in this volume (see Chapters 1 and 2), the social context of later life is one of the aspects of working with older adults that makes that work somewhat specialized. Older adults with chronic illnesses spend large parts of their lives within medical treatment settings (physicians' offices, hospitals, clinics, medical labs, skilled nursing facilities, etc.). These settings have a particular social ecology of their own and may be difficult to understand if the therapist has had little experience with the medical environment. Suggestions from psychotherapist-consultants often require time to implement. This time may not be available—in the sense that staff are already busy doing physical care and medical interventions, in the sense that the patient may not be there for many days, and in the sense that the staff to whom you speak may not be on duty for the next several days. Understanding the total workload, knowing the duration of time available before discharge, and knowing how to communicate directions in a multishift, rotating schedule environment will all be necessary if the therapist wishes to affect the patient's care. Suggestions will need to be simple, quick, related to medical care, and (probably) written in the chart.

In fact, it may be only marginally helpful to have work experience in medical settings unless the therapist has some ability to see the setting from the patient's point of view. Being a patient means being confronted with one's own physical limitations related to the illness; being defined as a patient also confronts one with tests, treatments, and other regimens that are constant reminders of the physical body. Depending on the previous attitude toward the physical body, this may require some reorganizing of the sense of self (see Sherman, 1991). That is, in our culture many people are inclined to think of themselves as primarily mind, spirit, or will and to take the body for granted. Until chronic illness makes being a patient a career, even early adulthood experiences with acute illness may be seen as interruptions in life and may challenge these nonphysical views only briefly and then be readily forgotten.

Medical settings themselves are designed primarily with acute illness in mind, and both their physical and social aspects are less pleasant when confronted often and regularly. It makes little difference how staff interact with you if you are there seldom and then briefly. Older adults are more sensitive to social interaction styles in these environments in large part because they spend more time there. They are also more keenly aware of the mistakes that are made in such settings. The therapist needs to listen carefully to the patient's viewpoint and to try and "see with a patient's eyes" when in a medical setting. For example, one test I use is to consider how complex a physical environment would be to navigate in if I were visually impaired, limited in ambulation, or cognitively frail. A "patient's-eye" understanding of these settings with their formal and informal social rules is an important part of working with older adults in psychotherapy.

Finally, medical settings confront patients not only with their own illnesses but with those of the other patients. One of the most frequent topics that comes up in working with the depressed chronically ill is the depression that comes from constant exposure to those who are even more ill than the client and to the frequent deaths of people who share hospital rooms or who have been met and befriended in hospitals or other medical settings.

THE THERAPIST'S REACTION
TO PHYSICAL ILLNESS

Discomfort with physical illness is fairly common among therapists. Although this point was made in Chapter 4 with regard to societal and countertransferential reactions to illness, here the discussion considers discomfort that is rooted in lack of skills or poor training. Training that is focused on younger adults does not provide much experience in working with people who are ill. The same type of training is likely to include learning that talk about physical symptoms either is a distraction from the real work of therapy or should be interpreted as having emotional significance. Although there are times in therapy when older adults use physical problems to avoid therapeutic work or when physical symptoms are emotion equivalents, there are more times when being able to converse about physical illnesses and the medical care system is essential to building rapport or is an integral part of understanding the illness and/or its treatment as a major stressor for the older client.

A common deficit in skills when working with older adults is the therapist's reluctance to discuss the facts of the illness with a client who is also avoiding the topic. When the avoidance is a failure to cope that is causing or maintaining an emotional disturbance, it is essential that the illness and its effects be discussed in therapy. It is also common that the older client avoids discussing illness because he or she has learned that most people cannot handle it. In this instance, the client avoids the topic to protect the therapist—not a desirable situation. The most common source of the therapist's reluctance is the feeling that it is unkind to confront the client with the realities of functional losses and disability. This feeling seems to be enhanced when the client is very old or very frail in appearance. In effect, one feels that therapy is supposed to help people feel better, and confronting physical illness does not feel helpful; in fact, it often feels a bit harsh or cruel. In part, this appraisal of the situation is the therapist's way of avoiding an unpleasant task. If this stance is not challenged and overcome, the client is cheated out of therapy and out of a chance to improve emotionally. It requires some experience of success with clients of this sort to feel better about the likely outcome of the confrontation.

Summary

This chapter has introduced important concepts and skills that can be used in helping older clients cope with the specific challenges of chronic illness and disability. Though accepting the loss of functioning is an important first step, in this model of thinking about therapy with older adults it is *only* a first step. The following steps include understanding the specific illness, not overgeneralizing from specific illness to global aging, and using therapeutic skills and techniques to enhance functioning, explore and improve emotionality, and understand and cope with medical treatments and health care settings, which can be stressors in themselves. The emphasis in this type of work switches from the age of the patient to the nature of the illness, its prognosis, and the pros and cons of its treatments. Readings on health psychology are given in the suggested readings for this chapter. In the next chapter, we turn to understanding the life review process and its place in psychotherapy with older adults.

Suggested Readings

Carstensen, L. L., & Edelstein, B. A. (1987). *Handbook of clinical gerontology.* New York: Pergamon.

Frazer, D. (1995). The interface between medicine and mental health. In B. G. Knight, L. Teri, J. Santos, & P. Wohlford (Eds.), *Mental health services for older adults: Implications for training and practice* (pp. 63-72). Washington, DC: American Psychological Association.

Haley, W. E. (in press). The medical context of psychotherapy with the elderly. In S. H. Zarit & B. G. Knight (Eds.), *Psychotherapy with the elderly: Effective interventions for older adults.* Washington, DC: American Psychological Association.

Hartke, R. J. (Ed.). (1991). *Psychological impacts of geriatric rehabilitation.* Gaithersburg, MD: Aspen.

Jarvik, L. F. (1988). *Parentcare: A commonsense guide for adult children.* New York: Crown.

Kemp, B., Brummel-Smith, K., & Ramsdell, J.W. (Eds.). (1990). *Geriatric rehabilitation.* Boston: Little, Brown.

Lichtenberg, P. A. (1994). *A guide to psychological practice in geriatric long-term care.* New York: Haworth.

Smyer, M. A., Cohn, M. D., & Brannon, D. (1988). *Mental health consultation in nursing homes.* New York: New York University Press.

Zarit, S. H., & Knight, B. G. (Eds.). (in press). *Psychotherapy and the elderly: Effective interventions for older adults.* Washington, DC: American Psychological Association.

8

Life Review in Psychotherapy
With Older Adults

Life review with older adults has a long-standing, though not always clear, role in psychotherapy with older adults. One of Freud's (1905/ 1953) objections to working with older adults—not discussed much anymore—was that there was simply too much life history to work through in psychoanalysis. Robert Butler (1963) observed that therapists often pathologized the tendency of older adults to reminisce and argued that reminiscence was a natural and healthy psychological activity. Later, Lewis and Butler (1974) described life review therapy as an effective method with older adults and with other adults in important developmental transitions. Erikson (1963) described adult developmental stages and argued that there were important transitions and develop-

AUTHOR'S NOTE: In addition to clinical work and the authors cited here, two sources have inspired and shaped this chapter. First, I have co-taught a summer class on Psychological Development Through Autobiography at the University of Southern California's Leonard Davis School of Gerontology with Marlene Wagner. She and the students have stimulated and shaped my thinking about the chapter. Second, the metaphor of the therapist as editor was suggested to me by an article on editing biographies by Peter Davison "To Edit a Life," *Atlantic Monthly,* October 1992, pp. 92-100.

mental stages past childhood, ending with the theme of integrity versus despair in the final stage in later life.

The success of reminiscence and life review therapies is another matter and may still be an open question. Early reports have been mixed (Haight, 1988, 1992; Rattenbury & Stones, 1989), although it is encouraging that the more clearly therapeutic uses of life review have shown significant results (Fry, 1983). Historically, it is of interest that both Erikson and Butler cautioned that life review can have negative outcomes of despair and depression and would not have predicted success for unguided life review processes.

In what follows, it is the clearly therapeutic use of life review that is the central focus of discussion. This is intended to omit unguided reminiscence as a naturally occurring activity and reminiscence groups in activity centers and long-term care centers in which the purpose is primarily socialization. (In passing, it is of some concern and curiosity to me that many reminiscence groups in long-term care probably include persons with significant memory impairment who are likely to be making up rather than recalling the past lives they reminisce about.) It is also my intention to omit autobiography groups as either a literary activity or a personal growth activity for nonclients. These omissions are made to simplify and focus the discussion that follows, not to criticize these other activities.

The Role of Life Review

Unlike the preceding chapters, which were problem focused, this chapter on life review with older adult clients is about helping clients understand life, understand aging, and reconstruct their self-concept. In the concluding chapter of the case histories volume (Knight, 1992), I argued that life review most commonly arises in therapy when one is working with grieving clients (who must construct a new view of themselves that extends past the death of the loved ones) and when "new" emotions must be integrated into the self. Some physical traumas that result in chronic illness and disability require a new view of the self as a person lacking abilities that have previously been taken for granted. For some older clients, aging itself poses what Kastenbaum (1964b) called the crisis of explanation: "How did *I* become an older adult?" Finally, as is true in therapy with younger adults, the presence of severe character disorder may require a life historical approach in therapy.

In what follows, it is assumed that the focus of life review is primarily on the creative development of self-concept, perceived here as our ideas about who we are, who we have been, and who we will be (Markus & Herzog, 1991). Whitbourne (1985) argued for a life span construct that is more explicitly developmental and unified than the Markus and Herzog formulation, which has the potential for multiple self-concepts. Whitbourne also argued for a future component, the scenario, as well as a past component, the life story.

The self-concept is thus a created cognitive schema that is strongly affected by social roles and expectations (see both Whitbourne, 1985, and Markus & Herzog, 1991). Though undoubtedly affected by developmental processes, the created life span construct is also influenced by culture, social roles, historical changes, and the events of one's life. In what follows, cohort, age-graded roles, and social context will be considered along with maturation as influences on the client's understanding of personal development.

Self-concepts both guide and are affected by coping with environmental changes. Inaccurate or outdated self-concepts can lead to anxiety if people are not able to predict reasonably accurately what they will do or what will happen to them (see Kelly, 1955) or to depression if people evaluate themselves negatively (e.g., if their lifetime achievements do not match adolescent goals that they still endorse as valid). In therapy, the purposive goal is generally the reduction of dysphoria rather than historical accuracy.

The next section describes maturation in an adaptation of Erikson's stages to life review work with older adults. After that, the possibilities of using social gerontological concepts to understand the life span construct and its role in therapy are explored.

Erikson and Developmental Stages

Erikson has described eight developmental stages in the life cycle that cover infancy to late life (see Table 8.1). As can be seen, five of the eight occur by adolescence, leaving three to cover the period from young adulthood to old age. Erikson's intellectual and psychological focus was on childhood and adolescence, although he became more interested in old age in his own later years (Erikson, 1978; also Erikson, Erikson, & Kivnick, 1986). His work is of great importance in extending the notion of development past childhood and into the adult years and in the assertion

TABLE 8.1 Erikson's Eight Developmental Stages

Age	Conflict
Infant	Trust vs. mistrust
Toddler	Autonomy vs. shame
Child	Initiative vs. guilt
Schoolchild	Industry vs. inferiority
Adolescent	Identity vs. confusion
Young adult	Intimacy vs. isolation
Middle-aged adult	Generativity vs. stagnation
Young-old adult	Integrity vs. despair

SOURCE: Erikson (1963).

that there are developmental conflicts in adulthood that can be the loci of unfinished business in late life, as well as the more commonly thought-of childhood conflicts.

In its strongest version, this theory encourages us to look for unresolved developmental conflicts throughout the life span when confronted with an older client. If it is assumed for the sake of exposition that one must work through the themes in order, then the focal theme will be the one whose negative emotion predominates in the client's internal life. In this view, a client who is 75 may still be 11 (industry versus inferiority) or even 2 (autonomy versus shame) in terms of internal emotional maturity. This view also argues that it is no better to be 70 and still struggling with generativity versus stagnation than to be 45 and still struggling with intimacy versus isolation. It is explicitly not the case that everyone who is 60 or more is necessarily at the final stage of integrity versus despair. Nor do external indications of compliance in social roles argue for successful completion of a stage: That is, being married does not mean having worked through intimacy versus isolation. This approach, especially in this strict interpretation, can guide psychotherapy to work on lifelong issues of immaturity and can guide questioning about life history to probable times in the life span when important events occurred that resulted in arrested development.

For example, Rose in the case histories volume (Knight, 1992) seemed to have formed an intimate connection with her first husband. On the other hand, though she had children, she seemed less connected to them and did not seem to have resolved the generativity issue either through her children or through work. Her striving for work had more of the flavor of industry versus inferiority: "If I can't work, then I'm nothing." Within this strict interpretation of stage theory, this observation would lead us to question the authenticity of the intimate connection with the first husband, who had been dead for several years prior to the beginning of therapy. Because there was no other evaluation of this relationship available, it was possible that the relationship and the first husband might have been idealized as part of unresolved grief.

Harold seemed to have gotten stuck in conflicts with his father and failed to form a separate identity. Even at 80, he was unaware of who he was, unattached to his accomplishments, and not very connected to wife or children. Even his sexuality seemed adolescent or preadolescent: He wanted to look at and talk to young women, but even his fantasies did not seem to extend to touching.

Lana appeared to be stuck much earlier. Not allowed to express anger at her father and develop her own sense of initiative, she got angry repeatedly at physicians who failed to care for her. All following stages were also blocked, and she was plagued by inferiority, was confused about roles and identity to the point of not recognizing the difference between emotions and physical symptoms, and had childlike relationships with her lovers and her own (now adult) children.

Although there are clearly strengths, the life stage approach has problems as well. Within its own terms, one has to wonder if three stages are sufficient to describe adult life. Erikson et al. (1986) also raised this point, framing it in terms of the greater number of older adults who live a couple of decades or more past 60, when the integrity stage is thought to be reached. My own clinical experience suggests the need either for more stages or for a different kind of analysis of adult life so as to account for the richness and complexity of older adults' life stories.

The theory also seems not to account for important variations in adult life histories. Are women's lives the same as men's (see Helson, Mitchell, & Hart, 1985)? Do cultural and class differences create different patterns for life stories? Do people who choose not to marry remain adolescent in their development? Do people who choose not to have children remain immature and hamper their chances of handling generativity well? Are the lives of lesbians and gays somehow less mature than those of heterosexuals? To comprehend these and other varieties of adult life experience, it is helpful to move out of purely intrapsychic development to biopsychosocial models such as life span developmental psychology and the life course perspective in gerontology (Bengtson & Allen, 1993).

The Life Course
Perspective in Gerontology

The life course perspective is an emerging worldview in gerontology that provides a framework for thinking about adult development in biological and sociological terms and in broader psychological terms than those of intrapsychic theories. Bengtson and Allen (1993) used the metaphor of different clocks to explain the various influences on people's lives.

THE BIOLOGICAL CLOCK

The biological clock, so obviously important in childhood development, tends to provide the model for many psychological perspectives, including Erikson's. After the attainment of adult maturity, this clock would appear to slow down and perhaps also become less salient. There are biological changes that are interpreted as signs of middle age and aging: wrinkled skin, grey hair, and mild to moderate changes in vision, hearing, reaction time, attention, and memory. Menopause provides a more dramatic marker for many women, although its meaning and apparent impact vary dramatically. In general, these biological markers of aging influence the self-concept more because of their socially defined value as symbols of aging than because of inherent significance. Gray hair is not debilitating, but our reaction to it may be. The loss of the capacity to bear children after menopause may be seen as liberating or as tragic, depending on the individual's life story and the cultural values that shaped it. These markers provide the individual with signposts that declare the onset of middle age or old age; they may be the occasion of starting to take seriously the approach of the end of life.

The greater prevalence of disease and disability in later life influences our perception of later life and older people; however, as noted in earlier chapters, the meaning of late life should not rest on overgeneralization of disease to normative aging. Struggling with illness and other limitations of the body is an important theme of life stories but is not inherently age specific. In the case histories, John is 20 years younger than Harold and far more disabled.

THE COHORT CLOCK

The historical clock provides a important context and source of variation in people's stories. As measured by cohort membership, this clock tells us when different groups of individuals enter the stream of historical time. This difference in entry into the flow of time becomes an important source of observed differences among people. In work with older clients, the concept of cohort membership can be useful in understanding the social forces that helped to shape the client's identity. Knowing the historical period in which the client was an adolescent and young adult can be helpful in understanding the social milieu in which identity was first formed.

Cohort membership rather than position in the life cycle accounts for many differences between young and old people in values, musical taste, life experience, perceptions of current trends, beliefs about health, and so forth. One indication of advancement to middle age is the awareness of a cohort of adults later born than oneself who are developing a different sense of the world and their place in it. It can help older adults understand and appreciate themselves to recall that their opinions are not the result of *growing* older but are the result of life experiences that later born generations did not share.

Expectations for a typical life cycle change over time and over cohorts (Hagestad, 1990; Hagestad & Neugarten, 1985). It is important to understand the client's life within the framework of what was normative for his or her cohort rather than what is normative for one's own cohort (e.g., in some earlier born cohorts, divorce was more stigmatized and early marriage less stigmatized than would be true now). Riley (1985) called the error of assuming that other cohorts age like our own "cohort-centrism." At the same time, it can be helpful to clients whose lives did not go as expected to question the origin of the expectations rather than accept them as implicit rules for human development. For example, Frances in the case histories volume (Knight, 1992) had always felt bad about not being raised in a normal family. (She was illegitimate when the term had considerable meaning and stigma, and she was raised by a foster family.) It was more helpful for her to question the values of the cohort in which she was raised, in the light of later standards, than to continue to judge her life against unattainable normality.

FAMILY TIME

Another type of clock is the family clock. Where are we in the successive generational structure of our own families? How many surviving generations are older? How many are younger? This family context can help determine how old we feel, how alone we feel, and what kinds of aging issues are being dealt with. Becoming a parent and watching children grow up gives a sense of adulthood and maturation. Watching parents become old confronts the adult children with their own future aging. Families have their own unfolding stories across successive generations, and the client's place in (or outside of) that story has important influences on the self-concept.

AGE-LINKED ROLES

Within these larger contexts is the playing out of age-graded social roles (see Neugarten & Hagestad, 1976). We have ideas, rules, and even laws that prescribe sequences and appropriate ages for different activities. In the career sphere, the sequence is school, work, retirement. In the family life sphere, the sequence is dating, marriage, child raising, empty nest marriage, postretirement marriage. The family sequence may be intertwined with ending and re-forming family: dating, marriage, child raising, divorce, single parenthood, dating, remarriage, blended-family formation, all intermingled with school and work. As noted by Neugarten and Hagestad, these role changes are often accompanied by a sense of doing something "on time" (at an appropriate age) or "off time" (too early or too late). This sense of timing may vary by cultural background, cohort membership, gender, and so forth (Hagestad, 1990).

These age-linked roles and the accompanying sense of appropriate timing pose an important conceptual challenge to the notion of stages of adult development. At least for individual clients engaged in self-understanding, and quite possibly for stage theorists of adult development as well, it is easy to misconstrue changes in these roles for transitions across developmental stages. Getting married, divorced, and remarried clearly involves role changes and significant life experiences that will shape the life span construct, but is it maturation? Similarly, career-oriented people construct a developmental view of their work histories, but would they be less mature if their work histories were different (e.g., if they had stayed in a particular job rather than moving on to the next)? Much of what is written about midlife developmental transitions may really be about midcareer issues when potential in a given career track no longer appears limitless and one has either reached the highest rung of the career ladder or can see where it is.

Thinking of such changes in social role terms tends to emphasize the potential for variation and creativity, whereas stage theories tend to imply a correct order, timing, and path to maturity. In strict Eriksonian terms, many adults in current U.S. society must be failing to resolve intimacy and generativity, given choices not to marry or not to have children. Although a view of much of modern American society as immature or adolescent is not wholly without merit, the counterpoint is to ask whether a 1950s view of normal development should still hold. Erikson himself (1978) noted that his examples were generally upper-class, creative people.

Even this version is too simple. Different kinds of people have different social roles open to them and different senses of what is on "time." One must be alert to such influences as gender, religion, country of origin, ethnicity, social class, and sexual orientation and more (Hagestad, 1990; Hagestad & Neugarten, 1985; Helson et al., 1985). Along with cohort membership, these help shape identity and influence the particular life experiences that make up each individual client's life. These markers, along with cohort membership, help us to place the client in a social and historical context and can guide the kinds of questions that should be asked to be certain that important shaping influences are not missed. For example, an English-Scotch man, born in 1920 in a small midwestern farming town to a middle-class, mainline Protestant family, who discovers while in military service that he is gay has a very different life story from that of an Italian, Catholic immigrant woman born in 1930 who goes back to work to support her children after her husband is killed in an industrial accident. These differences are due, in part, to differing gender, ethnicity, religion, and class distinctions that shape both the experiences available to people and their perceptions of those events.

SUMMARY

These concepts from the life course perspective and from social gerontology more generally broaden the potential basis for comprehending and guiding the creation of the client's life span construct beyond the unfolding of intrapsychic stages. This view reminds us that markers of development are often biological, although their meaning may be socially defined or highly personal. The sense of maturation is in large part determined by position in family constellations and the timing of age-graded social roles. These notions of developmental maturity in turn are influenced by cohort membership, gender, class, ethnicity, religion, and so on. To make this general analysis more specific and to encourage comparison with the earlier writings, in the next section we revisit and revise the life review of Dr. Borg from the Bergman film *Wild Strawberries.*

Revisionist Reflections
on Dr. Borg's Life Cycle

Ingmar Bergman's film *Wild Strawberries* has long been associated with life review and stage theories; Robert Butler (1963) mentioned it in his discussion of the normative nature of reminiscence in older people, and Erikson (1978) analyzed it to give an example of his stage theory of life span development. To continue the tradition and to clarify the foregoing attempt to integrate life course and social gerontological concepts with the life review method, I reconsider Dr. Borg's life here.

STAGE THEORY:
THE STRONG VERSION

If one takes the strong version of stage theory, as Erikson (1978) clearly did not, one can begin by questioning whether Dr. Borg is actually dealing with issues of integrity versus despair. In fact, there is ample reason to think that he is stuck considerably earlier in the life cycle. There is no evidence of his having successfully resolved intimacy; in fact, much of the story is focused on the complete failure of his marriage and the reasons that his childhood love Sara married his brother rather than Isak Borg. Although others consider him a success, Borg seems not to feel that generativity has been positively resolved: He sees himself as deserving the title of honorary idiot rather than the honorary doctorate, and his relationship with his son is cold and distant.

There are grounds for wondering about earlier stages as well. In this view, the opening dream is significant, not for the confrontation with death, but for the signs of identity confusion: the faceless man in the street, confronting himself in the coffin as neither clearly dead nor alive. The dream examination portrays him as feeling inferior and incompetent in his profession: unable to remember the first duty of a physician, to use a microscope, or to tell whether a patient is dead or alive. In the same dream, the examiner pronounces him "guilty of guilt," perhaps pushing his developmental arrest back even further. The analysis does not have to stop at this point, but the principal conclusion here is that Dr. Borg provides an example of an older adult who is struggling with developmental issues from earlier stages of life. As is always true in such persons, the picture is one of an individual who has conformed with adult behaviors and roles (work, marriage, parenthood, etc.) but has done so with the intrapsychic maturity of a child (or adolescent or young adult).

COHORT THEMES

The film was made in 1959 in Sweden, and Dr. Borg is 78 years old (Erikson wrote 76, the film states 78). He was therefore born in 1881 and would have come to maturity around the turn of the century. In placing Dr. Borg in the context of his cohort, his values and sense of identity (however incomplete) would have been influenced by the sociohistorical context of the cohort reaching young adulthood in Sweden in 1900. Because I know nothing about that cohort, it is not possible to fill in many details. One can guess that Dr. Borg's formality, insistence on his son's repaying the loan as a matter of principle, and attitude toward women's smoking may all be related to cohort membership. One question that arises from the story, but is not directly addressed, is whether having a child at 40 years of age (Isak Borg is 78; his son is 38) would have been significantly "off time" in this cohort. If so, it would be useful to explore the reasons for late fatherhood. If not, it may be of less clinical importance.

The differences between 1959 in Sweden and the current era in the United States provide other illustrations of cohort changes. The women are portrayed in relatively traditional stereotypical feminine roles. The change in women's roles can be seen in comparing Borg's mother, his daughter-in-law Marianne, and the young hitchhiker Sara. The young people, who appear to be late adolescents or young adults, are referred to and treated as children. Isak Borg would have seen changes of similar magnitude across his life span and probably would have approved of some more than others.

FAMILY TIME

If Borg is to be taken as an icon of the older adult reviewing his life before dying, what are we to make of his still-living mother? At 95, she would be closer to death than he. Though we know nothing of what happened to the father, the mother's long life may suggest that Dr. Borg, who has no obvious chronic illness or physical frailty, may have a couple more decades of life ahead of him.

We also are told that Borg was one of 10 children and the only one left living. This fact in itself is likely to have contributed to a sense of loneliness and of the closeness of death. If Isak Borg were available for therapy, his reactions to the loss of his nine siblings and his father would be an important theme to follow up. As an issue in the family dynamics, it is of interest that only Isak and his son Evald visit the matriarch.

We can also infer that Dr. Borg is 17 years younger than his mother and had his son at 40 and that now his son will have his first child at 39. Is this a reaction to the family setting in which Isak Borg grew up? Perhaps the coldness of his mother made him unwilling to have or uninterested in having children, a response that was then transmitted to his son. Although not entirely clear in the film, it is possible to infer that Evald, after the age of 8, was raised by Isak (and probably by Agda, the housekeeper) as a single parent: Toward the end of the examination dream, there is a reference to Isak's wife having been dead for 30 years. This theme is not explored in the movie, but one would want to find out more in therapy. In any case, Isak Borg will have his first grandchild when he is 79, rather late in the life cycle. The therapist would want to know how he feels about this.

AGE-GRADED ROLES

There is only a little to go on here other than the questions raised already about whether his fathering of Evald was "on time" or not. Dr. Borg's career is only indirectly described. He clearly was in clinical practice in his early career years and then moved to research. His own evaluation of his life work is ambivalent: He describes his early career as drudgery and seems to disagree authentically with the assessment of his later career that led to the honors ceremony. On the other hand, the encounter with the gas station owner who remembers his clinical practice years later with great fondness and gratitude seems to inspire him to wonder if he made the wrong choice. We have no clues as to when he made this change or why. Clearly, this is a topical domain of importance that would benefit from further exploration in therapy. For this analysis, the important point is that the career decisions were choices made in a given context rather than a developmental unfolding.

In terms of other socially defined roles, Dr. Borg is male, Swedish, and quite wealthy. Clearly, his options would have been different had he been female or born to a middle-class or poor family. His religious values, a frequent theme in the film, seem to have contributed to his difficulties with his childhood sweetheart, his wife, and most other people. The exploration of the way in which his personal issues influenced the expression of these values so as to alienate family and friends would require great care and tact in counseling. Having him consult with his pastor or priest about his interpretation of these values might well be an important adjunct to the therapeutic process.

SUMMARY

This review of Dr. Borg's life cycle has argued for a more dismal view of Borg's maturation. It has also suggested numerous questions to pursue about the context in which Isak Borg's life was lived: cohort, familial, career choices, class, and religion. As the movie ends, there are hopeful signs that Dr. Borg is moving toward a reconstruction of his life story that will move him along developmentally: He is warmer toward Marianne and Agda, makes steps toward communicating with Evald, has begun to reconstruct his failures in relationships. What about his future?

Because Borg is neither dead nor even frail or ill at the end of the movie, his reconstructed life story should lead to a future scenario as well. What could life hold for Isak Borg? It seems likely that he could, with some work, reconcile with Evald and Marianne and assume a full role as grandfather in the new family's life. A renewal of his romance with Sara (stated to be 75 and quite beautiful) or a new marriage is not out of the question. It is not clear what his vocational or avocational activities are at this point in his life, but he is clearly intellectually vigorous and could continue his previous work or explore some new avenues. The latter may be preferable given his ambivalence about past achievements. In any case, life review is not an end in itself, but rather a process that improves the life history as a step toward coping with the present and creating the future (see Whitbourne, 1985).

Strategic Issues for the Therapist Guiding a Life Review

The preceding discussion has argued for conceptualizing the life review process in therapeutic terms. The developmental approach to life review has been presented in a strong form that argues that older adults may be stuck at earlier stages of life in adulthood or childhood conflicts. This developmental approach has been supplemented by the sociological approach to the life course, which emphasizes the social contexts of cohort and family as well as viewing life stages as movement through social roles. This movement through roles may be roughly age linked but is often interpreted in developmental terms even when the paths through roles are highly varied and unsystematic (see, for example, the comments of Hagestad, 1990, on women's work lives and the misperception of male management roles as age linked).

In what follows, several strategic issues for the therapist guiding a life review are explored. The first is the question of whether life review should be attempted with a particular client. The next issue is posed by the impossibility of getting a truly complete life history from any client, and especially an older one who has more decades of adult life to review than the younger adult client. The impossibility of completeness in the review leads to the metaphor of the therapist as editor of the life history. Finally, it is argued that the life review is not an end in itself but should lead to a revised scenario; for older adults as well as younger ones, the point of therapeutic life review is preparation for the future.

WHEN TO REVIEW THE CLIENT'S LIFE

When to review the client's life will depend on the assessment of the client's problem and therefore on the theoretical framework of the therapist. My own values on this point were shaped by early exposure to Bandura's argument in *Principles of Behavior Modification* (1969) that the therapy should aim for the minimal change necessary to achieve the client's goals. Bandura used the metaphor of auto repair to argue that psychodynamic approaches always overhaul the engine even when a tune-up would have fixed the problem. Although I might take the argument less far than Bandura, I would agree that using life review (and other life historical approaches) for every client is unnecessary.

In the conclusion of the case histories volume (Knight, 1992), I noted that life review frequently arises during grief work, at least partly from the need to redo the life history so that it supports a future without the deceased in it. Major functional limitations may call for a life review to understand the future without the ability to see, to hear, or to walk. I also argued that major new realizations, such as the recognition of previously blocked emotion, may require life review to understand how the ignoring of this emotion shaped life up to this point and how incorporating it may change the future. The connection of life review to role transitions (recognized by Lewis & Butler, 1974, though framed in developmental terms) likewise is implied by the need to change the life history to absorb the new role and to support a new scenario that includes this role and future possibilities implied by it.

This listing is not intended to be exhaustive. Older adults do have many problems that do not require life review. Most rehabilitative counseling does not include life review; the client's existing self-concept supports the needed changes in health behaviors or mood. Many acute depressions, phobias, and anxiety states in later life do not require historical work. Many family problems require no life review or only very focused reviews of past problems and good times in the particular relationship. Chronic and recurrent problems may need a longer term frame of analysis including life review. When in doubt, the short-term approach can be tried first; the longer term life review can be used when clearly needed or as it arises naturally in the therapy.

A COMPLETE LIFE HISTORY

If one decides to do a life review, the length and complexity of the lives of older clients place pragmatic limits on how complete the review can be. Clearly, no therapist attempts minute-by-minute recall, even with young clients. However, with decades of a human life to cover, it is possible to see a client for a year or two, amass a large and detailed history, and still discover that major parts are missing. Because life reviews are motivated in part by a desire to encourage the incorporation of avoided negative topics into the life history (see Fry, 1983), some gaps are motivated, and the existence of these gaps is an important clue to what topics need to be explored.

One key to the discovery of gaps is to develop a time line for the client's life history as it is known. If years or decades are unaccounted for, these missing eras need further exploration. Clients can seem to be loquacious and open in their reminiscence and still neglect whole decades of their lives. Problematic work histories can be deleted, marriages that failed painfully may be omitted, estranged children may not be mentioned, and so forth.

A second type of check on completeness is a check on the domains of the client's life experience that are known. These should include

1. Family of origin, including significant developmental issues for client
2. Educational experiences
3. Client's perception of cohort membership and influence on identity
4. Sexual development and history
5. Love history
6. Marriage(s)
7. Children and other aspects of family or families of adult life
8. Work history and client's evaluation of it
9. Client's sense of ethnicity, gender, social class as influences on life

age and important changes in body
/spiritual history or life view/worldview
... experiences of death
13. Sense of the future (e.g., how much time is left and what things are left to accomplish)

After a reasonable period of time or reasonable diligence of inquiry on the therapist's part, one should have at least a general impression of these areas. If there are gaps, the therapist should question whether the gap is appropriate given the focus of the therapy or what is known about the client's life. Absent themes, like gaps in time, may be important clues to areas that the client is reluctant to bring up and therefore are guides to sensitive areas in the client's life.

THE THERAPIST AS EDITOR

Because completeness is not possible, the therapist will make choices for the client about what is important to cover and will make choices with the client about what should be emphasized in building up the life history. If we recognize the life history itself as a created schema of the self rather than a complete and veridical account (Sherman, 1991; Whitbourne, 1985), the therapist can be seen as editing the client's writing of the life history. This editing may take the form of deleting material ("You tend to focus on your failures; let's talk about successes you've had"). As discussed in the previous section, it can mean exploring deleted material ("I realized that I only know about your current job, what did you do before that?"). It often means reframing the material that is presented ("You view your life as highly stressed, but what strikes me is how well you cope with it all").

The therapeutic aim of the life review will determine the scope and focus of this editing. If the aim is to help the client feel better, then the editing may well focus on positive aspects of the client's past history. If the aim is changing long-standing patterns of behavior that are not well understood by the client, the editing may focus on discovering hidden, negative elements of the client's life history. A client struggling with current stressors may be guided to recall previous successful coping. Older adults seeking to understand what it means to be old in our society may be guided to see continuity with earlier aspects of their lives, to deemphasize age itself as a major explanation for current problems, and to plan futures that incorporate recent changes into ongoing stories.

THE FUTURE:
LIFE AFTER LIFE REVIEW

Life reviews are never complete when they are finished. The individual has future time left, and there is need for consideration of the scenario as well as of the life history (see Whitbourne, 1985). In research on possible selves, Ryff (1991) noted that older adults see more concordance among past, present, future, and ideal selves than do young and middle-aged adults. They also see future selves as stable or negative compared to the present self, whereas young and middle-aged adults expect improvement in the future. This contrast in views of the future in older people may imply a change of perspective for the therapists working with older clients: There is less future time to project improvement into, and the future is often thought of as limited in time and perhaps negative in outcome. It is, of course, not clear whether it is the older client or the younger adult client whose view is unrealistic.

Planning the scenario is often limited by unrealistic assumptions about the amount of time left. Life expectancy charts show an average future life expectancy of 14 to 18 years at 65, 9 to 11 years at 75, and 5 to 7 years at 85. This often represents considerably more time than the client (and perhaps the therapist) is assuming is left.

In fact, when time is known to be limited by life-threatening illness and/or when frailty is predictable in the near future due to progression of known disease, planning for the remainder of life typically takes on greater urgency. Deciding what issues and what unfinished business in life and relationships should be resolved is of greater urgency when the time is known to be limited. In this sense, planning for the future requires more therapeutic energy for frail clients than for healthy older clients.

The construction of scenarios or of future selves can have meaning for the not yet old as well. In planning for the future, adults rarely plan past the period of work and family raising in middle age and on into the postretirement lifestyle. Large-scale studies of the life course suggest that retirement takes up a large percentage of the life span, that we spend more time in the child-parent relationship as adults than as children, that widowhood is a predictable role for women, and that most of us will be frail for a few years prior to death (see Hagestad, 1990).

We might, for example, choose to resolve childhood or adolescent conflicts with parents differently if we did it with the awareness that we would be connected to our parents for more decades in the future than the two spent as their actual child. Parents might treat a daughter-in-law differently if they were aware that she was a very likely choice as their future caregiver. Because we may spend two or three decades retired, some thought should be given to postretirement life as well as to work and family life. Psychotherapy for younger adults, as well as for older adults, should take the future as seriously as the past.

Summary

This chapter concludes the consideration of frequent topics in psychotherapy with older adults: grief, chronic illness, and life review. These topics were highlighted as frequent issues that are thought to make work with older adults different from work with younger clients. It is worth noting again that these topics are not specific to older adults: Younger adults can grieve, become ill or disabled, and review their lives. Further, older adults are not limited to these topics: Older adults in therapy often discuss marital problems, conflicts with children, depression, phobias, drinking problems, and the other myriad concerns that can afflict human beings of any age.

In the next and final chapter, the question of whether therapy with older adults is a specialty is addressed. Some common ethical issues in working with older adults are examined. The potential relationship of the psychotherapy integration movement to work with older adults is noted. Finally, the place of group and family therapy with older adults is explored.

Suggested Readings

Breytspraak, L. M. (1984). *The development of self in later life.* Boston: Little, Brown.

Disch, R. (Ed.). (1988). *Twenty-five years of the life review: Theoretical and practical considerations.* New York: Haworth.

Erikson, E. (1968). *Identity: youth and crisis.* New York: Norton.

Erikson, E. H., Erikson, J., & Kivnick, H. Q. (1986). *Vital involvements in old age.* New York: Norton.

Sherman, E. (1991). *Reminiscence and the self in old age.* New York: Springer.

Viney, L. L. (1993). *Life stories: Personal construct therapy with the elderly.* Chichester, UK: John Wiley.

9

Concluding Thoughts on
Psychotherapy With Older Adults

This volume has summarized my thinking about the need to adapt psychotherapy for work with older adults. Using the contextual, cohort-specific maturity/specific challenge model as a guide, the first two chapters discussed gerontology for therapists and adaptations based on each of these four dimensions. Fairly minimal changes were described based on maturational processes: the need to be aware of the client's greater maturity, a greater readiness for therapy based on expertise in relationships, a need for slower pacing of speech and possibly for simpler language. Cohort effects suggested larger adaptations that may need to be made with some of today's older adults, perhaps not with future cohorts: less psychological jargon, adjustment to lower educational levels, less reliance on reasoning ability and visualization abilities, different word usage, and different worldviews and values. The specific social context of older adults was described as a potential source of complexity for the therapist and a potential source of misunderstandings between therapist and client.

The next two chapters addressed rapport building with older clients and the changes reported in transference and countertransference with older adults. Connecting with older adults seems to be difficult for many therapists new to work with the elderly. The need to be more active in explaining what therapy is and how it works has been characteristic of introducing psychotherapy to several populations not socialized to it, including lower-SES adults, ethnic minority groups, men, children, and the elderly. The changes in the therapeutic relationship when the client is older are among reasons that therapy may feel more different or more difficult with older clients when it does not in fact have to be.

Assessment has long been recognized as more complex with older clients (e.g., Zarit, 1980). The higher prevalence of neurological diseases, the higher co-morbidity with medical illness, the higher prevalence of iatrogenic disorders, and the different social context combine to make this the case. I have argued for years that, given an accurate assessment, the psychotherapy need not be as specialized as the assessment. However, the need for accurate assessment and the need to have continuous feedback between assessment and treatment may combine to make it essential that therapists working with older clients have a high level of competence in assessment.

After assessment, the principal focus for specialized knowledge is the specific challenges of later life that make up much (but not all) of therapy with older adults. These challenges include grief work and coping with chronic illness and disability. In addition, the need to do life review implies a need for a life course perspective that can guide the therapist through the task of helping older clients to see accurate patterns in their lives and to attribute perceived changes correctly to maturation, cohort differences, specific challenges, or the social context of older adults in our culture, as appropriate.

So how specialized is psychotherapy with older adults? On the one hand, the answer would appear to be that psychotherapy with older adults can be very much like psychotherapy with younger adults. Most, if not all, systems of psychotherapy have been used successfully with older adults (see Chapter 2), and the modifications reported have generally been minor (see Zarit & Knight, in press). This answer is likely to be most appropriate for therapists who see some older adults and who attract older clients who fit a profile similar to that of the younger clients in their practices.

More age-specialized practices or practices that include clients with problems that are rooted in later life, earlier born cohorts, or the social context of the aged are likely to require more specific expertise. The higher the baseline prevalence of dementia in the client load, the greater the need for expertise in assessment. If more clients need grief work or rehabilitation counseling, expertise in these topical areas is needed. The greater the exposure to older clients, the more likely it is that countertransference specific to the elderly will play a role in inhibiting the exercise of therapeutic skill. If clients are struggling with questions about their personal maturational process, the therapist will need to be equipped to guide life review and to distinguish maturational changes from stable cohort differences. Therapists who work primarily in nursing homes need some expertise in all of these issues plus expertise in nursing home consultation (Lichtenberg, 1994; Smyer, Cohn, & Brannon, 1988). In short, the more specialized the contact with older adults, the more specialized the therapist should be.

A paradox inherent in the question of specialization in working with older adults is that one may well require some degree of specific expertise and supervised experience with older adults to treat them as one would anyone else. My repeated experience as a teacher and as a consultant to colleagues is that the result of specialized training or consultation is the awareness that one can think about older clients and do therapy with them in much the same manner as with younger clients. This awareness often seems to require the acquisition of considerable knowledge about aging and experience with older clients so as to unlearn prejudices/stereotypes that inhibit the use of therapeutic skills with older clients.

An important element of treating older adults like other clients is to extend to them the same ethical standards as are used with younger clients. In the next section, some common ethical issues arising with older adults are addressed.

Ethical Issues With Older Clients

CONSENT

Competent older adults have the right to consent to, or refuse consent for, psychotherapy and other mental health treatments. Informed consent means being aware of what is being offered and the pros and cons of accepting or refusing. I have done considerable outreach work with older adults (see Knight, 1989) and continue to feel that outreach and education about psychotherapy are needed in the community of older adults. The purpose of this education is make certain that the potential client knows what she or he is refusing when turning down therapy (or consenting to when accepting therapy). The decision to refuse should be respected, but one should also work to be certain that the older adult is refusing on an informed basis. I have had potential clients change a refusal to consent when informed that the therapy would be short term, that there was a sliding-scale fee structure, that therapy did not involve inpatient commitment, and that they would decide what the goals would be.

The influence of others can complicate consent. Older adults are often brought into therapy by family members. It remains important to be certain that the older client consents to, or refuses, the therapy independently of the desires of the family. It is not uncommon for therapists and other helping professionals to join with family members in cajoling or compelling a passive older person into assistance to which she or he has not consented. Insistence on obtaining the older client's consent is an important part of building rapport with that client. If the family members want assistance and the older adult refuses, the family members could seek therapy on their own behalf.

A common complication for consent occurs when the older adult is dementing. The issue of when a dementing older adult is incapable of giving consent and who then can give consent is far from settled at this time (see Grisso, 1994, for a more in-depth discussion). For the purposes of this discussion, the following points should be kept in mind: (a) Older adults without dementia can give or refuse consent, (b) older adults with dementia maintain the ability to give or withhold consent until as yet undefined points in the progression of the illness, and (c) those undefined points depend on the decision to be made. It seems unlikely that psychotherapy would be possible with dementing individuals who can no longer give consent. Some behavioral interventions would be, and appropriate ethical safeguards should be maintained.

CONFIDENTIALITY

Older adults in psychotherapy deserve full confidentiality, as do younger adults. My own experience has been that the confidentiality of older adults is violated frequently with regard to sharing therapy progress with family members and with other helping professionals involved with the elderly client. I have never heard a good explanation offered for the impulse to share with family members. It would appear that therapists often identify with younger family members and feel that they are on the same side trying to help the older adult. In general, it has seemed to me that family is exactly where clients do not want confidences shared.

The desire to share with other helping professionals is often justified in terms of the need for interdisciplinary cooperation and coordination of different agencies to help the older client. Although this is a good and valid principle, the client should consent to the sharing of information, including of course the information that she or he is a client. In over 15 years of working with older adult clients, I have had very few refuse to sign releases to share information with other helpers. In all but a few cases, the refusals were based on sound reasons that were important material for therapy.

As with consent, a common values conflict with regard to confidentiality involves the older person who is moderately to severely cognitively impaired and may be in some danger. In such cases, it may be allowable to contact others. It is important, in my view, to recognize that these are exceptions to the general rules and to think through the exceptions with care. For some individuals, continued freedom and autonomy may be worth the risk of injury or the certainty of a substandard living environment.

BENEFICENCE VERSUS AUTONOMY

This last example involving violation of confidentiality for the good of the cognitively impaired older client raises the more general values conflict of beneficence versus autonomy. Gilhooly (1986) and Fitting (1984, 1986) have each written extensively about these two ethical principles and about situations involving older clients that present conflicts between these two ethical goals. *Beneficence* refers to the aim of doing good for others, whereas *autonomy* refers to the aim of allowing individuals to direct their own lives. Conflicts clearly arise with the cognitively impaired elderly because their autonomy is presumed to be impaired. Even when the cognitive incapacity does interfere with autonomy in the present, it may still be possible to ascertain what the demented person's wishes have been in the past and to act according to those wishes. If autonomy is to be set aside, the question arises as to who decides what is in the demented person's best interests: for example, one or another family member, a professional person, the residential facility in which the demented person resides, or the director of a research program. It is easy to imagine in each instance that the substitute decision maker might act for his or her own good rather than in the best interests of the demented older adult.

The more curious abrogations of autonomy occur when the older client is not thought to be demented. For example, there is considerable discussion of decision making by older adults regarding refusing or ceasing medical treatment when the decision to do so is likely to lead to death. Such discussions tend to focus on doing good for the patient, with the debate being over whether we think it is better for the patient to preserve life or to choose an earlier, perhaps easier, death. Concern for the patient's autonomy is not always clearly articulated in these debates. In the case histories volume (Knight, 1992), instances are presented (e.g., Agnes and Bea) in which the client decided on one course of action in the therapy room and then did something else after leaving. Such decisions are complex and highly personal, and it may be psychologically necessary to "try on" one point of view for a while to realize that one actually wants to do the opposite. An analogous situation in therapy is that individuals in unhappy marriages may decide to divorce and then reverse the decision and decide to work on the marriage after mentally exploring what it would mean to divorce. It may be quite easy for professionals (and family) to influence such decisions by strongly expressing their own view or by endorsing strongly an apparent decision before the client has time to try it on and reject it. The concern for autonomy argues that it should be the client's decision rather than the therapist's sense of what is good for the client that should rule in each case.

FIDELITY

Fitting (1984, 1986) also discussed the principle of fidelity in the sense of faithfulness to the therapeutic relationship and its attendant professional obligations. This issue is likely to arise with older clients because much work with older clients is at the behest of someone else: family, physician, institutional care facility. Although the referring source may often act primarily as an aid in achieving contact to effect a change that the client would want (e.g., alleviation of depression), there are many instances when the therapist is being asked to fix the older adult to meet the specifications of the referral source. Mother should be less demanding of my time; the patient should be less dependent on the physician; the nursing home patient should complain less about nursing staff. In earlier chapters (e.g., Chapter 4), the tendency to identify with persons in the family who are nearer the therapist's age than the client was discussed as a countertransference problem. Here the ethical issue is being raised that acting on the older adult in the service of someone else may violate the principle of fidelity to the older adult as the client. If, for example, an older woman is referred by her daughter with the expectation that mother will become less demanding, the therapist may come to the conclusion that the mother's best interest and psychological health are better served by becoming more assertive, which the daughter may perceive as more demanding. Whose goals dictate the course of the therapy?

Carstensen (1990) have raised a variation on the question of fidelity to the older client by noting that the absence of an understanding of normal aging may cause us to inappropriately treat older clients like younger and middle-aged ones. In their example, no therapist would treat for anxiety an infant who cried when strangers held him or her. We often assume that older adults need intervention if their social activity level is low by young adult standards. Fidelity to the older adult client means using his or her frame of reference for what is hurting and what needs to be changed, not our sense of what would bother us if we had the same current life experience.

For many older adults in nursing home settings, the situation will be complicated by advanced dementing illness, inability to communicate, and the probable absence of autonomy. The therapist's interventions should still be controlled by beneficence and by fidelity to the individual patient's best interests, which may well be different from goals that would be dictated by the institutional setting under principles of cost-effectiveness, efficient use of staff time, and so forth. For example, Baltes and her associates (e.g., Baltes & Reisenzein, 1986) have shown that dependency is encouraged in nursing homes because it is more efficient to provide the same level of care for everyone than to encourage achievement of individualized optimal levels of independence.

The question is "Who is the client?" and whether we are honest with the older adult and with ourselves about the answer. At a minimum, informed consent would mean that the older person should, whenever possible, understand whom the therapist is working for and what the goals of the intervention are. The therapist should also be clear about these same aspects of the assignment and should actively wonder about the ethical implications of undertaking to change older adults for a third party. It is my intent to argue, not that such intervention is always unethical, but that therapists should always be wondering whether a given intervention at the behest of a third party is ethical. To the extent that managed care and other attempts to control costs of health care come to dominate psychological services as well (see Knight & Kaskie, 1995), these concerns can only increase in the future.

Toward an Integrative
Therapy With Older Adults

In the nearly 10 years since the publication of the first edition of *Psychotherapy With Older Adults,* the field has grown and matured. As can be seen in this edition, far more has been written that is relevant to working with older clients. The field has expanded in a steady developmental fashion as more persons have been trained in working with older adults and has shown a quantum jump in growth with the extension of Medicare reimbursement to clinical psychologists and clinical social workers. It is no longer necessary in most settings to debate whether psychotherapy is possible with older adults. The current question is whether it needs to be modified and how much.

With few exceptions, the psychotherapeutic interventions described for older adults are still quite rooted in conventional systems of psychotherapy. Most people writing about psychotherapy with older adults are clearly identifiable as cognitive-behavioral, family systems, interpersonal, psychodynamic, and so forth (e.g., Zarit & Knight, in press).

Outside of the geropsychotherapy sector, there has been a considerable trend over the last decade or so toward integration of therapy systems (e.g., Beutler & Clarkin, 1990; Prochaska & Norcross, 1994; Saltzman & Norcross, 1990). Such integration is generally based on the observation of common factors across systems, attempts at theoretical integration, or systematic attempts to use what works, technical eclecticism, usually combined with some attempt to match technique to the client's problems or other characteristics (see Lazarus & Beutler, 1993). Integrative theorists have not paid much attention to older adults either: The oldest client discussed in Saltzman & Norcross's (1990) case-based presentation of integrative dialogue was 44.

This volume could be understood as a first step toward applying integrative therapy principles to older adults. Much of this discussion of psychotherapy has attempted to be neutral with regard to systems of therapy. The larger questions about the use of psychotherapy with older adults are not, in my view, system specific but are common across therapy systems. The answers about adaptations needed in psychotherapy with older adults have not generally been specific to the systems of psychotherapy. Indeed, my suggestion has been that such answers ought to be based on scientific gerontology as applied to the specifics of the psychotherapeutic situation. The contextual, cohort-based maturity/specific challenge model provides a framework that can guide that application.

This volume is integrative in a different manner as well. The chapters covering specific challenges in later life use different techniques that are rooted in differing therapeutic traditions for each specific challenge. As noted in the chapters, grief work is virtually a therapeutic system in its own right, working with chronic illness and disability is mainly described in terms of the use of cognitive-behavioral strategies, and the discussion of the life review draws on psychodynamic techniques and principles. Clearly, more empirical and conceptual work is needed to clarify the appropriate use of these and other therapeutic approaches in addressing the problems of later life. Even this first step improves upon the traditional notion that therapy in later life is always about helping depressed older clients cope with generic losses. The integrative approach argues that, like other adults, older clients have a variety of specific problems that require particular therapeutic approaches for their resolution.

Toward Prospective Therapy?

The application of the life course perspective to psychotherapy has the potential to change the conventional conceptualization of therapies as present centered or past centered. The life course perspective in gerontology poses the question of whether psychotherapy can be prospective as well as retrospective. In addition to solving current problems and resolving conflicts from earlier stages of life, should therapists pose the question to all clients of planning for their future life into old age?

At present, we could only sketch out what some of the questions may be for prospective therapy. Issues of physical health and preventive approaches to health become more important if one considers the length of the life span and the amount of time that one can be disabled or chronically ill. The question here is not so much how long life will be as how healthy one wants to be while living out the life span.

The healthy maintenance of family relationships may take on greater importance as one considers the number of decades that will be spent together and the greater reliance on family predicted by socioemotional selectivity theory (Carstensen, 1993). The individuation conflicts of adolescent and young adult may take on different meaning for all participants if the full future life span is considered in addition to the need to alter the small-child-to-parent relationship of the past. The dominance of career in clients' self-concepts is put into a different perspective if the probable length of postretirement life is considered. The time frame for resolving problems, working out personal issues, and maturation may seem less pressing if one takes seriously the full span of adult life. In summary, gerontology and the life course perspective present the possibility of therapies focused on projecting the scenario well into the future and thus the current goal of providing grounds for constructing the probable future as well as for solving current problems and finishing old business from troubled childhoods.

Closing Notes

My work has focused largely on individual psychotherapy rather than group or family therapies. In what follows, I hope to make it clear that this is due to factors that have shaped my experiences as a therapist rather than to any conviction on my part about the relative importance of these approaches.

With regard to group therapy with older adults, my own experience has been that it has been more difficult to get older adults to participate in group psychotherapy than in individual psychotherapy. In my experience, I have been able to form psychotherapy groups only from current and former clients in individual psychotherapy. Conversations with other therapists have led me to believe that this phenomenon is not specific to older adults but may be regionally specific. I have heard similar reports from colleagues throughout southern California but have had quite different reports from colleagues in other parts of the United States. This reluctance has been less of a problem with self-help groups and with discussion groups around psychological themes in senior centers and in other aging-network settings.

In principle, it seems to me that group psychotherapy and group work of other kinds can be quite helpful to older adults. As is true at other ages, many problems have a strong interpersonal theme, and the ability to work on these themes in the group setting should be quite useful. Advocates for group therapy need to address the question of what factors determine older adults' receptivity to this approach. A second caution is that the effectiveness of group therapy has often been assumed rather than demonstrated. A meta-analysis of psychosocial interventions with caregivers suggested that group approaches were less effective than individual ones (Knight et al., 1993). More research is needed on this point.

Group work is not discussed in more depth here due to my relative paucity of experience with it. Also, other authors have written on this subject, including Toseland (1990), whose *Group Work With Older Adults* provides good coverage of group dynamics and the range of groups used in working with older adults.

Similarly, I have said little about families and the importance of family approaches in working with older adults. The social demography of southern California makes the likelihood of getting all of a late-life family system into one room quite small. My own use of family systems theory has largely been in understanding the family context of the individuals with whom I have worked and in understanding that the first referred client may not be "the real client." In this sense, it has been in the spirit of Bowen's observations on doing family therapy with the individual client. I have often taken the opportunity to see family members during vacation visits, when they drive the older client to a session, or (with the client's consent) when they show up during a home visit. As with group therapy, others have written more extensively about the older family, including Qualls (1988, in press), Bumagin and Hirn (1990), and Carter and McGoldrick (1989).

Summary

The contextual, cohort-specific maturity/specific challenge model provides an image of the older adult client as a mature human being facing specific problems in a given societal and familial context and with the values and views of an earlier born cohort. The specific problems, rather than the client's age, determine the techniques and goals of psychotherapy. Cohort differences and context may necessitate adaptations in therapy or may simply make the therapy feel different to the therapist. Working with older clients in therapy is challenging and rewarding for the therapist, who may well find that learning about later life in the intimate context of psychotherapy is a maturing experience.

References

Abraham, K. (1953). The applicability of psychoanalytic treatment to patients at an advanced age. In S. Steury & M. L. Blank (Eds.), *Readings in psychotherapy with older people* (pp. 18-20). Washington, DC: Department of Health, Education, and Welfare. (Original work published 1919)

American Psychiatric Association. (1980). *Diagnostic and statistical manual of mental disorders* (3rd ed.). Washington, DC: Author.

American Psychiatric Association. (1987). *Diagnostic and statistical manual of mental disorders* (3rd ed., Rev.). Washington, DC: Author.

American Psychiatric Association. (1994). *Diagnostic and statistical manual of mental disorders* (4th ed.). Washington, DC: Author.

Anthony, J. C., & Aboraya, A. (1992). The epidemiology of selected mental disorder in later life. In J. E. Birren, R. B. Sloane, & G. D. Cohen (Eds.), *Handbook of mental health and aging* (2nd ed., pp. 27-73). San Diego: Academic Press.

Atkinson, R. M., Ganzini, L., & Bernstein, M. J. (1992). Alcohol and substance-use disorders in the elderly. In J. E. Birren, R. B. Sloane, & G. D. Cohen (Eds.), *Handbook of mental health and aging* (2nd ed., pp. 516-556). San Diego: Academic Press.

Baltes, M. M. (1995). Dependency in old age: Gains and losses. *Current Directions in Psychological Science, 4,* 14-18.

Baltes, M. M., & Reisenzein, R. (1986). The social world in long-term care institutions: Psychosocial control towards dependency? In M. M. Baltes & P. B. Baltes (Eds.), *The psychology of control and aging* (pp. 315-344). Hillsdale, NJ: Lawrence Erlbaum.

Bandura, A. (1969). *Principles of behavior modification.* New York: Holt, Rinehart & Winston.

Bandura, A. (1977). *Social learning theory.* Englewood Cliffs, NJ: Prentice Hall.

Barrett, T. R., & Wright, M. (1981). Age-related facilitation in recall following semantic processing. *Journal of Gerontology, 36,* 194-199.

Beck, A. T., Ward, C. H., Mendelson, M., Mock, J., & Erbaugh, J. (1961). An inventory for measuring depression. *Archives of General Psychiatry, 4,* 561-571.

Bengtson, V. L., & Allen, K. R. (1993). The life course perspective applied to families over time. In P. G. Boss, W. J. Doherty, R. LaRossa, W. R. Schumm, & S. K. Steinmetz (Eds.), *Sourcebook of family theories and methods: A contextual approach* (pp. 469-498). New York: Plenum.

Bengston, V. L., Reedy, M. N., & Gorden, C. (1985). Aging and self-conceptions: Personality processes and social contexts. In J. E. Birren & K. W. Schaie (Eds.), *Handbook of the psychology of aging* (2nd ed., pp. 544-593). New York: Van Nostrand Reinhold.

Bengtson, V. L., & Robertson, J. (1985). *Grandparenthood.* Beverly Hills, CA: Sage.

Beutler, L. E., & Clarkin, J. F. (1990). *Systematic treatment selection: Toward targeted therapeutic interventions.* New York: Brunner/Mazel.

Beutler, L. E., Scogin, L., Kirkish, P., Schretlen, D., Corbishley, A., Hamblin, D., Meredith, K., Potter, R., Bamford, C. R., & Levenson, A. I. (1987). Group cognitive therapy and Alprazolam in the treatment of depression in older adults. *Journal of Consulting and Clinical Psychology, 55,* 550-556.

Blessed, G., Tomlinson, B. E., & Roth, M. (1968). The association between quantitative measures of dementia and of senile change in the cerebral grey matter of elderly subjects. *British Journal of Psychiatry, 114,* 797-811.

Botwinick, J. (1984). *Aging and behavior* (3rd ed.). New York: Springer.

Breytspraak, L. M. (1984). *The development of self in later life.* Boston: Little, Brown.

Brody, C. M., & Semel, V. G. (1993). *Strategies for therapy with the elderly: Living with hope and meaning.* New York: Springer.

Bumagin, V. E., & Hirn, K. F. (1990). *Helping the aging family.* Glenview, IL: Scott, Foresman.

Buschke, H., & Fuld, P. A. (1974). Evaluating storage, retention, and retrieval in disordered memory and learning. *Neurology, 24,* 252-254.

Butler, R. N. (1963). The life review: An interpretation of reminiscence in the aged. *Psychiatry, 119,* 721-728.

Butler, R. N. (1975). *Why survive? Growing old in America.* New York: Harper & Row.

Butler, R. N., & Lewis, M. I. (1991). *Aging and mental health* (4th ed.). St. Louis: C. V. Mosby.

Carstensen, L. L. (1990, November). *Normal aging: Implications in assessment and treatment.* Invited paper presented at the meeting of the Association for the Advancement of Behavior Therapy, San Francisco.

Carstensen, L. L. (1993). Motivation for social contact across the life span: A therapy for socioemotional selectivity. In J. Jacobs (Ed.), *Nebraska Symposium on Motivation, 1992: Developmental perspectives on motivation.* (vol. 40). Lincoln, NE: University of Nebraska Press.

Carstensen, L. L., & Edelstein, B. A. (Eds.). (1987). *Handbook of clinical gerontology.* New York: Pergamon.

Carter, B., & McGoldrick, M. (Eds.). (1989). *Changing family life cycle: A framework for family therapy* (2nd ed.). Boston: Allyn & Bacon.

Christensen, H., Hadzi-Pavlovic, D., & Jacomb, P. (1991). The psychometric differentiation of dementia from normal aging: A meta-analysis. *Psychological Assessment, 3,* 147-155.

Costa, P. T., & McCrae, R. R. (1985). Hypochondriasis, neuroticism, and aging: When are somatic complaints unfounded? *American Psychologist, 40,* 19-28.

Costa, P. T., & McCrae, R. R. (1988). Personality in adulthood: A six-year longitudinal study of self-reports and spouse ratings on the NEO personality inventory. *Journal of Personality and Social Psychology, 54,* 853-863.

Costa, P. T., McCrae, R. R., & Arenberg, D. (1983). Recent longitudinal research on personality and aging. In K. W. Schaie (Ed.), *Longitudinal studies of adult psychological development* (pp. 222-265). New York: Guilford.

Costa, P. T., Zonderman, A. B., McCrae, R. R., Cornoni-Huntley, J., Locke, B. Z., & Barbano, H. E. (1987). Longitudinal analysis of psychological well-being in a national sample: Stability of mean levels. *Journal of Gerontology, 42,* 50-56.

Covey, H. C. (1992-1993). A return to infancy: Old age and the second childhood in history. *International Journal of Aging and Human Development, 36,* 81-90.

Craik, F. I. M., & Trehub, S. (1982). *Aging and cognitive processes.* New York: Plenum.

Crook, T., Bartus, R. T., Ferris, S. H., Whitehouse, P., Cohen, G. D., & Gershon, S. (1986). Age-associated memory impairment: Proposed diagnostic criteria and measures of clinical change. Report of a National Institute of Mental Health Work Group. *Developmental Neuropsychology, 2,* 261-276.

DeBerry, S. (1982). The effects of meditation-relaxation on anxiety and depression in a geriatric population. *Psychotherapy: Theory, Research and Practice, 19,* 512-521.

De Rivera, J. (1984). Development and the full range of emotional expression. In C. Z. Malatesta & C. E. Izard (Eds.), *Emotion in adult development* (pp. 45-63). Beverly Hills, CA: Sage.

Derogatis, L. R., & Spencer, P. M. (1985). *The Brief Symptom Inventory.* Baltimore: Johns Hopkins University Press.

Dye, C. J. (1978). Psychologists' role in the provision of mental health care for the elderly. *Professional Psychology, 9,* 38-49.

Erikson, E. (1963). *Childhood and society* (2nd ed.). New York: Norton.

Erikson, E. (1968). *Identity: Youth and crisis.* New York: Norton.

Erikson, E. (1978). Reflections on Dr. Borg's life cycle. In E. H. Erikson (Ed.), *Adulthood: Essays* (pp. 1-24). New York: Norton.

Erikson, E. H., Erikson, J., & Kivnick, H. Q. (1986). *Vital involvements in old age.* New York: Norton.

Field, D., & Millsap, R. E. (1991). Personality in advanced old age: Continuity or change? *Journals of Gerontology: Psychological Sciences, 48,* P299-P308.

Fisher, J. E., & Carstensen, L. L. (1990). Behavioral management of the dementias. *Clinical Psychology Review, 10,* 611-629.

Fitting, M. D. (1984). Professional and ethical responsibilities for psychologists working with the elderly. *Counseling Psychologist, 12,* 69-78.

Fitting, M. D. (1986). Ethical dilemmas in counseling elderly adults. *Journal of Counseling and Development, 64,* 325-327.

Folstein, M., Anthony, J. C., Parhad, I., Duffy, B., & Gruenberg, E. (1985). The meaning of cognitive impairment in the elderly. *Journal of the American Geriatric Society, 33,* 228-275.

Folstein, M. F., Folstein, S. E., & McHugh, P. R. (1975). "Mini-Mental State": A practical method for grading the cognitive state of patients for the clinician. *Journal of Psychiatric Research, 12,* 189-198.

Frankfather, D. (1977). *The aged in the community.* New York: Praeger.

Frazer, D. (1995). The interface between medicine and mental health. In B. G. Knight, L. Teri, J. Santos, & P. Wohlford (Eds.), *Mental health services for older adults: Implications for training and practice* (pp. 63-72). Washington, DC: American Psychological Association.

Freud, S. (1953). On psychotherapy. In J. Strachey (Trans.), *The complete psychological works of Sigmund Freud* (Vol. 6, pp. 249-263). London: Hogarth. (Original work published 1905)

Fry, P. S. (1983). Structured and unstructured reminiscence training and depression in the elderly. *Clinical Gerontologist, 1,* 15-37.

Gallagher-Thompson, D., & Thompson, L. W. (1995). Issues in geropsychological training at the internship level. In B. G. Knight, L. Teri, J. Santos, & P. Wohlford (Eds.), *Mental health services for older adults: Implications for training and practice* (pp. 129-142). Washington, DC: American Psychological Association.

Garfield, S. L. (1978). Research on client variables in psychotherapy. In S. L. Garfield & A. E. Bergin (Eds.), *Handbook of psychotherapy and behavior change* (pp. 191-232). New York: John Wiley.

Gatz, M., & Hurwicz, M. (1990). Are older people more depressed? Cross-sectional data on Center for Epidemiological Studies Depression scale factors. *Psychology and Aging, 5,* 284-290.

Gatz, M., & Pearson, C. G. (1988). Ageism revisited and the provision of psychological services. *American Psychologist, 43,* 184-188.

Gatz, M., & Smyer, M. A. (1992). The mental health system and older adults in the 1990s. *American Psychologist, 47,* 741-751.

Gendlin, E. (1978). *Focusing.* New York: Everest House.

Genevay, B., & Katz, R. S. (1990). *Countertransference and older clients.* Newbury Park, CA: Sage.

Gilewski, M. J., Farberow, N. L., Gallagher, D., & Thompson, L. W. (1991). Interaction of depression and bereavement on mental health in the elderly. *Psychology and Aging, 6,* 67-75.

Gilhooly, M. L. M. (1986). Ethical and legal issues in therapy with the elderly. In I. Hanley & M. Gilhooly (Eds.), *Psychological therapies with the elderly* (pp. 173-197). New York: New York University Press.

Goldfarb, A. I., & Sheps, J. (1954). Psychotherapy of the aged III: Brief therapy of interrelated psychological and somatic disorders. *Psychomatic Medicine, 16,* 209-219.

Goldfried, M. R., & Davison, G. (1994). *Clinical behavior therapy* (2nd ed.). New York: Holt, Rinehart.

Goldstein, A. P. (1973). *Structured learning therapy: Toward a therapy for the poor.* New York: Academic Press.

Grisso, T. (1994). Clinical assessments for legal competence of older adults. In M. Storandt & G. R. VandenBos (Eds.), *Neuropsychological assessment of dementia and depression in older adults: A clinician's guide* (pp. 119-140). Washington, DC: American Psychological Association.

Gurin, G., Veroff, J., & Feld, S. (1960). *Americans view their mental health.* New York: Basic Books.

Gutmann, D. (1987). *Reclaimed powers: Toward a new psychology of men and women in later life.* New York: Basic Books.

Gynther, M. D. (1979). Aging and personality. In J. N. Butcher (Ed.), *New developments in the use of the MMPI* (pp. 39-68). Minneapolis: University of Minnesota Press.

Haan, N., Millsap, R., & Hartka, E. (1987). As time goes by: Change and stability in personality over fifty years. *Psychology and Aging, 1,* 220-232.

Hagestad, G. O. (1990). Social perspectives on the life course. In R. H. Binstock & L. K. George (Eds.), *Handbook of aging and the social sciences* (3rd ed., pp. 151-168). San Diego: Academic Press.

Hagestad, G. O., & Neugarten, B. L. (1985). Age and the life course. In R. H. Binstock & E. Shanas (Eds.), *Handbook of aging and the social sciences* (2nd ed., pp. 35-61). New York: Van Nostrand.

Haight, B. (1988). The therapeutic role of a structured life review process in homebound elderly subjects. *Journal of Gerontology, 43,* 40-44.

Haight, B. K. (1992). Long-term effects of a structured life review process. *Journals of Gerontology: Psychological Sciences, 47,* 312-315.

Haley, W. (in press). The medical context of psychotherapy with the elderly. In S. H. Zarit & B. G. Knight (Eds.), *Psychotherapy with the elderly: Effective interventions with older people.* Washington, DC: American Psychological Association.

Haley, W. E., & Pardo, K. M. (1989). Relationship of severity of dementia to caregiver stressors. *Psychology and Aging, 4,* 389-392.

Hall, C. M. (1981). *The Bowen family theory and its uses.* New York: Jason Aronson.

Harris, L., & Associates (1975). *The myth and reality of aging in America.* Washington, DC: National Council on Aging.

Hartlage, S., Alloy, L. B., Vazquez, C., & Dykman, B. (1993). Automatic and effortful processing in depression. *Psychological Bulletin, 113,* 247-278.

Helson, R., Mitchell, V., & Hart, B. (1985). Lives of women who became autonomous. *Journal of Personality, 53,* 257-285.

Hinze, E. (1987). Transference and countertransference in the psychoanalytic treatment of older patients. *International Review of Psycho-Analysis, 14,* 465-473.

Hultsch, D. F., & Dixon, R. A. (1990). Learning and memory in aging. In J. E. Birren & K. W. Schaie (Eds.), *Handbook of the psychology of aging* (3rd ed., pp. 259-274). San Diego: Academic Press.

Hussian, R. A., & Davis, R. (1985). *Responsive care: Behavioral interventions with elderly persons.* Champaign, IL: Research Press.

Jung, C. J. (1933). *Modern man in search of a soul.* New York: Harcourt Brace Jovanovich.

Kaplan, E., Goodglass, H., & Weintraub, S. (1983). *The Boston Naming Test* (Rev. ed.). Philadelphia: Lea & Febiger.

Kastenbaum, R. (1964a). The reluctant therapist. In R. Kastenbaum (Ed.), *New thoughts on old age* (pp. 137-145). New York: Springer.

Kastenbaum, R. (1964b). The crisis of explanation. In R. Kastenbaum (Ed.), *New thoughts on old age* (pp. 316-323). New York: Springer.

Kaszniak, A. W. (1990). Psychological assessment of the aging individual. In J. E. Birren & K. W. Schaie (Eds.), *Handbook of the psychology of aging* (3rd ed., pp. 427-445). San Diego: Academic Press.

Kelly, G. A. (1955). *The psychology of personal constructs.* New York: Norton.

Klingner, A., Kachanoff, R., Dastour, D. P., Worenklein, A., Charlton, S., Gutbrodt, E., & Muller, H. F. (1976). A psychogeriatric assessment program: Clinical and experimental psychologic aspects. *Journal of American Geriatrics, 24,* 17-24.

Knight, B. G. (1986a). Management variables as predictors of service utilization by the elderly in mental health. *International Journal of Aging and Human Development, 23,* 141-148.

Knight, B. G. (1986b). Therapists' attitudes as an explanation of underservice to the elderly in mental health: Testing an old hypothesis. *International Journal of Aging and Human Development, 22,* 261-269.

Knight, B. G. (1988). Factors influencing therapist-rated change in older adults. *Journal of Gerontology, 43,* 111-112.

Knight, B. G. (1989). *Outreach with the elderly: Community education, assessment, and therapy.* New York: New York University Press.

Knight, B. (1992). *Older adults in psychotherapy: Case histories.* Newbury Park, CA: Sage.

Knight, B. (1993). Psychotherapy as applied gerontology: A contextual, cohort-based, maturity-specific challenge model. In M. Smyer (Ed.), *Mental health and aging* (pp. 125-134). New York: Springer.

Knight, B. (1994). Providing clinical interpretations to older clients and their families. In M. Storandt & G. R. VandenBos (Eds.), *Neuropsychological assessment of dementia and depression in older adults: A clinician's guide* (pp. 141-154). Washington, DC: American Psychological Association.

Knight, B., & Kaskie, B. (1995). Models for mental health service delivery to older adults: Models for reform. In M. Gatz (Ed.), *Emerging issues in mental health and aging* (pp. 231-255). Washington, DC: American Psychological Association.

Knight, B., Kelly, M., & Gatz, M. (1992). Psychotherapy with the elderly. In D. K. Freedheim (Ed.), *The history of psychotherapy* (pp. 528-551). Washington, DC: American Psychological Association.

Knight, B. G., Lutzky, S. M., & Macofsky-Urban, F. (1993). A meta-analytic review of interventions for caregiver distress: Recommendations for future research. *Gerontologist, 33,* 240-249.

Koenig, H. G., George, L. K., & Schneider, R. (1994). Mental health care for older adults in the year 2020: A dangerous and avoided topic. *Gerontologist, 34,* 674-679.

Labouvie-Vief, G. (1985). Intelligence and cognition. In J. E. Birren & K. W. Schaie (Eds.), *Handbook of psychology and aging* (2nd ed., pp. 500-530). New York: Van Nostrand Reinhold.

Labouvie-Vief, G., DeVoe, M., & Bulka, D. (1989). Speaking about feelings: Conceptions of emotion across the life span. *Psychology and Aging, 4,* 425-437.

Langer, E. J., & Rodin, J. (1976). The effects of choice and enhanced personal responsibility for the aged: A field experiment in an institutional setting. *Journal of Personality and Social Psychology, 34,* 191-198.

LaRue, A. (1992). *Aging and neuropsychological assessment.* New York: Plenum.

LaRue, A. (1995). Neuropsychology and geropsychology. In B. G. Knight, L. Teri, J. Santos, & P. Wohlford (Eds.), *Mental health services for older adults: Implications for training and practice* (pp. 53-62). Washington, DC: American Psychological Association.

LaRue, A., Dessonville, E., & Jarvik, L. F. (1985). Aging and mental disorders. In J. E. Birren & K. W. Schaie (Eds.), *Handbook of the psychology of aging* (2nd ed., pp. 664-702). New York: Van Nostrand Reinhold.

Lasoki, M. C., & Thelen, M. H. (1987). Attitudes of older and middle-aged persons toward mental health intervention. *Gerontologist, 27,* 288-292.

Lazarus, A. A., & Beutler, L. E. (1993). On technical eclecticism. *Journal of Counseling and Development, 71,* 381-385.

Lehman, D. R., Ellard, J. H., & Wortman, C. B. (1986). Social support for the bereaved: Recipients' and providers' perspectives on what is helpful. *Journal of Personality and Social Psychology, 54,* 438-446.

Lewinsohn, P. M., Youngren M. A., & Grosscup, S. J. (1979). Reinforcement and depression. In R. A. Duprue (Ed.), *The psychobiology of the depressive disorder: Implications for the effects of stress.* (pp. 291-316). New York: Academic Press.

Lewinsohn, P. M., Munoz, R. F., Youngren, M. A., & Zeiss, A. M. (1978). *Control your depression.* Englewood Cliffs, NJ: Prentice Hall.

Lewinsohn, P. M., Rohde, P., Seeley, J. R., & Fischer, S. A. (1993). Age-cohort changes in the lifetime occurrence of depression and other mental disorders. *Journal of Abnormal Psychology, 102,* 110-120.

Lewis, M. I., & Butler, R. N. (1974). Life review therapy: Putting memories to work in individual and group psychotherapy. *Geriatrics, 29,* 165-172.

Lichtenberg, P. A. (1994). *A guide to psychological practice in geriatric long-term care.* New York: Haworth.

Light, E., & Lebowitz, B. D. (Eds.). (1991). *The elderly with chronic mental illness.* New York: Springer.

Light, L. L. (1990). Interactions between memory and language in old age. In J. E. Birren & K. W. Schaie (Eds.), *Handbook of the psychology of aging.* (3rd ed., pp. 275-290). San Diego: Academic Press.

Lorion, R. P. (1978). Research on psychotherapy and behavior change with the disadvantaged. In S. L. Garfield & A. E. Bergin (Eds.), *Handbook of psychotherapy and behavior change* (pp. 903-938). New York: John Wiley.

Malatesta, C. Z., & Izard, C. E. (1984). The facial expression of emotion: Young, middle-aged, and older adult expressions. In C. Z. Malatesta & C. E. Izard (Eds.), *Emotion in adult development* (pp. 253-273). Beverly Hills, CA: Sage.

Markus, H. R., & Herzog, A. R. (1991). The role of the self concept in aging. *Annual Review of Gerontology and Geriatrics, 11,* 110-143.

Matarazzo, J. D. (1972). *Wechsler's measurement and appraisal of adult intelligence.* Baltimore: Williams & Wilkins.

Mattis, S. (1976). Mental status examination for organic mental syndrome in the elderly patient. In L. Bellak & T. B. Karasu (Eds.), *Geriatric psychiatry* (pp. 79-121). New York: Grune & Stratton.

McCall, P. L. (1991). Adolescent and elderly white male suicide trends: Evidence of changing well-being? *Journals of Gerontology: Social Sciences, 46,* S43-S51.

McCrae, R. R., & Costa, P. T. (1984). *Emerging lives, enduring dispositions.* Boston: Little, Brown.

McIntosh, J. L., Santos, J. F., Hubbard, R. W., & Overholser, J. C. (1994). *Elder suicide: Research, theory, and treatment.* Washington, DC: American Psychological Association.

McKhann, G., Drachman, D., Folstein, M., Katzman, R., Price, D., & Stadlan, E. M. (1984). Clinical diagnosis of Alzheimer's disease: Report of the NINCDS-ADRDA Work Group. *Neurology, 34,* 939-944.

Menninger, K. A., & Holzman, P. S. (1973). *Theory of psychoanalytic technique.* New York: Basic Books.

Miller, N. E., & Cohen, G. D. (Eds.). (1987). *Schizophrenia and aging.* New York: Guilford.

Myers, W. A. (1984). *Dynamic therapy of the older patient.* New York: J. Aronson.

Myers, J. K., Weissman, M., Tischler, G., Holzer, C., Leaf, P., Orvaschal, H., Anthony, J., Boyd, J., Burke, J., Kramer, M., & Stoltzman, R. (1984). Six month prevalence of psychiatric disorders in three communities. *Archives of General Psychiatry, 41,* 959-967.

Nemiroff, R. A., & Colarusso, C. A. (1985a). Adult development and transference. In R. A. Nemiroff & C. A. Colarusso (Eds.), *The race against time: Psychotherapy and psychoanalysis in the second half of life* (pp. 59-72). New York: Plenum.

Nemiroff, R. A., & Colarusso, C. A. (1985b). Issues and strategies for psychotherapy and psychoanalysis in the second half of life. In R. A. Nemiroff & C. A. Colarusso (Eds.), *The race against time: Psychotherapy and psychoanalysis in the second half of life* (pp. 303-330). New York: Plenum.

Nemiroff, R. A., & Colarusso, C. A. (Eds). (1985c). *The race against time: Psychotherapy and psychoanalysis in the second half of life.* New York: Plenum.

Neugarten, B. L. (1977). Personality and aging. In J. E. Birren & K. W. Schaie (Eds.), *Handbook of the psychology of aging* (pp. 626-649). New York: Van Nostrand.

Neugarten, B., & Hagestad, G. O. (1976). Age and the life course. In R. H. Binstock & E. Shanas (Eds.), *Handbook of aging and the social sciences* (pp. 35-57). New York: Van Nostrand.

Newton, N. A., Brauer, D., Gutmann, D. L., & Grunes, J. (1986). Psychodynamic therapy with the aged: A review. *Clinical Gerontologist, 5,* 205-229.

Niederehe, G. (1986). Depression and memory impairment in the aged. In L. W. Poon (Ed.), *Handbook for clinical memory assessment of older adults* (pp. 226-237). Washington, DC: American Psychological Association.

Niederehe, G., Gatz, M., Taylor, G., & Teri, L. (1995). Clinical geropsychology: The case for certification. In B. G. Knight, L. Teri, J. Santos, & P. Wohlford (Eds.), *Mental health services for older adults: Implications for training and practice* (pp. 143-152). Washington, DC: American Psychological Association.

Orne, M. T., & Wender, P. H. (1968). Anticipatory socialization for psychotherapy and behavior change. *American Journal of Psychiatry, 124,* 1201-1212.

Patterson, R. L., Dupree, L. W., Eberly, D. A., Jackson, G. M., O'Sullivan, M. J., Penner, L. A., & Kelly, C. D. (1982). *Overcoming deficits of aging.* New York: Plenum.

Perlick, D., & Atkins, A. (1984). Variations in the reported age of a patient: A source of bias in the diagnosis of depression and dementia. *Journal of Consulting and Clinical Psychology, 52,* 812-820.

Peterson, C., Seligman, M. E. P., & Vaillant, G. E. (1988). Pessimistic explanatory style is a risk factor for physical illness: A 35 year longitudinal study. *Journal of Personality and Social Psychology, 55,* 23-27.

Phifer, J. F., & Murrell, S. A. (1986). Etiologic factors in the onset of depressive symptoms in older adults. *Journal of Abnormal Psychology, 95,* 282-291.

Poon, L. W. (1985). Differences in human memory with aging: Nature, causes, and clinical implications. In J. E. Birren & K. W. Schaie (Eds.), *Handbook of the psychology of aging* (2nd ed., pp. 427-462). New York: Van Nostrand Reinhold.

Powers, S. M., & Powers, E. A. (1991). *Factors which predict older adults' knowledge of psychological difficulties and of mental health services.* Final report submitted to AARP Andrus Foundation, Greensboro, NC.

Prochaska, J. O., & Norcross, J. C. (1994). *Systems of psychotherapy: A transtheoretical analysis* (3rd ed.). Pacific Grove, CA: Brooks/Cole.

Qualls, S. H. (1988). Problems in families of older adults. In N. Epstein, S. E. Schlesinger, & W. Dryden (Eds.), *Cognitive-behavioral therapy with families* (pp. 215-253). New York: Brunner-Mazel.

Qualls, S. H. (in press). Family therapy with aging families. In S. H. Zarit & B. G. Knight (Eds.), *Psychotherapy with the elderly: Effective interventions with older people.* Washington, DC: American Psychological Association.

Qualls, S. H., & Czirr, R. (1988). Geriatric health teams: Classifying models of professional and team functioning. *Gerontologist, 28,* 372-376.

Radloff, L. (1977). The CES-D Scale: A self-report depression scale for research in the general population. *Applied Psychological Measurement, 1,* 385-401.

Rando, T. (1984). *Grief, dying and death.* Champaign, IL: Research Press.

Rapp, S. R., Parisi, S. A., Walsh, D. A., & Wallace, C. E. (1988). Detecting depression in elderly medical inpatients. *Journal of Consulting and Clinical Psychology, 56,* 509-513.

Rattenbury, C., & Stones, M. J. (1989). A controlled evaluation of reminiscence and current topics discussion groups in a nursing home context. *Gerontologist, 29,* 768-771.

Rechtschaffen, A. (1959). Psychotherapy with geriatric patients: A review of the literature. *Journal of Gerontology, 14,* 73-84.

Reding, M., Haycox, J., & Blass, J. (1985). Depression in patients referred to a dementia clinic: A three-year prospective study. *Archives of Neurology, 42,* 894-896.

Reisberg, B. (1981). *Brain failure.* New York: Free Press.

Reisberg, B., Ferris, S. H., Franssen, E., & Kluger, A. (1986). Age-associated memory impairment: The clinical syndrome. *Developmental Neuropsychology, 2,* 401-412.

Reisberg, B., Shulman, E., Ferris, S. H., de Leon, M. J., & Geibel, V. (1983). Clinical assessments of age-associated cognitive decline and primary degenerative dementia: Prognostic concomitants. *Psychopharmacology Bulletin, 19,* 734-739.

Rickard, H. C., Scogin, F., & Keith, S. (1994). A one year follow up of relaxation training for elders with subjective anxiety. *Gerontologist, 34,* 121-122.

Riley, M. W. (1985). Age strata in social systems. In R. H. Binstock & E. Shanas (Eds.), *Handbook of aging and the social sciences* (2nd ed., pp. 369-414). New York: Van Nostrand.

Rodin, J. (1986). Aging and health: Effects of the sense of control. *Science, 233,* 1271-1275.

Rodin, J., & Salovey, P. (1989). Health psychology. *Annual Review of Psychology, 40,* 533-579.

Rorsman, B., Hagnell, O., & Lanke, J. (1986). Prevalence and incidence of senile and multi-infarct dementia in the Lundby Study: A comparison between time periods 1947-1957 and 1957-1972. *Neuropsychobiology, 15,* 122-129.

Rosen, A. (1971). Detection of suicidal patients: An example of some limitations in the prediction of infrequent events. In L. D. Goodstein & R. I. Lanyon (Eds.), *Readings in personality assessment* (pp. 375-383). New York: John Wiley.

Rosen, J. T. (1990). Age-associated memory impairment. *European Journal of Cognitive Psychology, 2,* 275-287.

Rosenthal, H. R. (1959). Psychotherapy of the aging. *American Journal of Psychotherapy, 17,* 55-65.

Roth, M. (1955). The natural history of mental disorders in old age. *Journal of Mental Science, 101,* 281-301.

Rotter, J. B. (1954). *Social learning and clinical psychology.* Englewood Cliffs, NJ: Prentice Hall.

Rybash, J. M., Hoyer, W. J., & Roodin, P. A. (1986). *Adult cognition and aging.* New York: Pergamon.

Ryff, C. D. (1991). Possible selves in adulthood and old age: A tale of shifting horizons. *Psychology and Aging, 6,* 286-295.

Sadavoy, J., & Fogel, B. (1992). Personality disorders in old age. In J. E. Birren, R. B. Sloane, & G. D. Cohen (Eds.), *Handbook of mental health and aging* (2nd ed., pp. 433-462). San Diego: Academic Press.

Salthouse, T. A. (1985). Speed of behavior and its implications for cognition. In J. E. Birren & K. W. Schaie (Eds.), *Handbook of the psychology of aging* (2nd ed., pp. 400-426). New York: Van Nostrand Reinhold.

Salthouse, T. A. (1991). *Theoretical perspectives on cognitive aging.* Hillsdale, NJ: Lawrence Erlbaum.

Saltzman, N., & Norcross, J. C. (Eds.). (1990). *Therapy wars: Contention and convergence in differing clinical approaches.* San Francisco: Jossey-Bass.

Schaie, K. W. (Ed.). (1983). *Longitudinal studies of adult psychological development.* New York: Guilford.

Schaie, K. W. (1990). Intellectual development in adulthood. In J. E. Birren & K. W. Schaie (Eds.), *Handbook of psychology and aging* (3rd ed., pp. 291-310). San Diego: Academic Press.

Schaie, K. W., & Parham, I. A. (1976). Stability of adult personality: Fact or fable? *Journal of Personality and Social Psychology, 34,* 146-158.

Schneider, L. S. (1994). Meta-analysis from a clinician's perspective. In L. S. Schneider, C. F. Reynolds, B. D. Lebowitz, & A. J. Friedhoff (Eds.), *Diagnosis and treatment of depression in late life: Results of the NIH Consensus Development Conference* (pp. 361-374). Washington, DC: American Psychiatric Press.

Schofield, W. (1964). *Psychotherapy: The purchase of friendship.* Englewood Cliffs, NJ: Prentice Hall.

Schulz, R. (1982). Emotionality and aging: A theoretical and empirical analysis. *Journal of Gerontology, 37,* 42-51.

Schulz, R., & Hanusa, B. H. (1978). Long-term effects of control and predictability-enhancing interventions: Findings and ethical issues. *Journal of Personality and Social Psychology, 11,* 1194-1201.

Scogin, F., & McElreath, L. (1994). Efficacy of psychosocial treatments for geriatric depression: A quantitative review. *Journal of Consulting and Clinical Psychology, 62,* 69-74.

Scogin, F., Rickard, H. C., Keith, S., Wilson, J., & McElreath, L. (1992). Progressive and imaginal relaxation training for elderly persons with subjective anxiety. *Psychology and Aging, 7,* 419-424.

Semel, V. G. (1993). Private practice. In C. M. Brody & V. G. Semel (Eds.), *Strategies for therapy with the elderly: Living with hope and meaning* (pp. 93-138). New York: Springer.

Settin, J. M. (1982). Clinical judgement in geropsychology practice. *Psychotherapy: Theory, Research and Practice, 19,* 397-404.

Sherman, E. (1981). *Counseling the aging.* New York: Free Press.

Sherman, E. (1991). *Reminiscence and the self in old age.* New York: Springer.

Sherman, J. (1992). *Medicare's mental health benefits: Coverage, utilization, and expenditures.* Washington, DC: American Association of Retired Persons.

Shibayama, H., Kasahara, Y., & Kobayashi, H. (1986). Prevalence of dementia in a Japanese elderly population. *Acta Psychiatrica Scandinavica, 74,* 144-151.

Siegler, I. C. (1983). Psychological aspects of the Duke Longitudinal Studies. In K. W. Schaie (Ed.), *Longitudinal studies of adult psychological development* (pp. 136-190). New York: Guilford.

Sloane, R. B., Staples, F. R., & Schneider, L. S. (1985). Interpersonal therapy versus nortriptyline for depression in the elderly. In G. D. Burrows, T. R. Norman, & L. Dennerstein (Eds.), *Clinical and pharmacological studies in psychiatric disorders* (pp. 344-346). London: John Libbey.

Smith, G., Ivnik, R. J., Petersen, R. C., & Malec, J. F. (1991). Age-associated memory impairment diagnoses: Problems of reliability and concerns for terminology. *Psychology and Aging, 6,* 551-558.

Smyer, M. A., Cohn, M. D., & Brannon, D. (1988). *Mental health consultation in nursing homes.* New York: New York University Press.

Smyer, M. A., & Downs, M. (1995). Psychopharmacology: An essential element in educating clinical psychologists for work with older adults. In B. G. Knight, L. Teri, J. Santos, & P. Wohlford (Eds.), *Mental health services for older adults: Implications for training and practice* (pp. 73-84). Washington, DC: American Psychological Association.

Smyer, M. A., & Gatz, M. (1983). *Mental health and aging: Programs and evaluations.* Beverly Hills, CA: Sage.

Spielberger, C. (1984). *State-Trait Anxiety Inventory: A comprehensive bibliography.* Palo Alto, CA: Consulting Psychologists Press.

Storandt, M., & Hill, R. D. (1989). Very mild senile dementia of the Alzheimer's type: 2. Psychometric test performance. *Archives of Neurology, 46,* 383-386.

Storandt, M., & VandenBos, G.R. (Eds.). (1994). *Neuropsychological assessment of older adults: Dementia and depression.* Washington, DC: American Psychological Association.

Stroebe, M., & Stroebe, W. (1991). Does "grief work" work? *Journal of Consulting and Clinical Psychology, 59,* 479-482.

Teri, L., & Gallagher-Thompson, D. (1991). Cognitive-behavioral interventions for treatment of depression in Alzheimer's patients. *Gerontologist, 31,* 413-416.

Teri, L., & Lewinsohn, P. M. (Eds.). (1983). *Clinical geropsychology: New directions in assessment and treatment.* New York: Pergamon.

Thompson, L. W., Gallagher-Thompson, D., Futterman, A., Gilewski, M. J., & Peterson, J. (1991). The effects of late life spousal bereavement over a 30 month period. *Psychology and Aging, 6,* 434-441.

Toseland, R. W. (1990). *Group work with older adults.* New York: New York University Press.

Troll, L. E. (1980). Grandparenting. In L. Poon (Ed.), *Aging in the 1980's* (pp. 475-484). Washington, DC: American Psychological Association.

Trzepacz, P. T., Baker, R. W., & Greenhouse, J. (1988). A symptom rating scale for delirium. *Psychiatry Research, 23,* 89-97.

Turk, D. C., Meichenbaum, D., & Genest, M. (1983). *Pain and behavioral medicine.* New York: Guilford.

Veroff, J., Kulka, P. A., & Douvan, E. (1981). *Mental health in America.* New York: Basic Books.

Waxman, H. M., Carner, E. A., & Klein, M. (1984). Underutilizing of mental health professionals by community elderly. *Gerontologist, 24,* 23-30.

Weiner, I. B. (1975). *Principles of psychotherapy.* New York: John Wiley.

Weissert, W. (1983, November). *Estimating the long-term care population.* Paper presented at the meeting of the Gerontological Society of America, San Francisco.

Whitbourne, S. K. (1985). The psychological construction of the life span. In J. E. Birren & K. W. Schaie (Eds.), *Handbook of the psychology of aging* (2nd ed., pp. 594-618). New York: Van Nostrand.

Wisocki, P. A. (1991). *Handbook of clinical behavior therapy with the elderly client.* New York: Plenum.

Woodruff, D. S. (1985). Arousal, sleep, and aging. In J. E. Birren & K. W. Schaie (Eds.), *Handbook of the psychology of aging* (2nd ed., pp. 261-295). New York: Van Nostrand Reinhold.

Woodruff, D. S., & Birren, J. E. (1972). Age changes and cohort differences in personality. *Developmental Psychology, 6,* 252-259.

Worden, W. (1992). *Grief counseling and grief therapy* (2nd ed.). New York: Springer.

Wortman, C. B., & Silver, R. C. (1989). The myths of coping with loss. *Journal of Consulting and Clinical Psychology, 57,* 349-357.

Yesavage, J., Brink, T., Rose, T., Lum, O., Adey, V., & Leirer, V. (1983). Development and validation of a geriatric depression screening scale: A preliminary report. *Journal of Psychiatric Research, 17,* 37-49.

Zarit, S. H. (1980). *Aging and mental disorders.* New York: Free Press.

Zarit, S. H., & Knight, B. G. (Eds.). (in press). *Psychotherapy with the elderly: Effective interventions with older people.* Washington, DC: American Psychological Association.

Zeiss, A. M. (in press). Behavioral and cognitive behavioral treatments: An overview of social learning. In S. H. Zarit & B. G. Knight (Eds.), *Psychotherapy with the elderly: Effective interventions with older people.* Washington, DC: American Psychological Association.

Zelinski, E. M., Gilewski, M. J., & Schaie, K. W. (1993). Individual differences in cross sectional and 3-year longitudinal memory performance across the adult life span. *Psychology and Aging, 8,* 176-186.

Zelinski, E. M., Gilewski, M. J., & Thompson, L. W. (1980). Do laboratory memory tests relate to everyday forgetting? In L. W. Poon, J. L. Fozard, L. S. Cermak, D. Arenberg, & L. W. Thompson (Eds.), *New directions in memory and aging: Proceedings of the George A. Talland Memorial Conference* (pp. 519-537). Hillsdale, NJ: Lawrence Erlbaum.

Index

About the Author

Bob G. Knight, Ph.D., is the Merle H. Bensinger Associate Professor of Gerontology and Psychology at the Andrus Gerontology Center, University of Southern California (USC). In that position, he serves as Director of the Tingstad Older Adult Counseling Center and Co-Director of the Los Angeles Caregiver Resource Center. In Fall 1995, he was a visiting professor at University of Sheffield, England. Prior to joining the faculty at USC, he managed the Senior Services program at Ventura County (California) Mental Health Services (1980-1988). He has published extensively in mental health and aging, including the first edition of *Psychotherapy With Older Adults* (Sage, 1986; available in French and Dutch translation), *Outreach With the Elderly* (1989), and *Older Adults in Psychotherapy: Case Histories* (Sage, 1992). He received his Ph.D. in clinical psychology from Indiana University at Bloomington. His professional experience in working with older adults began at the Urban League of Madison County, Indiana, where he organized and served as first president of the Madison County Council on Aging in 1973.